Beyond the Sun

The History, Teachings and Rituals
of the Last Golden Dawn Temple

NICK FARRELL

© Nick Farrell, 2017

Foreword © Peregrin Wildoak 2017

This edition first published in Great Britain in 2017 by Skylight Press,
210 Brooklyn Road, Cheltenham, Glos GL51 8EA

All rights reserved. Except for the quotation of short passages for the purposes of criticism and review, no part of this publication may be reproduced, stored in a retrieval system or transmitted, in any form or by any means, electronic, mechanical, photocopying, recording or otherwise, without the prior consent of the copyright holder and publisher.

Nick Farrell has asserted his right to be identified as the author of this work.

Designed and typeset by Rebsie Fairholm
Publisher: Daniel Staniforth
Cover artwork by Rebsie Fairholm

www.skylightpress.co.uk

Printed and bound by Lightning Source, Milton Keynes
Typeset in Minion Pro and Mr Eaves.

British Library Cataloguing in Publication Data:
A catalogue record for this book is available from the British Library.

ISBN 978-1-908011-96-1

To the circle of Whare Ra Adepts who,
by putting up with a young, annoying magician
with too many questions, helped create the
Magical Order of the Aurora Aurea

And to Tony Fuller
who gave much support to this edition.

PRAYER OR ASPIRATION TO ISIS

Hermetic Version of a Sanskrit Gayatri
(May be used by such as feel in sympathy with its sentiments & languages)

Hail to Thee ! O Thou mighty Mother Isis ! Unveil !
Thou Soul of Nature, who giveth Life and Energy to the Universe.
From Thee all things do proceed,
Unto Thee all must return,
Thou dost spring from that Glorious Sun of Tiphareth, which is shrouded from the profane.
Lead us to the Truth
Make us to do all our duty,
As we travel upwards and onwards to the Kingdom of Divine Love
Where we shall see God face to face.

Sent out to members of the Golden Dawn by W. Wynn Westcott
December 12th 1892.

CONTENTS

Foreword by Peregrin Wildoak — 11
Introduction — 14

Dr Robert Felkin: Mighty Medicine Man & Victorian Hero — 21
Felkin & Havelock North Work — 51
The Twilight of the Dawn — 72
Whare Ra & Me — 94

Second Order Rituals & Commentaries

6=5 Ritual — 103
6=5 Ritual Commentary — 125
Experience of 6=5 Ritual — 148
6=5 Teaching Material — 150
7=4 Ritual — 187
Commentary on the 7=4 Ritual — 200
Experience of the 7=4 — 213
The Rite of the Link — 216

Light in Extension: Papers inspired by the 6=5 and 7=4

Attuning to Chesed — 231
Becoming the Star Child — 233
The Cross and 16 Nails — 243
Inner Temples — 247
Additional Whare Ra Material — 251

References — 276
Index — 278

ABOUT THE AUTHOR

Nick Farrell has been initiated into six different traditions which have their roots in the Golden Dawn. His first group was Builders of the Adytum in New Zealand. Later he worked with former members of the last Golden Dawn temple to close its doors, Whare Ra, in New Zealand and was a member of the still thriving side order, the Order of the Table Round. He moved to the United Kingdom and for many years followed Dion Fortune's Inner Light tradition through the Servants of the Light and David Goddard's Pharos Group. Later he joined Chic Cicero's Hermetic Order of the Golden Dawn, helping that order to establish itself in the United Kingdom.

In 2009, he founded the Magical Order of the Aurora Aurea, with his wife Paola. It is an International Order based in Rome with a correspondence course and temples working to bring Magic into the 21st Century.

More information can be found on the Order's website:

www.auroraaurea.com

or his Blog
www.nick-farrell.blogspot.com

ACKNOWLEDGEMENTS

This book was only possible thanks to the work of researchers and those who follow the Golden Dawn path, both in New Zealand and overseas. My own involvement with former Whare Ra people was personal and related to the people I had met and the stories they told. These formed the basis of the original edition of this book. In this version I had a number of people help me establish the truth behind some of those stories. This enabled me to flesh out details that I could not otherwise have had and enable it to be a little more "hard hitting" and accurate. So, thanks to Darcy Kuntz, Tony Fuller, Peregrin Wildoak, Pat Zalewski, Christine Zalewski, Mike Burden, Yvette Reece, Roel van Leeuwen, Robert Gilbert, Robert S. Ellwood and Ellic Howe.

FOREWORD

Peregrin Wildoak

THIS IS a dangerous book: possibly the most dangerous Nick Farrell has ever written. This is quite a statement considering Nick has previously tackled such daring topics as the creation of talismans, journeys to inner planes, advanced magical practices, shamanism, and perhaps most perilous of all, forming magical groups with real human beings whose foibles are only marginally less challenging than confronting a demon before breakfast.

What makes this particular work so dangerous is that it covers an area of advanced group magic that is rarely discussed properly and even more rarely conducted appropriately. It concerns the so called 'higher' grades of magic, beyond the state of consciousness symbolised by the unifying power of the Sun. Its province is therefore both of an exalted quality and also likely to attract those people within modern magic looking for more advanced and higher works for various personal reasons. And sadly some of these people will think that by reading and possibly enacting (without due care and preparation) the ceremonies Nick presents and discusses, they will have 'achieved' such grades and lofty states of consciousness and spiritual development.

The appropriate response to anyone actively seeking these grades is to deny them access. This is clearly indicated in one of the foundational texts of modern western esotericism, *the Chymical Wedding of Christian Rosenkreutz*, where the hero of the story is clear he is not worthy of an invitation to the wedding of a great Queen, only to find he is called forward while those convinced of their worth are denied.

In practical terms this translates in most magical and esoteric Orders to the practice of admission to the higher grades *by invitation only* – and only if the candidate is deemed to have the right attitude and dedication by their superiors – regardless of other qualities, skills and accomplishments. This was the practice in Whare Ra, the New Zealand temple that Nick draws these important ceremonies and commentaries from and is a crucial aspect of all genuine magical organisations.

There are many potential problems in presenting these ceremonies, all of which Nick is aware of. Of course they have been reproduced in part before, and this publication by Skylight Press will correct some errors and expand greatly on the inner side of the ceremonies, the magic that makes them actually work.

The renaissance of the Golden Dawn since the early 1980s – however we view this phenomenon – has reached a point where many temples and groups are requiring and looking for ceremonial motifs and processes 'beyond the Sun'. This book is, in part, a way of providing some solid and sensible approaches to this task, through methods and ideas formulated and honed down by the longest lasting Golden Dawn temple in the world.

This last point should be framed for what it is: remarkable. One of the unfortunate consequences of the development of western magic into self-dependent and self-determined groups (not to mention the bloody mindedness of many magicians) is that groups and Orders seldom last long. Wisdom is often passed to new generations of magicians in piecemeal fashion only and modern generations of magical groups actually rely more on books and personal 'on-the-spot' ideas more than they care to admit.

In complete contrast to this approach, Nick draws on the texts and wisdom of an Order that not only lasted but flourished in thinly populated New Zealand towns for 60 years. This book, in a real sense, is a continuation of that tradition. Another aspect of the book is the correction of the attitude towards Dr Robert Felkin, co-founder of the Whare Ra temple. Often unfairly derided for his 'astral junketing' and reliance on inner plane communication, Nick's treatment of Dr Felkin is deeper and more respectful, showing a practical depth and deep commitment to service and spirit unexplored previously.

Included here also are many interesting aspects of the history of Whare Ra, the Cromlech Temple and the Golden Dawn tradition in general. Much of this has never been published before and Nick reproduces letters, original documents and oral history to flesh out the story of the Golden Dawn in the antipodes, which is where the grades beyond the Sun were worked most often and most comprehensively.

Realistically of course, no one is expecting groups of magicians across the globe to pick this book up and work the ceremonies within verbatim. They are being provided by Nick in order to prompt people and groups to use the deep symbolism and methods contained within them as part of their own exploration and creation. And really, there is nothing like this book out there already, as one of its strengths is the inclusion by Nick of papers on the symbolism and inner aspects of the ceremonies as well as personal accounts by those who have been initiated through them.

Nick is no stranger to presenting the inner aspects of ritual, and his tireless insistence of the importance of these vital aspects of ceremonial and magical work makes me consider him one of the more significant bearers of the magical tradition today. Since the publication of my own work on the inner workings of the Golden Dawn, *By Names and Images,* I constantly receive messages from magicians stating there is no equivalent teaching in their Orders. This has been the case for pretty much every public Order – apart from Nick and Paola's *Magical Order of the Aurora Aurea.* This tells me something and that 'something' can be found in this wonderful book on the higher reaches of the Golden Dawn.

So, sit down, put your feet up and enjoy the read – then come back a second time, and a third time – with notebook in hand and start to pull apart the ceremonies and the commentaries. Engage deeply with the book; think about it, experiment a little, imagine a lot – then and only then you will travel beyond the Sun; thanks to Nick and Paola Farrell and the Whare Ra temple.

Peregrin Wildoak
Perth, Australia, March Equinox, 2015

INTRODUCTION

IN THE 1980s, Patrick Zalewski blew the lid off the established Golden Dawn magical tradition by revealing that the Order had continued to exist in New Zealand until the late 1970s. Until then, it had been widely believed that the Order of the Golden Dawn had died in the 1940s after Israel Regardie published a big chunk of its rituals and teachings in his four-volume *Golden Dawn*[1] book.

Zalewski revealed that not only had one important branch of the Golden Dawn continued, but also it had prospered and was producing new teaching and training at least until the early 1970s, when it suffered a terminal decline. This long lost group was not called the Order of the Golden Dawn, but Smaragdum Thallasses,[2] which means "Emerald of the Sea" in Ancient Greek. It was more commonly known by its adepts by the name of its temple building – Whare Ra.

In his book *Secret Inner Order Rituals of the Golden Dawn*,[3] Zalewski released the 6=5 and 7=4 rituals of Whare Ra as well as an unknown ritual called the Rite Link, along with a brief history of the Order in New Zealand. With hindsight, this announcement should have created a bigger storm amongst those who were already using made-up lineage and high grades as a way to attract people into their modern Golden Dawn-style orders. After all, Whare Ra was a real "Golden Dawn Order" that had a real historical connection to the historical magical group which attracted such members as Allan Bennett, Algernon Blackwood, Aleister Crowley, Florence Farr, Dion Fortune, Maud Gonne, Paul Case, Annie Horniman Arthur Machen, Gustav Meyrink, E. Nesbit, William Sharp, Evelyn Underhill, Charles Williams, A. E. Waite and W. B. Yeats. It should have created a stream of wealthy Americans heading over to New Zealand attempting to buy high grades from the adepts that were left alive. However, it did not.

---

1 Regardie, I. (1971). *The Golden Dawn*. St. Paul: Llewellyn Publications.
2 Smaragdum Thallasses was sometimes spelt Smaragdum Thalasses by its members and in its official paperwork.
3 Zalewski, Patrick J. *The Secret Inner Order Rituals Of The Golden Dawn*. Phoenix, AZ: Falcon Press, 1988. Print.

Introduction

The reason for this was mostly that Whare Ra really was, and had always been, a real magical order. Even after it closed, those adepts who were still living were never going to give out its secrets or lineage to those who did not demonstrate that they had the right qualities. Even those with the power to do so were not going to give grades to those who had not undergone the same extensive training that they had.

That does not mean that they did not train or initiate people, but those who were lucky enough to receive any information had to work for it. Real magical training is never about papers, or even rituals, it is about doing. If you were doing something, then the Whare Ra adepts would notice you and help. They were good at hiding from the lineage hunters and others who wanted to leech off the Golden Dawn name without doing the herculean amount of work required.

The impact of the Zalewski book was also muted by the actions of his publisher, Falcon Press, which made a pig's ear of publishing it. Important chunks of the rituals were missing so that they could not be performed correctly. Many in the Golden Dawn community wondered if this had been done deliberately to protect Falcon Press' own attempt at creating an American Golden Dawn Group. This was confirmed for me when I was contacted by a member of that particular temple who signed himself a 7=4 and ordered me to stop mentioning Whare Ra as only he had the magical rights to the lineage.

All this had a comedic effect. After the book was released, a number of lineage hunters and occult paper collectors contacted Zalewski claiming that they held the 7=4 grade from Whare Ra. They asked him to hand over copies of any teaching material that he might have which they were lacking. One "adept" was asked by Zalewski to prove that he had a right to the 6=5 grade by telling him the number of clauses in the oath and their meaning.

"That is easy," said the would-be 'exempt adept'. "There were three clauses in the oath and they represented the supernal triad, or the white triangle, which was placed on the altar of the 0=0."

As you will see in this book, there were five clauses to the 6=5 oath. These symbolise the sphere of Geburah to which the grade was attributed. The publisher had deleted two of the clauses and so the "adept" had initiated himself from Pat's book.

Over the years, I collected the correct ritual material and some of the teaching material of these grades. I have also penned some of my own ideas about the nature of these grades which I have included in this book.

I had hoped that Zalewski would reprint corrected rituals, but he has, reasonably enough, become involved with fleshing out the Golden Dawn tradition and is less interested in historical curiosities. I fully understand his viewpoint on this as I am going through a similar procedure with my own Magical Order of the Aurora Aurea.

Included in this book are the published experiences of those who have been through these grades, including William Butler Yeats. A group claimed that it was using some new "unpublished Golden Dawn grade rituals" and it described a person going through their "new rite" and their experiences. The experiences were copied from Yeats' experiences of the 6=5 ritual, which he had experienced as a member of the proto-Smaragdum Thallasses group, the Stella Matutina.

There will be those who feel that this material should remain secret, but there is much in these rituals which needs to be studied and used. The 21st century has shown how a ritual or system of magic can be greatly improved by being shared and discussed. It has also proved that putting information in the public domain does not diminish its power. The idea that a published ritual is somehow destroyed or "profaned" is based on the concept that people can know or experience a ritual by reading it and somehow destroy its effects with their own negative thinking.

This is incorrect.

Publication cannot re-create the inner conditions of a rite; it can only give pointers to the ideas behind them.

The much-published 0=0 ritual has managed to keep its "secrets from the profane" despite being published in full in the 1940s. I am still amazed people believe that it is possible to pick up Israel Regardie's *Golden Dawn* and initiate people. Some modern Golden Dawn leaders even insist that it is possible to rope large numbers of people together to initiate them at once, or that the candidate does not even have to be in the room for their own initiation. All this indicates that they have not even scratched the surface of the mysteries of the Golden Dawn rite (or even read the published material).

Over the years, I have initiated several people who have thought that because they had read the Golden Dawn ritual they knew what to expect. One told me that it was exactly like craft masonry, for example. But they soon discovered that what you might have read of a ritual is the tip of the iceberg of a magical experience. You not only have the words, you have the interaction of godforms, energy and power which no book can describe. Intellectually you might understand the ritual, but during a well-prepared initiation, your mind shuts down and you become disorientated and confused. One person told me although he knew that if he was walking around the circle there would be knocks that would surprise him, when they happened he still jumped out of his skin. People join my Order from those that use the same ritual. Their former Golden Dawn group might have done the same rite, but they would have done it differently.

I have conducted hundreds of 0=0 rituals and I still see new things, or ideas, emerge from it every time it is performed. Not only that, the ritual energy changes for each candidate. Godforms which are aggressive for one candidate can be passive for another and this can change the whole flavour of the ritual. On occasions where one initiation was worked after another, only the words have remained consistent.

Thus, the chance of anyone understanding the 6=5 or 7=4 material by reading or doing it is remote. If they can do it, then they deserved the grade anyway. The papers I have provided in this book are to provide ideas for a serious student to discover.

Whare Ra grades protected themselves from the lineage and grade hunters. They can only be awarded to a candidate by someone who has obtained the Rite of the Link. That was awarded in Whare Ra after the 7=4 ceremony. I know of people who hold the link and they are few. I also know of those who have obtained the grade, and link, without contact with Whare Ra. They are even rarer.

Specific Whare Ra 6=5 and 7=4 rituals are being performed by only two modern Golden Dawn orders (which I will not name). Zalewski's own Order does not work them, and the Magical Order of the Aurora Aurea has no plans to use them in their current form. For an Order that works those grades, they have their use and they create an effect. A group that has opened itself to those levels might be guided by their own contacts to something else and expand on things that are hinted at in these grades.

Included in this book is a history. After I wrote my Golden Dawn history in *King over the Water*[4] and *Mathers' Last Secret*[5] I swore that I would not write another history of the Golden Dawn. I feel fairly strongly that it is time that people stop looking towards the Golden Dawn's past and start focusing on its future. Those who look too

---

4   Farrell, N. (2012). *King over the Water*. Dublin: Kerubim Press.
5   Farrell, N. (2011). *Mathers' Last Secret Revised – the rituals and teachings of the alpha et omega*. [S.l.]: Rosicrucian Order of the.

much to tradition lose sight of the magic and become re-enactment groups. However, I felt it important for this material to put the history of Whare Ra, which is unknown outside New Zealand, into some context.

Felkin is an unjustly maligned figure in the history of the Golden Dawn. While far from perfect, he has been a figure of fun for all the main Golden Dawn historians, particularly Francis King. King, who tried desperately to get a Golden Dawn order together himself,[6] and failed, attacked what he thought was Felkin's obsession with Inner Plane communications and searches for secret chiefs in Europe as the First World War was brewing. For King, Inner Plane communications were just "Astral Junketing"[7] and were something to be mocked as coming from the unconscious mind of the medium.

However, everyone within the Golden Dawn tradition used inner plane communications to a greater or lesser extent. Samuel Mathers, Florence Farr, Wynn Westcott, John Brodie-Innes, Paul Case, all held channelling sessions to obtain esoteric information. If Felkin was mad, then they were all mad. If it was coming from Felkin's unconscious mind, then the entire Golden Dawn system was built on it. While this occult technique continued to be developed in the United Kingdom, it has been banished by those who follow King and Regardie, particularly in the United States – to their detriment.

I understand their reluctance. Inner Plane communication is a badly used tool. It has been possible for the chief of an order to outsource responsibly for unpopular decisions to the 'contact' who that chief was supposed to 'serve.' Many contacts had a nasty habit of repeating the unconscious garbage of the person channelling them. Contacts have insisted that a person carry out all sorts of atrocities against innocent members of their group, based on the channeller's fears.

However, that did not mean that Inner Plane contacts do not exist, simply that those who used them did so incorrectly. Much magical work includes building relationships with inner plane beings and often the message is blocked. Ironing the kinks out of this particular

---

6   In his otherwise well researched book *Ritual Magic in Great Britain* (King, F. (1970). *Ritual magic in England*. London: Spearman.), King created a fake historical temple for his own group to claim a lineage without having to worry about others having the paperwork. I have it on a very reliable source that King's Order built the equipment and even posed for photographs that were used in some of King's books but only held a few meetings before collapsing in acrimony.

7   See King, Francis (1989). *Modern Ritual Magic: The Rise of Western Occultism*.

tool of magic has been limited because those using it obscure it in mummery or elitism. They often refuse to admit that a little bit of psychology would help them sort the wheat from the chaff.

What I have tried to do with this edition of the book is cover more of Felkin's early history, which discounts any chance of him being the clown of the Golden Dawn. Seeing his early history as a Victorian adventurer, missionary and explorer you can't but help feel that any biographer uninterested in 20th century occult politics would have painted a different picture. Names such as Gordon of Khartoum and Mackay of Uganda are woven into Felkin's life, making him historically significant in the Age of the British Empire. His medical work in New Zealand and contributions to saving lives during the Spanish Flu epidemic in Hastings made him a hero there too. Yet if you believe King, for a brief part of his life in England he took leave of his senses and retired into a fantasy world, which is coincidentally the time when he happens to be the key player in the Golden Dawn in Europe.

This book is a collection of material from many different sources which I have collected throughout the years. Some of it, such as the 6=5 ritual and material, comes from Percy Wilkinson's collection. This collection was divided between a friend of mine and another who was less forthcoming with providing access. Darcy Kuntz also found a fascinating magazine article on Felkin in Africa which I have mined for details.

I have included my own 6=5 and 7=4 writings in this book, not because I think that they are of a high level, but because they might help the reader understand something about working beyond the Sun of Tiphareth.

This book will be somewhat of a milestone because after sending it off to the printers, I will be at last able to stop writing about other people, and get back to presenting my own magical material.

Thanks also to Pat Zalewski and Tony Fuller for providing me with some additional information.

Nick Farrell
Rome
2017

⟨ I ⟩ DR ROBERT FELKIN: MIGHTY MEDICINE MAN & VICTORIAN HERO

"Adventurers and their exploits have always had a great interest for Englishmen, and it is the love of adventure and travel inbred in us which has built up our mighty Empire — an Empire on which the sun never sets, whose morning drum goes round the world."

EP Scott[8]

DOCTOR ROBERT William Felkin (1853-1926) has attracted some undeserved negative press for his work within the Golden Dawn, and the Stella Matutina, thanks mostly to unsympathetic modern biographers such as Francis King and Ellic Howe[9] who liked to mock his dependence on astral contacts with his secret chiefs. They portray him as silly, naïve, and neurotic – a suitable comedy character whose stupidity led to the decline of the later Golden Dawn tradition. His story was supposed to have ended with his move to New Zealand and leaving the Order in the unsafe and clinically insane hands of Christina Stoddard.[10]

But the real man was nothing like that. Felkin was a late Victorian 'Ripping Yarn' hero who, by his own direct and indirect work, was responsible for the Golden Dawn tradition's survival into the 21st century.

That is not to say that Felkin did not have his shortcomings. He had a drinking problem; he could be gullible and was a consummate spinner of his own history. Unlike Mathers, whose fatal flaws destroyed his good work, Felkin's shortcomings did not overshadow his contribution to the esoteric tradition. Felkin's approach to magic was built to evolve and lasted longer than many other magical orders.

---

8   Scott, E. P. *Stanley and his Heroic Relief of Emin Pasha*. Toronto: W. Bryce, 1890. Print.
9   Howe, Ellic. *The Magicians of the Golden Dawn*. London: Routledge and K. Paul, 1972. Print. (see Chapter 17)
10 Inquire Within, *Light Bearers of Darkness*. London: Boswell Print. & Pub. Co., 1930. Print.

Felkin was born in Beeston, near Nottingham, in 1853. He was named after his father who was a local lace manufacturer. Robert was educated at Wolverhampton Grammar School, where he had a meeting that was to change his life – he met the famous explorer Dr David Livingstone.[11]

David Livingstone was a pioneer medical missionary with the London Missionary Society who was later to become famous for going missing in central Africa and being found by the American explorer Sir Henry Morton Stanley.

Felkin was inspired to become a doctor and a medical missionary like his hero, although it did not happen directly. After he left school, he moved to Saxony where he worked for a relative who owned a large factory. Things were going well for him until, as he later told his Whare Ra students, a complete stranger came up to him and reminded him that he was supposed to be in Darkest Africa helping to "save the souls of the natives."

He returned to London and met with Alexander Murdoch Mackay (13 October 1849 – 4 February 1890) who was a Presbyterian missionary to Uganda, who wished him to go back with him when he was a little older. Mackay was making headway in Uganda with King Muteesa I of Buganda who wanted more missionaries in his kingdom. Muteesa, who reigned from 1856 to 1884, realised he needed Western technology if his kingdom were to survive and called for European missionaries to come to his country.

The famous "Mackay of Uganda" thought Felkin was too young to join him and arranged for him to study medicine for two years so that he might be more useful when he arrived. Mackay, who was an engineer, had managed to entrench himself with Muteesa with his feats of engineering, which were seen as magic. Felkin, Mackay reasoned, would be seen as a magical "medicine man."

Felkin was clearly talented at medicine and dedicated enough to learn quickly. By the age of 26 he travelled to Cairo, heading towards Uganda along the Nile.

It is difficult for a modern person to understand the mindset of British people attempting missionary work at that time. It was Victorian duty at its highest. Not only were missionaries expected to be brave, as death was a near certainty, but they were also expected

---

11 Dunn, P. M. 'Robert Felkin MD (1853-1926) And Caesarean Delivery In Central Africa (1879)'. *Archives of Disease in Childhood – Fetal and Neonatal Edition* 80.3 (1999): F250-F251. Web. 20 Mar. 2015.

to bring British culture and civilisation to those without it. Religion, while being important, was sometimes secondary to the adventure; Livingston who was billed as "Africa's greatest missionary" only converted one person. What appeared to be more important was the spreading of Empire, exploring with the chance of a death from some exotic disease. Such a death gave you the rare celebrity of both a spiritual and a humanist martyrdom and such stories were the fodder of the Victorian newspapers of the time. There was also a requirement to assist in the ending of the slave trade, which was still thriving in Africa. Mackay reported to the UK that his message had to compete with the rich selling cloth and guns for slaves. The going rate was a link of red cloth for one man, a gun for two men and 100 percussion caps for one woman. Mackay famously convinced King Muteesa that it was not right for him to sell his subjects.

On his arrival at Khartoum, Felkin met that ultimate martyr to the British Empire, Major-General Charles George Gordon (28 January 1833 – 26 January 1885). At the time, Gordon was well on the path towards his own dramatic death. He was Governor-General of the Sudan, where he did much to suppress revolts and the slave trade. Later, Gordon's own death would come because as a Christian evangelist he was determined to stand up to the Mahdi (Muhammad Ahmad), who was a Muslim. He died after a year's siege.

In an interview on his return[12] with the *Wild World Magazine* (1898), Felkin recounted his meeting with Gordon:

> "I well remember my first call at the palace of the Governor General. Our party entered the palace and of course we expected General Gordon to be standing ready to receive us. Apparently he was not, however, for the only person about the palace was a little man in short sleeves wearing a white apron, who was busy laying the table. We waited for a few minutes expecting the arrival of the great general but no one came. We were just debating amongst ourselves what move we should make under the circumstances when the active little waiter cast off his apron, put on his coat and then briskly declared he was going to receive us. Of course it was General Gordon… his experience was that the native servants never could set out the knives, forks, and glasses to the satisfaction of an Englishman. So he had undertaken to do it himself."

---

12   The interview was reprinted in *The Ruby Tablet* Vol I Number 4.

This should give an idea of the world in which Felkin was moving. His world was the ultimate place for British heroes, who usually ended up either being killed or dying of malaria. It was not a world for the flaky or the faint hearted. History was going on all around Felkin and he was meeting some of the key players in British colonial history.

Felkin remained friends with Gordon and had a collection of letters from him. He also had a map which Gordon drew for him which was helpful in finding his way up the Nile. Felkin wrote that Gordon was a great believer in casting lots and would settle some difficult decisions in this way.

Gordon, Felkin felt, had a fatal flaw in that he did not read or understand Arabic and he trusted too much in his 'native' servants to transmit critical information on his behalf. Felkin noticed that Gordon's staff were often playing their own political games.

"Had Gordon been able to speak or read Arabic with anything like fluency, he would never have put his name onto many of the letters he signed," reported Felkin.

Felkin was convinced that Khartoum would never have fallen if Gordon had listened to his suggestion of sending some of his troops from Berber to Suakin. He thought that they could have found water at any point simply by drilling for it.

Gordon was worried that the Abyssinians would block the Nile at the sixth cataract and divert it to the Red Sea. Apparently the Abyssinians had threatened as much as it would have only taken a ton of dynamite.

After leaving Gordon, Felkin's party became trapped in the Nile marshes for 40 days, in dense heat and tormented by mosquitoes.

"The air was alive with mosquitoes and their attacks by day as well as by night. Sleep was impossible," he later wrote.

Starved, they were rescued by Emin Pasha, the famous Austrian missionary. Pasha sent an army of "400 black soldiers" to hack a path through the marshes which allowed Felkin's party to escape.

Pasha was another European missionary who was rescued by Sir Henry Morton Stanley in the days when journalists were in Africa making news rather than just reporting it. Pasha was an influence on the young Felkin and taught him how to run an efficient missionary operation. His own life became threatened during the Mahdi revolt. The Emin Pasha Relief Expedition, led by Stanley, undertook to rescue Emin by going up the Congo River and then through the Ituri Forest. It cost the lives of two-thirds of the expedition and a battle before Stanley and Pasha arrived safe in Bagamoyo in 1890. All that was in vain however, as Pasha was killed by two Arab slave traders at Kinena Station in the Congo Free State when history moved on.

During this time, Felkin encountered African magic for the first time and found it fascinating. In fact in one interview he seemed as much interested in the magic of the region as in slavery. Until then magic was not a feature in his life, but he found "African medicine men and wizards" could do things that he could not explain. He said that some of them could transform themselves into lions, jackals and hyenas at night and travel extreme distances in a short time.

"They are also said to have the power of divination, to restore lost cattle, tell fortunes, and perform other miraculous feats. In the morning they return to their normal shape and can give information about what happened at any distance," he reported.

Felkin said he had ample opportunity to see the work of these medicine men. He said they would eat a root "known only to them" and go into a heavy sleep. The next day they would recount their dream.

As an example Felkin said there came a time when the Nile was blocked by a floating island of grass. The local m'log, or wizard, had been roaming the country at night in the form of a jackal. He had then travelled 250 miles on, found two steamers with mail for Felkin's party, and described the captain of one of the boats in minute detail. It was predicted that he would be here in a month.

"I ridiculed the whole thing as absurd... in fact 32 days later an Englishman did arrive in our camp bringing us letters from Khartoum... I am satisfied that this man had never even left his village."

After meeting Emin Pasha, Felkin's party left for Uganda where they were received by King Muteesa and his 7000 wives, 70 sons and 88 daughters. Felkin was given a job as the king's medical adviser and found that the king had an ego which he would not see the like of again until he dealt with Samuel Mathers.

The king felt that there was only one other person in the world more important than him and that was Queen Victoria, wrote Felkin. He also had a habit of asking Felkin to perform live vivisection on a person while he watched, and getting cross when the doctor said no. Felkin was also the first Westerner to record the use of Caesarean births in Africa – something which was considered far too advanced by the arrogant European doctors of the time.

He later told the Edinburgh Obstetrical Society on 9 January 1884 in a speech entitled *Notes on Labour in Central Africa*:

"So far as I know, Uganda is the only country in Central Africa where abdominal section is practised with the hope of saving both mother and child. The operation is performed by men, and is sometimes successful.[13]"

However, all was not well in Uganda. Felkin found that there were rivalries between the missionaries of the different churches. Of a particular concern to Felkin was Father Simon Lourdel Monpel, known as Père Mapeera, who was popular with the King. The Roman Catholics had arrived in 1879 and were a serious threat to the Anglicans.

According to Felkin, Muteesa thought it would be a splendid gesture to sort out all these arguing missionaries and cement his friendship to Rome by bumping off all the Anglicans. Felkin claimed that he was going to be one of the victims, but the King found him useful as a doctor. In *A Wayfaring Man*, a fictionalised biography written by his second wife Harriet and published in serial form between 1936 and 1949, Felkin claimed he warned the King that if he planned to murder him and all the Anglicans, the sun would turn dark the next day. Felkin had worked out that the region was due for a solar eclipse, so he was confident of his prediction. After the skies did go dark, the King's followers thought he was a mighty medicine man and left him alone.

It is all rubbish,[14] but it does indicate that Felkin was not above talking up his story and the amount of risk he personally felt.

The reality was much different than even a young Felkin could have predicted. Muteesa allowed Felkin to leave the country, conditionally upon him taking with him three of the King's envoys, whom he was commanded by King Muteesa to present to Queen Victoria.

Muteesa had not wanted to kill the Anglicans at all; he still saw the British as part of a modernisation programme for his kingdom and had been playing them both off against each other to see which side would win. Arguably, it was the Catholics who won; more than half the population of the region is still Catholic.

---

13   Felkin, RW (1884) Notes on labour in Central Africa. *Edin Med J* 29:922–930.
14   The story is too similar to that told by Mark Twain in *Connecticut Yankee at King Arthur's Court,* and besides there was no total eclipse in Uganda during the time that Felkin was there.

Felkin used to boast that he broke an old superstition that it was impossible for a white man to get to the Great Lakes and back to the Nile alive. He also claimed to be the first white man to measure the pygmies of Central Africa.

His next expedition was to Zanzibar, where he lived for a while before finally returning to Britain to continue his medical studies. Felkin then obtained his medical qualification, founded the Geographical Society, taught in London and lectured on the continent and in England on tropical diseases. His lectures on the subject were the first ever given.

He wrote more than 22 books or articles. He was joint author of such catchy titles as *Uganda and the Egyptian Soudan* (1882); *Notes on Labour in Central Africa* (1884), *Lectures on Diseases of the Tropics and Climatology* (1886); *Emin Pasha in Central Africa* (1888); *Foetal Malaria* (1889); *Ethrology and Climatology of Central Africa* (1892); *Hypnotism and Mural Reservation* (1893) and *The Emin Pasha Relief Operation* (1890).

He then interested himself in the Congo and obtained permission from the King of the Belgians, King Leopold II (1835-1909) to trade over an immense area. It would have involved working with Stanley who had been working with Leopold. Felkin was ready to set up the enterprise, but the British government withdrew the concessions and the project fell through.

Felkin had a narrow squeak. Although the enterprise would have been extremely profitable, Leopold was, even by colonial standards, a nasty piece of work who enslaved and murdered many. While involvement with the project did not harm Stanley's reputation in the UK, he personally felt bad about it and as the history of African colonialism was re-evaluated, Stanley's heroic image suffered. Felkin would almost certainly have been implicated in the king's wrongdoing and genocide, and be remembered for that instead of being a hero of the Golden Dawn.

In 1882 Felkin married his first wife, Mary Jane, who was the daughter of Samuel and Mary Mander of Wolverhampton. In 1886 he joined the Theosophical Society in Edinburgh. He was soon bored because it was lacking in terms of ritual, and in 1894 joined Brodie-Innes' Amen-Ra Temple of the Order of the Golden Dawn.

In 1903, Mary died and Felkin was crushed. He made a retreat to the monastery of the Mirfield fathers, the Community of the Resurrection, and even considered joining the order. Harriet Felkin later grudgingly admitted that Felkin had loved his first wife deeply. They had a son (Samuel) Denys and a daughter, Ethelwyn (1883-1962), who was to join the Stella Matutina and later publish a paper which many think is the bedrock of Western Tarot and certainly the Golden Dawn Tarot.

Several of the Mirfield fathers had an interest in Rosicrucian and Christian mysticism, and regarded Felkin as an eminent figure in that tradition. This fame would result in him being contacted by the Havelock North community.

In 1900, a schism occurred within the Order of the Golden Dawn. Mathers had gone too far in believing his own propaganda and had become autocratic to work with. After expelling Mathers and his supporters, a council led by the poet W.B. Yeats ruled a group which was already fragmenting. I have recounted the story of the revolt in my book *King over the Water*, but what was not clear was how Felkin found himself at the head of the order after the revolt. At that time Felkin was junior to John Brodie-Innes and only a Zelator Adeptus Minor (ZAM).

There were some political reasons for the choice: Felkin was closely linked to Brodie-Innes and other senior members who were the "magical faction" within the Order, while the "mystical faction" was focused on Arthur Waite. Felkin was a good leader, and to many in the order also a hero, who had gone to Africa and lived to tell the tale.

But there were some good magical reasons: Felkin was psychic and able to make contacts on the astral plane. Felkin apparently made contact with the Inner Masters of Brodie-Innes' Solar Order. Using his own medium, Felkin contacted the Hidden Masters of the Sun. Felkin also believed he received "impressional" and "astral" teaching from the Third Order. This greatly impressed John Brodie-Innes, who became a strong Felkin supporter and pushed him to the role of a Chief within the new ruling Triad established by the rebels.

It did not last long. After recovering from the revolt, the magical faction was overthrown by the more politically motivated masonic mystics led by Arthur Waite.

Felkin took most of the magicians out of the order, formed the Stella Matutina and set up the Amoun temple in London to replace the Isis Urania temple. Waite kept the Isis temple running and there was a signed agreement between the two orders which kept things civil.

One of Felkin's closest allies was Neville Meakin, who was considered the ritual genius who had turned the awful Mathers version of the Portal rite into something complex and spectacular. He will become important later in the story.

Felkin married again. If Mary had been the love of his life, then Harriet Miller Felkin (1872-1959) was his priestess. She spent a large amount of her life promoting him and his work. Harriet was the daughter of John Davidson, a Scottish Presbyterian minister who helped establish the University of Adelaide in Australia. Harriet was born in 1872 in Adelaide, but her father died when she was nine and she was packed off to live in the UK with relatives. She joined Felkin's branch of the Golden Dawn in May 1904, having met Felkin through an introduction from a member of the Edinburgh temple of the Golden Dawn. Felkin was looking for a companion for his daughter Ethelwyn after the death of Mary. There was 19 years age difference, but according to Harriet, the pair fell in love and they were married in 1908.

Harriet is one of those figures who history has largely ignored, but she was singularly powerful in the Golden Dawn history and for the Havelock North community. She also wielded terrific influence over decades. When people write the history of the Golden Dawn they tend to talk mostly about Felkin, but it is clear that Harriet was a strong woman who ruled her husband, the order, and also Felkin's ghost. Most of what we know about Felkin was written by his wife, who was a dedicated spinner of his life. She did little to cover up his weaknesses, and it is from her that we learn about his long struggle with alcoholism. She blamed it on a prescription given him by another doctor during his Edinburgh period, to take a "stiff dose of whiskey and quinine" whenever he felt a bout of the recurrent malaria coming on. His late wife Mary was also to blame because she "could not plan adequate meals on time, leaving him to come home from his medical calls cold and wet and unprovided for", wrote Harriet.

In fact, looking at his alcoholism and the time it appeared in his life suggests that he might have been suffering from post-traumatic stress syndrome following his missionary adventure, and was self-medicating from a bottle.

After his death, Harriet took control of the order and was the undisputed ruler of the temple. All of the Whare Ra people I met from that era looked upon Harriet as the fount of all occult wisdom.

Much of the history of the development of ideas at Whare Ra came from Harriet's own spiritual processes. It was from Harriet that more Eastern teaching about chakras and auras entered the order. She was particularly interested in the Seven Rays and the teachings of Alice A. Bailey.[15] These assign different colours and contacts to each of the seven rays. In later years she appeared to lose interest in this too and this teaching disappeared into the background.

She became a little eccentric later in life. She liked to haunt the gardens of Whare Ra dressed in a monk's robe.

She survived Felkin by 23 years and died in December of 1959, having been a member of the order for 55 years and a leader of it for 43. After her death, the order started to face its significant challenges.

SECRET CHIEFS

Felkin, like Samuel Mathers, believed that a magical order was controlled by astral masters or Secret Chiefs. If a group lacked these contacts then it was spiritually dead and could offer no new teaching or valid initiations. Unlike the others in the Order, such as Waite, who felt that issues like Secret Chiefs were best not worried about, Felkin wanted to find some connection with them. Much of what Felkin was reacting to was the 'spin' that Mathers had placed on his contacts with the Secret Chiefs. There was another good reason for Felkin to look for his secret chiefs and that was to do with egregores. Egregores are spirits which represent the totality of a magical order. They are similar to the concept of the Roman Lares. A temple will have one and so will an order. These enable a group to excel beyond the sum of its parts. The egregore will encourage them to behave in a positive way, but they are also problematic. If an egregore carries the totality of all its members, it means that it carries their shadows too. It will encourage members to follow the same lines that formed the group in the first place. If new information comes into the temple, it will be like putting new wine into old skins.

An egregore becomes contaminated with the influences of its leaders. If a leader goes mad for magical reasons then the egregore will attract the same astral forces to itself. Say a founder develops an ego problem; the egregore will then be susceptible to encouraging those same problems within the membership. If a leader sleeps with

---

15 Bailey, A. (1971). *A treatise on the seven rays.* New York: Lucis Publishing Co.

his students for grades, then they will, in turn, find situations where they will sleep with their students for grades.

The Golden Dawn egregore had been formed by those who wanted a quasi-masonic organisation without magic. Mathers had introduced magic into the group and the egregore did not like it. Then Mathers compounded the problem with his drinking, eccentricity and autocracy. Its egregore was in trouble.

The rebels did not hold their order together by hanging on to the old egregore. Felkin wanted the old order's rituals and teaching; he realised that he needed to create a new egregore which was astrally wired in such a way that the Golden Dawn egregore was not activated. The best way to do that was to find a spiritual lineage which did not require him to call upon Mathers and Westcott's order. Since historical roots were important, he would have to find a link to the astral masters which did not need the Golden Dawn.

Since the founding of the higher grades within the Golden Dawn, Samuel Mathers had claimed to be the only link between the Order and its mysterious Secret Chiefs and had managed to convince people that this was the case. However the only person who Mathers ever claimed was a secret chief and he met in the flesh was the conwoman Madame Horos; everything else he described was an "astral experience".

While he was in England, Samuel along with Moina Mathers made an astral contact with the Archangel Raphael, who used the motto *Lux E Tenebris (Light in Darkness)*. This was revealed in a letter to the head of the Bradford Temple, T.H. Pattison, who had picked up the same contact.[16]

This changed slightly when Mathers had to go to Paris and he needed to come up with a decent reason. Mathers had really moved to Paris to be with his artist wife, who had been paid by the heiress Annie Horniman to go to the city to set up a studio. Mathers allowed it to be put about that he was in France at the instructions of the Secret Chiefs to receive special teaching. This piece of spin was possible because Horniman did not want people to know that she was funding the Mathers and kept this secret until it became impossible to keep quiet about it.

At no point does Mathers appear to have met *LeT* or anyone in Paris, and all the notes that have come down to us from that

---

16   Farrell, Nick. *King over the Water: Samuel Mathers and the Golden Dawn.* Dublin: Kerubim, 2012, p.62. Print.

period refer to astral meetings. Yet Mathers was happy to leave the impression that the 5=6 ritual had come to him from these Secret Chiefs who he had met in Paris.

Felkin then had to obtain the same form of contact for his order, while at the same time partly discrediting Mathers. He wanted to build a grade structure beyond the 5=6; something the Golden Dawn was lacking and felt the only way to do that was to make a connection with the real Rosicrucians.

From the time that Felkin assumed leadership of the Stella Matutina, he became increasingly dependent on an astral group of teachers called "Sun Masters" who existed on the astral plane. These were mostly centred on another group run by Felkin's fellow rebel John Brodie-Innes, called Cromlech.

Cromlech, or the Sun Temple, was separate from the Golden Dawn and Stella Matutina which never-the-less had a close relationship (particularly in United Kingdom). Many members of the Golden Dawn and particularly the rebel faction were members, attracted to its mostly channelled teachings on magical subjects. It attracted a higher membership from the Clergy. Felkin's inner Order 'name' as a Chief in the Sun Order was 'Hakim', Arabic for 'Wise', which was mentioned by Mrs Felkin in her *Wayfaring Man* biography.

Cromlech described itself as a Rosicrucian Order, but it drew heavily on Mithraism, and also – depending on the specific ritual worked – Egyptian (one ritual extends some of the Golden Dawn 5=6 material), Kabbalah, Christianity (not Protestant), plus Celtic aspects and themes. There was some Indian material such as the Tatwas and the Nagas, which made for an unusual synthesis. Francis King claimed there was no magic in the order, but only saw some of the material, and in the higher Third Grade there were some magical practices. More famous amongst modern occultists are the Aura papers. The papers have taken on somewhat of a legend for being dangerously powerful, but this is mostly due to the fact that the majority have not been seen. Tony Fuller, who has all of them, said that some of the approximately 60 Aura papers are pretty tedious but others are excellent – very good material on the Elementals, polarities, and an interesting series on the 'Exempt Adept'.

There were no overt references to Christianity in the rituals, although some of the papers do mention approvingly the Eastern Orthodox, Roman Catholic Church and Anglo-Catholic traditions.

King only had access to the badly typed versions (partly condensed) made by Gerald Yorke. The Cromlech and Beltane rituals were complex and hard to stage as they involved things like coloured fires, Naga of Fire, Naga of Water etc. There was also quite a heavy feminine emphasis throughout with the use of priestesses and the emphasis upon Isis and Nephthys.

The Sun Masters had correctly tipped Felkin off that Mathers had not received the Ritual of the 7=4 and therefore could not advance anyone beyond 6=5. He was also warned against working with Mathers. His connections reinforced his position as leader in the Stella Matutina. However, in 1906 Felkin lost his contacts with the Sun Masters only to see them start speaking through Brodie-Innes. In fact, he largely depended on Brodie-Innes to bring through new material.

But this dependence caused Felkin some problems. Like many channellers before him, Brodie-Innes used the fact that the Sun Masters were speaking through him to control Felkin. For example, as Felkin was trying to find a 6=5 ritual, the Sun Masters started to tell him that as a 5=6 he was not allowed to have that material. This placed him in a Catch 22, in that he could not write the Higher Grades until someone else bestowed them upon him.

In 1907 he journeyed to Egypt and conducted two vision journeys. One was in Philae on November 16 and the other was in the Great Pyramid at Giza. He wrote a report where the astral and the material overlap. It is common for vision experiences to be described like this. Indeed in *King over the Water* Mathers described his meetings with his Secret Chiefs in a similar manner and caused considerable confusion among those who believed that his meetings were literal and on the earth plane. These visions are important, and appear to be the sources of some of the techniques in the 6=5 and 7=4 rituals.

Notes on Experiences in Egypt
PHILAE 16:11:07

We landed on Philae and walked over to the ancient landing place with steps leading to the water's edge. I was directed to go down to the steps and on coming up them, to salute by placing one hand right on the steps and the left touching my forehead. As I came through the archway at the top, a host of presences appeared to crowd around me. "This," he said, "is where from ancient times the Kings and rulers assembled to do homage to the Most High, not only those of Khem, but of every nation. For to each of us are given a nation to teach and rule over, but ever must we remember our allegiance to the All-Ruler. For those who sought to forget this and who would rule on their own power came doom. These are the 'False Gods' and their nations perished."

Then I came to the great course and made the signs in succession before advancing. As I approached the Inner Gateway, two priests clad in white met me. I have the L.V.X and I.A.O. signs,[17] and they blindfolded me and led me up to the next Gateway: there I was handed over to another guide who demanded of me the signs. I hesitated and was told that it was the sign of the Hanged Man[18] [large space] which I then made, upon which they brought me to the entrance of the sanctuary. They removed the bandage from my eyes and directed me to make the sign of the Fool,[19] "For," said they, "The Fool is the Adept who hath cast the burden of material things behind him and Bes – who is to the child souls – a god, since to him belongeth material good, joy and laughter and earthly love – to the Adept becometh but a demon, seeking to drag him down from the spiritual but succeeding only in tearing the rags of his earthly desires."

So I put on the form of the Fool and therewith advanced alone to the altar, whereon I was directed to place my hands crossed at the wrists. Then one standing beyond the altar said to me "Behold," and I beheld a silver chalice. "Pour forth now thy blood wherein lieth concealed the sacred ichor, into the cup that it may become the living Lotus whence ariseth the White Serpent of Pure Wisdom. Now there is a mystery."

Then blood was taken from my right arm between the wrist and the elbow and poured into the chalice, and behold the chalice became a lotus blossom whence arose a serpent of White Light.

Then said the Concealed One: "See now, sacrifice is indeed a necessity, but it must be the sacrifice of that which you value.

"For from of old have the nations offered blood sacrifice and many have made a mockery of it, offering the life blood of their enemies which they rejoiced to shed. Nevertheless without the shedding of blood there is no remission of sin.

---

17   The word 'signs' has been circled by hand and an arrow has been drawn to place the word after the L.V.X. In other words he did the L.V.X. signs and vibrated the I.A.O. formula. These are Golden Dawn signs.
18   This is a sign from the Cromlech Temple.
19   This is another sign from the Cromlech Temple.

"God is Love, God is Light, and God is Life. You say the first two so often that you regard them almost as commonplace, but rarely do you say the last: yet of the last alone it is possible to say inversing – God is Life, Life is God. Love is not God, nor is Light, but wheresoever life is – from the mightiest Archangel in the heaven of Heavens down to the mollusc or lichen which can scarce be distinguished from the rock whereon it dwells – there is God.

"Death, negation, is evil, it is of the Devil. Therefore when man partook of the knowledge of evil, death was the inevitable penalty. Now life dwelleth in the Blood, wherefore is Blood sacred. For this reason the Jews were forbidden to eat blood; for this reason also under the new dispensation it becomes lawful for true Christians to eat. Nevertheless it should always be considered a sacrament. For the 'vital organs' can not only claim the title because they promote the circulation of this sacred fluid. The heart, the brain, the lungs, these three are indispensable and correspond to the Supreme Triad. To the Eternal Trinity. For the brain is the father, the heart is the mother and the lungs are the spirit, the word. For the brain is the seat of the intellect, and the heart is the seat of the emotions, but with the lungs we inspire the air wherewith to vibrate the Sacred Names. All these three are bound together in the blood which courses unceasingly from one to another even as the universal currents which ye name the 'Tatwas' pass through the uttermost spaces from one person to another; but should this bond of movement cease death must ensue: and should the Universal Current pause, yea but for a moment of time, annihilation would instantly result.

"Therefore must the Christ shed his most holy blood at the four extremities of the Universe and finally at his Heart, wherefrom gushed forth that unfailing spring of Life in which whosoever bathes will receive Eternal Life."

* * * * *

"There are three paths – the intellectual, the emotional, and the inspirational. The True Adept must transverse them all and since in the fourth dimension it is possible to be in two different places at once, therefore it is possible for the adept to transverse the three simultaneously. Many women tread the emotional, some also the inspirational. Many men follow the intellectual and some the emotional but only a few can follow all three. True balance and equilibrium lie not in cutting off but training and developing all powers, turning the force from evil to good. Atrophy of a part must inevitably weaken the whole. It is not by negation but by affirmation that the highest becomes obtainable, not by repression but by direction."

* * * * *

"Understand therefore that the City of the Grail is Man himself. For the outer citadel with its yellow streets and houses and people going to and fro is the body of man with his cells and activities. Ever building up and ever falling into decay for [drawing of a square, earth Tatwas] Earth with the material and the castle set upon a hill is as the Intellect and Reason which orders and rules the body. For if man were to obtain perfection, his body would obey his mind as a well-trained steed obeys his master, and the Chapel, which can only be reached by a narrow bridge spanning a cleft, is the soul which is apart from and yet united to the mind but can only be reached interiorly as is shown by the Hall of the Quest, and within the ever living sanctuary of the soul dwells the spirit and the Christ, drawing down the Divine White Brilliance from above and shedding the Rose Light around it. That this sanctuary must maintain this Holy Gift it must ever be alive to the light and colour of the Universe and this may be seen in the many coloured windows of prismatic light. And around flows the Great Current which at once unites and separates each from the other."

Notes on Experiences in Egypt

The Great Pyramid

On our arrival we went up to see and touch the Pyramid. I sat at its foot in the gathering dust and heard music as of copper or bronze gongs inside. I was conscious that there were priests within it. Before me I saw the flood fade away and great stretches of sand reached for miles to the banks of the Nile.

The next morning I climbed up it. The sun rose when I was two thirds up. Again the sheet of water below gave place to billows of golden sand, waterless, treeless and empty of life save for a solitary pilgrim trudging wearily along, a staff in his hand. The pilgrim came alone always, and generally on foot, rarely on a camel, never on horseback or a donkey. He wore a linen robe the colour of the desert. He went first to the Temple of the Sphinx where he stayed till a suitable time, probably the next New Moon.

The following day I visited the Temple of the Sphinx. When the Candidate arrived at the temple he was greeted by a fair youth with a bowl or "iota" of clear sparkling water in his hands. The Candidate must however turn away from the tempting draught neither tasting thereof, nor suffering his feet or hands to be bathed therein.

An aged priest now led him across the threshold and drew him to the doorway on the right hand side of the passage. The door was closed behind him and behold he was in a vault or a charnel-house and confronted with death and corruption. Upon this he must gaze unmoved till the door again opened and he was free to step back into the passage. Thence he was led by a veiled woman to the central hall where the assembled Adepts greeted him. There was a way out through lengthy and careful examinations. Some in writing, others by speech or gesture. He was then taken to a small bare cell where he might repose and meditate. Next morning before sunrise he was summoned forth through the central hall, across the court of the Well, first to the right hand room wherein in a niche above his head stood the statue of an Ape, a type of bestial man. Live apes were in the room also; facing the statue was a great window through which shone the coming dawn. In this the niche was occupied by a statue of the highest type of manhood, Osiris, and as the candidate gazed upon that divine face, the first rays of the rising sun fall upon the sculptured features. Here there were beautiful youths chanting the morning hymn to the accompaniment of stringed instruments.

The third day he was taken to an inner changer whereto the light of day never penetrated. Here he must give some proof of his magical powers as might be demanded of him. Here perchance he was commanded to make a dry stick blossom, or his staff to become a serpent, but certainly and invariably must he call down the Divine White Light so that the darkness of the chamber be illumined therewith. Here also was death, but beautiful and peaceful, and he might be required to bring the dead to life. Should he do this, it was permitted to him to ask of them such secrets as he desired to have revealed to him.

All these things were done by degrees with many hours of solitude and meditation between. When his time was accomplished the Candidate was led forth to the hall under the Sphinx and there left. Since his arrival he had tasted no food and his only bed had been the stone floor of his cell. As he stepped into the Hall he found himself standing on a narrow strip of stone pavement beyond which stood tables laden with every delicacy of food and drink. The floor was strewn with scented rushes, soft music played, couches and divans invited repose; fountains sparkled in the radiance of unseen lamps; beautiful maidens, their lips scarce veiled by the gauzy draperies smiled upon him as they floated to and fro in a rhythmic dance; all that could appeal to the senses enticed him: but he must remain on the stone pavement, seated with his legs crossed under him in the attitude of meditation. If he remained steadfast and rejected all these allurements then gradually the light faded and the hall became dark. Then another temptation came. He was offered illimitable knowledge if he would renounce the path, if he would listen to the teachings and obey the guidance of the Tempter (Typhon or Apophis). Long the whispering went on in the darkness but as it was met again and again (seven times) with stern refusal it died away at last to utter silence.

Then, as it were, a veil was withdrawn from the further end of the hall and a great panorama passed slowly before the Candidate's eyes. Beautiful countries, fertile lands, mountains with gold and jewels at the hearts, busy cities, thrones and palaces: "All these things shall be yours if you will but stretch out your hand. Why should your pursue the long and arduous road? Of what good is suffering and sacrifice? Live and rejoice as you were born to do." But the Candidate held fast to the faith that was in him and at the last this also passed away and in the silence and the twilight that succeeded he stretched himself on the stone pavement and peace more profound than sleep fell upon him.

As he was roused by a light touch and a shadowy figure veiled in glimmering folds stood by him; he arose in silence and she led him by a narrow but not low passage; other passages branched off from it but of these he took no heed and presently they emerged into the open air, the Pyramid towering in front of them.

They now ascended the steep slope leading up to the entrance and were met about half-way up by five priests, the fifth of who came forward and demanded all the signs, which being given he grasped the candidate's wrists firmly in the 5=6 grip and drew him up the path to the door. Here three figures were partly visible, one above the apex and one on either side of the base of the doorway.

Now the veiled woman had passed beyond the Hierophant and when they reached the doorway she put forth her right hand and touched the great stone, which thereupon swung around in silence and gave access to the interior. The procession now moved forward, first the veiled woman, or Sybil, then the Hierophant, moving backwards and drawing after him the candidate, the four priests going two by two. This passage is only 3.5 feet high and slopes downwards rather steeply. The floor is of polished marble with very slight hollows or footholds and from these the walls emanated a faint phosphorescent glimmer so that the candidate could see one step before him and the gleam of the Sybil's robe beyond the Hierophant. Thus they passed down the long low passage to the place of the Trial by Fire. Here stood a gigantic metal figure with outstretched arms. The candidate was directed to place himself in the huge hands; indeed this seemed the only possible way of avoiding the leaping white flames in the midst of the chamber, for it seemed as though those great hands could lift him safely across the fire. Did he however follow this counsel he must perish, for the figure would throw him down into the furnace within it. If he refused and chose to walk boldly through the midst of the flames, he emerged unscathed upon a narrow ledge of rock beyond, with a passage leading up to the Well of the Waters of Life. Here he was at length permitted to drink before mounting the ladder which bought him to the passage of the Queen's chamber. Here another low passage is to be crept through still in the same order, and then he found himself in the Queen's Chamber or Place of Regeneration.

Here, let into the floor, stood a great stone tank; a soft light filled the room; at the foot of the tank now stood the Sybil, partly unveiled, a brush in her hand whereof the brush was made of a pungent herb bound with flax, the handle being of iridescent crystal. The Hierophant stood behind the Candidate, the priests two on either side of him. His old ragged, sand coloured garment was loosened and slipped from him. The Hierophant grasped his head and neck, two priests his arms and shoulders, two his ankles and thighs and so they lowered him into the tank. Three times was he submerged in the sacred waters; then sat upright while the priests with their ankhs uplifted in their left hands poured forth over him water from slender beakers. Finally the water in the tank was drained away and the Sybil sprinkled him five times with the brush in her right hand dipped into a "silver stoup" which she held in her left. After this he was raised by the four priests, dried with five towels (one blue, one red, one yellow, one green and one pure white) and placed before the niche and his arms stretched out, his back to the niche. The Hierophant stepped forward bearing a gold dish filled with sandalwood oil in his left hand. Dipping the middle finger of his right hand into this, he anointed the Candidate's face and body in a peculiar manner. The four priests then stepped forward bearing garments, a silken tunic, a linen robe – both pure white, a heavily embroidered girdle fastening in the front with a gold clasp, the mantel on the head (the eyes were great emeralds or cats' eyes) on his right shoulder. He was then turned to face the niche before which hung a violet silk curtain; the tank was closed, the Sybil and the five priests bade him farewell, each giving him a peculiar sign and whispering a single word in his ear and withdrew, leaving him alone. He must now answer three questions, one of the past, one of the present and one of the future – what was, what is, what shall be, and having received the answers, the curtain before him was for one moment parted and in the midst he found himself standing face to face with the Black God.

It was now his task to follow the directions contained in the farewells of the Sybil and the priests in order that he might reach the King's Chamber. The first told him how to leave the Queen's Chamber. The second how to avoid the stumbling block, the third how to ascend the gallery, and the remaining three those words of power by the utterance of which he might pass the three ultimate barriers.

Having by aid of these directions traversed the second passage leading to the great gallery, avoided the stumbling block and climbed to the gallery itself, he stood before a seemingly impassable wall of rock, alone and in semi-darkness. Now he must pause, regulate his breathing and vibrate the first world of Power. As the Vibrations echoed, behold the great gallery, behind the wall before him, was slowly withdrawn, being raised by invisible means. Bending low he stepped forward and found himself on the right side of a narrow, oblong cell, confronted by one of those three whom he had dimly discerned on first approaching the Pyramid. To him he gave certain signs, and from him he received the Lotus Wand and sandals. Now again he must vibrate a Name, and again the wall was raised and he passed inwards into the second recess. This time he stood on the left and the greeting figure to the right, gave the sign and received the Tet and a ring, the jewel of which was engraved with a secret symbol. This was placed on the forefinger of his right hand.

The barriers now surmounted, the third master cast over his head the loop of his ankh and therewith drew him into the King's Chamber, the other two following and taking their places on the square rush mat near the door. Thus standing they made their passage and circumambulated around him, leading him by degrees nearer and nearer to the Pastos, chanting and vibrating certain words, while behind the curtains with which the chamber was draped, acolytes sounded the sistern[20] and harp. At last they reached the side of the Pastos and a sudden silence and darkness fell. Unseen hands raised and lowered him into the Pastos. His hands were crossed on his breast, the lotus in his left, the phoenix in his right, the Tet lower down so as to cover the lower part of his body.

---

20 Should be 'sistrum'.

For a space, absolute darkness and silence possessed him: he was as an atom suspended in the midst of space; he was nothing and around him was nothingness.

But slowly the darkness passed away. Around him he beheld strange radiant beings, and his soul hovering over the Pastos knew that he himself was an Osiris, crowned by Isis, with Nephthys at his feet, on his right hand Hathor, on his left Set, on his right Horus, on his left Anubis. The Universe was reflected there and he was the centre of all things. But Osiris slain was not and could not be the end of all things and his soul cried aloud in the silence that it might behold that which laid beyond. Then in answer to that cry he was drawn upwards. The solid stone above his head became as the thin air, and above he found himself face to face with Osiris Onophris, the Justified One, even Osiris [large blank here] the Ever Living and beyond veiled by the excess of Light, his Spirit cognised but could not see, Amoun the Infinite, Supreme, the Concealed One. Then for him, Time and Space were not, he was as God knowing both good and evil and he perceived that evil is but the shadow of matter cast by Infinite Light. Therefore it is said "The people who dwelt in Shadow saw a Great Light."

Now for myself as I lay in the Pastos I beheld the Mighty Ones and I spake with them. Yea in the New Name I demanded that they should grant me my desire and in ransom of I vowed a vow; and the name was given to me. And my soul and the astral abode there for three days and three nights but my body arose and departed. And on the third day in the evening I, even my body, climbed the outer wall of the Pyramid and as it climbed it called "Soul, my soul, return to me lest I perish." And again, "Soul, Soul, art thou there, come up Soul and return to me." And a third time as I reached the summit, "Soul, Soul, Soul, return to me." And behold my soul arose and came to me and I beheld it as one of the Shining Ones. Yeah it hovered against the sunset sky and its outspread wings were as the colours of the sky and its face shone. And I set to it, "Tell me my Soul, what hast thou seen and learnt in thy sojourn in the Place of the Mighty Ones?"

And my Soul answered, saying "I have seen Osiris, yea I have spoken with the Justified One, but that which I have learnt may not yet be told to thee. Yet if you will have patience it may be that even thou may learn and know."

Then I commanded my soul to return to me; and for a time it hovered there reluctant, but at last it folded its winds and passed into its dwelling. And I descended again to the houses of man.

Felkin was thoroughly excited by his experience at the Great Pyramid as he felt that it contained the formula for the 6=5 ritual that he had been waiting for. He went to a shop in Cairo and bought Brodie-Innes a statue of a Black Osiris which he probably saw as a sign that his vision was true.

However Brodie-Innes, while grateful for the statue, was less than impressed. Apparently neither were his Sun Masters who described Felkin's vision as being related to "another order" and a "shadow group" to their own.

However, if you read the above and weed out those parts of the vision which are clearly lifted from the bible or Crater Ropea[21] you can see the format of what became the 6=5, particularly in the final sequence (and what was supposed to be taking place). Although the vision is a little daft in places, it is worthwhile looking at it in reference to the resulting 6=5.

The two would continue to ask questions of the Sun Masters together and while they continued to give accurate answers when it related to the order or Brodie-Innes, the moment someone asked a question about Felkin, the Sun Masters were prone to slapping down the poor Doctor.

In 1908 Felkin freed himself from Brodie-Innes when he contacted an "Arab Teacher" called Ara Ben Shemesh ("Lion Son of the Sun"), one of the "Sons of Fire" inhabiting a Near Eastern "temple in the desert", who had been given special permission to contact and teach Western students.

His first contact with Ara Ben Shemesh was told in *A Wayfaring Man*, which describes how a conversation between Felkin and Waite was interrupted by the appearance of a "shadowy presence." Felkin called for Harriet, who was very clairvoyant, and she saw a tall man in Eastern dress, kuftan, galabieh and turban. He had a smooth olive face, and large dark eyes. The person, known as "the Chaldean," was seeking someone to help in uniting Eastern and Western teaching. While this sounded like Theosophy again, the spirit believed in Jesus Christ.

The Arab, as he came to be known, appeared to be a valid contact, but angered Brodie-Innes considerably. Behind Felkin's back, he started reaching out to Samuel Mathers in Paris, with the suggestion that he be given the 6=5 material. The change did not happen

---

21 Farrell, N. (2014). *The Hidden Path of Initiation*. Rome: Lulu.

overnight, with Brodie-Innes just visiting Mathers' London AO temple, which was being run by Edward Berridge. Brodie-Innes was apparently impressed with the standard of material that he received from Mathers, although he could not have been impressed with the 6=5 and 7=4 ritual, which was light years behind what Waite and later Felkin would produce. The Mathers ritual was a few pages long and mostly about exchanging passwords and grade signs.

Felkin started to pull back from the Sun Temple, but Brodie-Innes and his temple remained part of the Stella Matutina for a few years yet.

Another mystical teacher for Felkin was P. Ramanathan, the Solicitor-General of Ceylon, who wrote under the name of Shri Parananda. Ramanathan was certainly a real person with connections to the Golden Dawn, who even managed to impress Crowley. In his *Confessions*, Crowley wrote:

> "Ramanathan engaged Allan [Bennett] as private tutor to his younger sons. This gentleman was a man of charming personality, wide culture and profound religious knowledge. He was eminent as a yogi of the Shaivite sect of Hindus (he was a Tamil of high caste) and had written commentaries on the gospels of Matthew and John, interpreting the sayings of Christ as instructions in Yoga. It is indeed a fact that one of the characters who have been pieced together to compose the figure of "Jesus" was a yogi. His injunctions to abandon family ties, to make no provision for the future, and so on, are typical.
>
> "From this man, Allan learnt a great deal of the theory and practice of Yoga. When he was about eighteen, Allan had accidentally stumbled into the trance called Shivadarshana, in which the universe, having been perceived in its totality as a single phenomenon, independent of space and time, is then annihilated. This experience had determined the whole course of his life. His one object was to get back into that state. Shri Parananda showed him a rational practical method of achieving this. Yet Allan was not wholly in sympathy with his teacher, who, despite his great spiritual experience, had not succeeded in snapping the shackles of dogma, and whose practice seem in some respects at variance with his principles."[22]

---

22 p.237 Crowley, Aleister, and Aleister Crowley. *The Spirit of Solitude: An Autohagiography: Subsequently Re-Antichristened The Confessions of Aleister Crowley*. London: Mandrake, 1929. Print.

Felkin first saw Shri Parananda materialising out of steam at the Bad Pyrmont baths in Germany. He saw him as a dark Eastern man with a beard and large black eyes, wearing a flowing robe and a peculiar conical cap, who arranged with Felkin to meet him in exactly a month in the lounge of the Carlton Hotel in London. Felkin said this meeting took place in the flesh, which was certainly possible, and was the start of a series of conversations that lasted for several years. However, Shri Parananda would not have done as a Golden Dawn secret chief as Felkin believed in a literal lineage from the original Rosicrucian order. He reasoned, and was encouraged in this belief by the Order of the Golden Dawn's fictional history, that there was a real Rosicrucian order in existence on the continent which could give him teaching and the necessary legitimacy. This would require him to travel to Europe to find them.

The Golden Dawn's fictional history said that Wynn Westcott was given legitimacy by a Rosicrucian person called "Sprengel." The name Sprengel was written in the Golden Dawn cipher manuscripts, along with a contact address, but at no point was Sprengel identified as a woman, nor was her connection with the cipher documents revealed. Early Golden Dawn researcher Ellic Howe claimed that Westcott never contacted Sprengel and forged letters of legitimacy between the two of them.

If Westcott had done that, he was hardly going to confess to Felkin. But he was interested as the Doctor moved around Europe looking for Sprengel. After all, if he did find Sprengel it could cause some problems if "she" never mentioned giving him the rights to set up the Golden Dawn. Felkin believed that Sprengel and her order still existed deep under cover in Germany and probably could be found along with the tomb of Christian Rosencreutz.

In 1904 he received a letter from a Dr. Studtmann, who was a medical doctor from Hanover. Studtmann was looking for a cure that Felkin had invented for cancer which was based around taking clover tea-tablets. The patient then wrote to Felkin about her illness and signed the name Anna Sprengel. If you believe Howe, Felkin immediately assumed that Sprengel was the person who gave permission for Westcott and Mathers to start the Golden Dawn. The letter Felkin wrote back to her does not suggest that. In addition to questions about the cancer, Felkin asks if she has relatives in Ulm, Heidelberg or Nuremberg, which were places associated with the Sprengel myth. "It is very odd, but I once knew a Fräulein Anna

Sprengel who, I believe, must have died in 1894. Is it possible that this was a relative of yours?" he wrote.

It is not clear where Felkin had received "Anna" as the first name of the founder of his tradition. It is not written in any Golden Dawn paperwork and might have been channelled information. The new Anna Sprengel said that her namesake was not a member of her family. When Felkin tried to arrange to meet her, she replied in 1904 that she was out of town. She will appear later in the story.

In search of the Secret Chiefs, Felkin and Harriet travelled to Europe in 1906, 1910 and 1914. Those who like to mock Felkin's efforts, such as King and Howe, seem to think it amusing that someone could go looking for a myth and expect to find it. However, Felkin and his agent Meakin, who acted as a researcher and a scout, did a lot better than is realised. Writing in 1914, Felkin said that the reason he made his journeys was to establish the truth about the Golden Dawn Order. His plan was to either find a connection or drop his link with the Golden Dawn tradition. This seems unlikely. You do not usually spend a fortune looking for something you suspect might not be there. It is more possible that Felkin suspected something was true and was trying to prove it by finding a Third Order.

In 1906, he met a professor, his daughter and another man near Hanover who he was convinced were Rosicrucians. They did not tell him so of course, but told him that although he was a doctor he was not a Mason, nor did he belong to any occult association that they were familiar with, so they could not talk to him. Felkin rushed back to Edinburgh and was initiated into the Mary's Chapel Lodge of Freemasonry. Felkin was not particularly enthused by masonry, but he reasoned that if becoming a Freemason meant the Rosicrucians would talk to him, it was worth it. Once he had become a Master Mason, Westcott arranged for him to join the Societas Rosicruciana in Anglia (Rosicrucian Society of England) which was being run by Westcott.

In 1909, the Felkins became closer to Neville Gauntlett "Tudor" Meakin (1876-1912). Meakin is an extraordinary Golden Dawn character who would have become incredibly important if his life had not been cut short by illness. Born in Ambleside in 1881, Meakin's father, Henry Meyers Meakin, did not appear to be around. He was raised by his mother, Roberta Meakin, in the St. George's Cottage Home Orphanage in Ocle Pritchard, where she was the manager. He attended Fettes College in Edinburgh.

According to Patrick Benham (1993) in his book *The Avalonians*,[23] when he was 21, Meakin's stepfather, a Rev. Meakin, told him that his real name was Tudor and gave him some family papers, which showed he was Grand Master of the Order of the Table Round.

Meakin told Felkin that the order had been in existence since before the time of King Arthur and had passed through generations of the Tudor family. There was a break of three hundred years until the order was revived by Meakin's grandfather. The name 'Tudor' does not appear on any record and there is no proof that Meakin's grandfather, John Alexander Deverill Meakin (1805-1873) revived anything. Normally I would have suspected that it was a cover story from Meakin, who was capable of writing the rituals himself, but the dedication Meakin showed to preserving this order, even as he was dying, indicated that he believed it.

Neville was a creative writer who co-authored with Hugh Tempest Sheringham two books; one entitled *The Court of Sacharissa*,[24] which was published by Heineman in 1904, and *The Enemy's Camp*.[25] He also wrote an article called The Dream which was published in the *Occult Review*. He wrote *The Assassins – a Romance of the Crusades* under the name Neville Myers Meakin.

Meakin was a talented writer of rituals and is credited with having written the portal grade ritual after the rebels had removed Mathers. It is also possible he also wrote some of the minor tweaks to the o=o rendering them more poetic and less masonic, although there have been several claimants for this, including W.B. Yeats.

Meakin was suffering from tuberculosis and did not feel he had long to live. He met with the Glastonbury mystic Wellesley Tudor Pole (1884-1968). Meakin feared he would die without an heir and wanted a replacement for the Grand Mastership of the Order of the Table Round. Tudor Pole claimed Welsh royal blood, but had made a name for himself with his writings about the grail legends. Meakin visited the Oratory in Glastonbury in September 1910 and initiated Pole into the Order of the Table Round. In the meantime, he became interested in the Bahá'í movement and was starting to channel third order material from the secret chiefs. (Waite notes on

---

23 Benham, Patrick. *The Avalonians*. Glastonbury: Gothic Image, 2006. Print.
24 Sheringham, H. T, and Neville Meakin. *The Court Of Sacharissa*. New York: Macmillan, 1904. Print.
25 Sheringham, H. T, and Neville Meakin. *The Enemy's Camp*. London: Macmillan, 1906. Print.

March 16, 1911 that there was some cabbalistic information, but it could equally have been the outline of the SM 6=5 and 7=4 rituals.)

Meakin was in Cairo with the aim of finalising the visit of Abdu'l Baha. Baha was the head of the eldest son of Bahá'u'lláh, the founder of the Bahá'í faith. Abdu'l Baha was impressed with Meakin according to people present during these meetings. Meakin and Felkin might have considered Abdu'l Baha one of their secret chiefs. In her research[26] on Felkin and the Bahá'í faith Lil Osborn suggests that Bahá'í teachings, with their idea that they could be used to unify Eastern and Western spiritual systems, would have appealed to Felkin and Meakin.

In September 1911 Felkin met Abdu'l Baha in London and gave him two rings. It is not clear what the two talked about, but a letter exists written to Felkin's student Maurice Chambers from Abdu'l Baha when Chambers was in Egypt at the end of the First World War waiting to go home. In this letter, Abdu'l Baha remarks on Maurice's "teacher," mentioning that he had met him, "the honoured Felkin," in London. However, Meakin was also in Egypt as part of his pilgrimage to follow in the footsteps of Christian Rosencreutz. Shortly before he was due to initiate Felkin into the Order of the Table Round, he died on the 4th October 1912.

This caused a problem for both Pole and Felkin, who wanted to continue the Order of the Table Round. Pole had the best claim, as he was the only Tudor involved in the story. Felkin would later say that Meakin had given him the Grand Master job on his deathbed after clearing it with the surviving members of the family. However, that did not tally with what actually happened next. Felkin consulted Arthur Edward Waite (1857-1942) about the matter of the Grand Mastership of the Order of the Table Round and who should be running it. Waite had a copy of the rituals. If they ever had been an ancient order they had been recently reworked by a modern hand, most likely Meakin. The system had a structure similar to the Golden Dawn. It had three grades, with the Earth grade split into four subgrades, much like the Golden Dawn. It did not use any Golden Dawn techniques or anything that could have been associated with that system.

In the end, Felkin set up the Order of the Table Round as a side order of the Stella Matutina in New Zealand and just hoped that Pole

---

26 The *Extraordinary Life and Work of Robert Felkin – Baha'i Mage*. N.p., n.d. Web. 22 Mar. 2014 (http://bahai-library.com/osborn_life_robert_felkin)

would not find out about it. If Pole ever did, he did nothing about it and swiftly forgot about the Order.

Felkin returned to Europe in 1910 as part of a plan to introduce Westcott to the Anna Sprengel he had corresponded with before. Although the meeting did not take place, Westcott was clearly ready to attend – with good reason. Felkin had told him that she was the original founder's niece. Given the existing letters between them, it is hard to see how he reached this conclusion – there are clearly missing letters. Westcott believed the meetings would end any future speculation about Sprengel and in 1912 asked Felkin to write confirming that Sprengel had existed and he had authority to form the Golden Dawn.

This letter, which Westcott asked for and Felkin wrote, is an interesting piece of psychological history. Westcott, who had founded the order, required Felkin to prove he had the right to do so. The affidavit said that Felkin had been talking to Anna Sprengel's family; one of whom had been a patient of his. Felkin said the woman had been a patient once in 1904 and once in July 1910. Felkin was counting each time Anna Sprengel had written to him as "a medical consultation."

"Personal interviews with members of the Rosicrucian order on the continent in 1910 and 1912 had proved that Dr William Wynn Westcott was in correspondence with Anna Sprengel and had permission from her to form a society of the said G.D.," Felkin wrote.

Those 1910 and 1912 interviews were apparently with Dr Rudolf Joseph Lorenz Steiner (25 February 1861-30 March 1925). During his 1910 visit, Felkin was staying with Dr Marcus at Bad Pyrmont, near Hanover. As part of his Rosicrucian hunt, Felkin wanted to meet Dr. Hubbe-Schleiden, who had founded the German Theosophical Society. Hubbe-Schleiden published *Die Sphinx* which was the first significant occult publication in Germany. It turned out to be impossible to arrange a meeting with Hubbe-Schleiden, but the writer helpfully arranged for Felkin to meet Steiner.

Much has been made of the influence of Steiner's anthroposophy on Whare Ra. However, at the time that Felkin was meeting him, Steiner was the Secretary General of the German Theosophical Society and more interested in esoteric masonry and Rosicrucianism. Steiner and his followers have done an excellent job at airbrushing this part of his life from his history. It was not the anthroposophy founder that Felkin found but the head of the *Memphis and Misraim* rite. The Grand Master of the order for Germany and Austria was Theodore Ruess, a sex magician who, along with Carl Kellner, founded the *Ordo Templi Orientis* (O.T.O.), which in 1910 had just admitted one Aleister Crowley as its Great British head.

Although Steiner was still experimenting with ideas which would form the backbone of anthroposophy these were not shown to Felkin. Felkin could not stay in Berlin and sent Meakin to learn all he could from Steiner. Meakin went first to Berlin and seems to have thought it necessary to carry out a pilgrimage to all the places mentioned in the legend of Christian Rosencreutz. The Arab warned Felkin that Meakin was in trouble:

> "[Meakin] is consuming his forces by misdirected energies; his time has not yet come, but he is attracting the destructive forces instead of repelling them, and unless he ceases to do this he will die before his time, thereby missing the fulfilment of his destiny and vocation. Forcibly ejecting the demon of melancholy which is attracting the outward form of death… he must substitute a centre of Light in its place, and then he will attract the forces of life and get well."

It appeared that Meakin did not get the message and died.

Felkin went and visited Steiner himself in July 1912 and visited five "Rosicrucian temples" in different parts of the continent and was initiated into grades equivalent to the 8=3. He noted that the manuscripts used had to be memorised, so they had no copies of the rituals. Steiner apparently wanted Felkin to be the head of the Rosicrucian order in Great Britain. However, we only have Felkin's word for this.

Waite interviewed Steiner during a visit to England in 1912. Steiner confirmed that Felkin had "witnessed certain things" of a ceremonial kind. Waite inferred that Steiner was not going to commit to Felkin. In any event, Waite thought that Steiner was not as well connected to German Rosicrucians as Felkin thought.

When reading Felkin's letters to Westcott about his continental searches for Sprengel and the Secret Chiefs, it is impossible to tell if he is lying or has met the people he claimed. For example, Felkin claimed to have spent a lot of time and money in Paris trying to track down Mathers' Secret Chief Fr L.e.T.

Felkin claimed that L.e.T. was a Dr. Thiessen, who was apparently dead by 1909, and "well known in Martinism circles in Paris". Felkin claimed that Thiessen had been writing to Mathers, often through an intermediary. Felkin claimed that Thiessen acted in a similar manner to Sprengel in providing the 5=6 teachings and rituals to Mathers.

The Golden Dawn researcher Robert Gilbert said that Thiessen was "so well known" that he has not left a trace in the historic records and is unlikely to have existed. Mathers failed to mention him to anyone either, which is strange given that when he met Madam Horos and thought she was a real secret chief, he told everyone. A real secret chief with a proper address would have been proof to all doubters that Mathers had been well connected. If Thiessen had existed, it would have been difficult for Mathers not to have played that trump card.

Many see Thiessen as an attempt by Felkin to look for physical masters that were never there, and proof of how gullible he may have been. However, there is another possible scenario. The Thiessen story could have been part of a power play after the rebellion. Felkin claimed to have a letter written around 1900 using the Golden Dawn cypher, in which Thiessen said that he was withdrawing support from Mathers. This date coincided with Mathers' expulsion from the Golden Dawn and would mean that Samuel was no longer blessed by the Secret Chiefs.

Felkin was being clever and creating Secret Chiefs who were not there. He was following Westcott's technique and creating a lie. The only thing that went wrong with Felkin's lie and revealed his power play was that Westcott, from his dealings with Mathers, knew that Fr L.e.T was another name for the Archangel Raphael. When he saw the letter, written in cypher, Westcott was puzzled by the message. However, he kept it in case it ever became useful in his fight against Mathers. When he found a copy of the letter amongst Westcott's papers Howe thought it was a bad forgery from Crowley.[27]

The next part of the story sees Felkin and his wife taking a significant journey to the other side of the world.

---

27   p.236 Howe, E. (1985). *The Magicians of the Golden Dawn*. Great Britain: Routledge & Kegan Paul.

⟨ II ⟩ FELKIN & HAVELOCK NORTH WORK

On the east coast of the North Island of New Zealand is the small village of Havelock North. The village started as a disappointment. It was supposed to be a small city, but when the Wellington-Napier rail line went through the area in 1874 it bypassed Havelock North, which saw its population head to Hastings.

The town is dominated by TeMata Peak, which is a magical centre. Māori legend is that the Peak was the body of a giant, TeMata, from the Waimarama sea tribes. TeMata was bewitched into falling in love with Hinerakau, the daughter of a Pakipaki chief. The Pakipaki people demanded that Hinerakau make TeMata prove his devotion by accomplishing impossible tasks. His last task was to bite through the hills between the coast and the plains, so that people could come and go with greater ease. Eating that much Earth killed him.

The upper parts of the Peak in particular have a strong cultural importance to Māori. There is evidence of past settlement, including pā sites and other earthworks. The Karaka groves in the upper Te Hau Valley area and Moa bones found on the slopes suggest intensive Māori settlement.

In the Whare Ra order, there was a legend that TeMata Peak housed a Hogwarts for Tohunga or Māori magic leaders. This particular school taught white magic, while a rival school, close to what is now Cape Kidnappers, taught black magic. All Tohunga had to learn how to curse people and perform battle magic, the legends say, but only the good ones learnt to use white magic – which was all about healing.

In 1907 a Canadian, Reginald Gardiner, who had immigrated to New Zealand, settled in Havelock North. Gardiner was born in Australia but spent most of his childhood in England. He moved to New Zealand with his stepmother, and the family lived at Taradale. Gardiner had money too. As a youth, he joined the staff of the then newly formed New Zealand agricultural firm of Williams and Kettle. Later he worked as a partner of Frank Williams on a sheep station at Waipare, on the East Coast. Gardiner returned to England, where he met his future wife, a daughter of J.G. Scott who was the head of a Canadian railway company. They moved to Canada, and Gardiner was secretary to his father-in-law. Then he established a commission import business in Hastings and made his home in Havelock North.

In 1908, a meeting of more than 100 people was held to discuss cultural affairs in Frimley, with Reginald Gardiner as one of the main speakers. To give some indication of the interest, the entire population of Havelock North was fewer than 500 people; even allowing for interest from people outside the area, it was a good turnout.

This sparked the "Havelock Work," which held its first meetings in 1908. The Havelock Work was organised to remind European New Zealanders of their mostly British past and culture. This project was tiny and attended by only half a dozen to a dozen regulars and consisted mostly of readings from Shakespeare and Dickens in a church schoolroom. From this the group developed social afternoons and Wednesday night talent shows, then carving and drama classes, flower and fruit shows and arts and crafts exhibitions. Gardiner was responsible for the first New Zealand Morris dancing troupe, which was something of a blight in an otherwise remarkably karma free life.

In 1911 an Old English Village Fête was organised, opening with a procession of over 100 men, women and children in medieval costume and carrying banners. King Arthur and his court presided over Morris and folk dances, tourneys and plays, and there were stalls selling refreshments and crafts. In 1912 there was an elaborate re-enactment of a Shakespearean pageant, opening with a grand procession including someone dressing as Queen Elizabeth I. Entertainments included teas and games, sixteenth century songs and dances, music by the Hastings Town Band and other concerts, a production of *Much Ado about Nothing*, scenes from *Twelfth Night* and *The Merchant of Venice*. That weekend a ball was held in Shakespearean costume.

A magazine called *The Forerunner* was produced, with its first issue in 1909. It contained spiritual and Theosophical articles. In 1910, Gardiner took a leading part in the formation of the company that established the *Hawkes Bay Tribune* newspaper. He became the company's first chairman of directors and remained in the job for 48 years. He was around to see it merge with the *Hawkes Bay Herald* as the *Hawkes Bay Herald Tribune*. Gardiner was behind the trust that established Woodford House in Havelock North, which became one of New Zealand's leading educational institutions. He also helped establish Royston Hospital.

Most of the Havelock Work was what these days would be called "community identity." Its aim was to civilise the area by arranging meetings and village events. It focused on the arts and spirituality movement. Gardiner and his wife Ruth, and their friend Harold Large, believed that Eastern methods of spiritual training such as Theosophy were unsuitable for Westerners. However, they also felt that the church had lost the esoteric teachings of Jesus and his disciples. The feeling, which was common at the time, was that Jesus' teachings were to be found in Western esoteric occultism.

The three of them held daily meditations together, and were joined by Miss M.M. McLean and Reginald's sister, Miss Rose Gardiner. This formed an inner circle and the meditation group grew and began to incorporate simple ritual, calling itself the Society of the Southern Cross.

In 1910 the Mirfield Fathers sent a mission to New Zealand, preaching and conducting retreats. Miss McLean, who had met Father Fitzgerald in Britain, arranged for him to meet members of the Havelock prayer group, and he agreed to direct their spiritual work from Britain. Father Fitzgerald provided the group with an esoteric approach to Christianity, but they reached a point where he felt they needed personal instruction. He recommended Felkin for the task and within a week, the group cabled a £300 ticket for Felkin, Harriet and Ethelwyn to visit New Zealand for three months.

The Felkins' Arab contact was enthusiastic, and according to Stoddard, said that a move to New Zealand would give the Golden Dawn system a chance which it had not had for nearly a thousand years – a clear space in which to work.

"It will leave us free to form fresh symbols which have been unprejudiced by any previous tradition. It is most important that everything should be new, clean, and fresh; as far as possible we must try to discard recent errors and get the more accurate symbolism," the Arab said.

Felkin felt that the new venture was more important than his London operation. He wrote to Stoddard:

"[The Arab] is greatly impressed with the importance of virgin soil, no occult order has been there before, and the Theosophists only breaking the soil," he said.

His old missionary enthusiasm returned.

During this first visit to New Zealand in 1912, Felkin established the *Smaragdum Thallasses* temple of the Stella Matutina. The New Zealand order became known by the Māori name of Whare Ra or "the House of the Sun", which was the name of the Temple building. Over three months, Felkin initiated 12 people into the 5=6 grade of the Order. It is unclear if they used a vault, as it was unlikely that one could be built that quickly. Given that Felkin and his entourage were the only people who were allowed to see the vault before the ritual, it would mean that they would have to have painted one beforehand and brought it with them. It is not impossible, as the early vaults of the Golden Dawn were painted onto canvas and could be rolled up, stored or carried.

It is clear that the New Zealanders did everything they could to ensure that Felkin was encouraged to stay. They commissioned the architect James Walter Chapman-Taylor (24 June 1878-25 October 1958) to design a purpose-built temple, complete with magical vault, and two extra rooms on either side of the Mars and Jupiter walls so that further grades could be added to the Golden Dawn structure. These rooms were hidden behind the dais of the main hall behind concealed doors and thick brown curtains. No-one other than those of the correct grade knew they were there.

Judy Siers in her *The Life and Times of James Walter Chapman-Taylor*[28] said that the plans allowed for a 900 square metre building with more than half of that dedicated to temple space. The reinforced concrete construction was a new idea at a time when there was still strong resistance to any building material other than timber in earthquake-prone New Zealand.

'Whare Ra' was to be a very different building from a domestic home and the advantages of fire resistance, low maintenance, permanence and durability of concrete appealed, Siers wrote. "The reinforced walls were six inches thick and were poured by sections at a time into boxing of around a metre in height."

Chapman-Taylor was one of New Zealand's most important architects, who brought the influence of the Arts and Crafts Movement to New Zealand houses. However, it is telling that the rooms for the second order grades had already been literally cemented into the foundations of Whare Ra, before anyone believed that the 6=5 and 7=4 rituals had been written.

Felkin initiated enough members into the order during their stay. A trust had been set up to manage the monetary affairs of the order, and the building commissioned and sufficiently advanced. A Whare Ra legend, recounted to Tony Fuller, said that the village was well aware what was going on, because Felkin made the mistake of trying to get the local builders to swear an oath to keep the creation of the building secret. The concept of taking great lengths to keep it secret in a small rural New Zealand village was the equivalent of putting

---

28 Siers, Judy. *The Life and Times of James Walter Chapman-Taylor*. Napier, N.Z.: Millwood Heritage Productions, 2007. Print.

the news on the front page of the local paper – in fact at that point the "bush telegraph" would have been heard by more people.

Before Felkin left New Zealand to return to England, a Warrant was issued establishing the Smaragdum Thallasses Temple No. 49 of the Order of the Stella Matutina. The understanding was that Felkin would return.

There was a change in Felkin after that trip. His ideas about the way occult orders should work had been transformed, and the old model of simply studying material and doing a ritual every month was dismissed in favour of a more practical magical way of life.

"That trip to New Zealand taught me more clearly than any other experience the necessity for action in cooperation with study. It puts teaching into dramatic form and welds together those who work together. There is a great deal more in it than that of course, but these two aspects were strongly impressed on me when I watched a handful of people taking part in what to them was an entirely strange form of work. There is a type of mind in which dramatic action is not merely uncongenial, but definitely repellent. But for those that can accept it, here is a beauty and impressiveness which they can find nowhere else," he wrote.

What he was doing in New Zealand would have been impossible outside of a specialised community like Havelock North – or an actual commune. But this explains why when he returned to the UK he was less interested in what was happening to his Order there.

But it also did not mean his distrust of Mathers had lessened. A row had been brewing between Brodie-Innes and Felkin for some time. Brodie-Innes admitted Samuel and Moina Mathers into the Cromlech temple which resulted in Felkin resigning the moment he heard about it. On his return to the UK, Felkin broke completely with Brodie-Innes who defected his Stella Matutina temple entirely over to Mathers' AO.[29]

To see off any chance of his order following Brodie-Innes, Felkin asserted his authority over the Stella Matutina by saying that Steiner was a secret chief and had awarded him an 8=3. This made him

---

[29] Mathers and Cromlech benefited considerably from the defection. Both groups appear to have swapped papers, and Tony Fuller has several Cromlech papers with AO stickers on them. Brodie-Innes appeared to have been attempting to make Cromlech a Second Order for the AO. Cromlech had many of the names of the AO members – notably Dion Fortune's teacher Maiya Tranchell-Hayes. Tony Fuller did find some indications that Fortune was a member later in her life, which might have resulted in her interest in Polarity.

senior to both Mathers and Brodie-Innes. It was a moot point if this was necessary. It is not recorded if anyone defected from the Stella Matutina, but Felkin played the card he was given during his Steiner visits and that seemed to be enough for his followers.

Felkin must have suspected that if he went to New Zealand again there was a good chance he would not come back. That meant that he had to shore up as much as he could of his European Rosicrucian contacts while he had the chance. In 1914, the Felkins ignored the political landscape of Europe and again tried to meet up with Rosicrucian contacts in Germany.

According to Stoddard, their Arab contact let them down badly. The Secret Chiefs knew that war was coming, but told Felkin it would not be until a year later. His Arab teacher said to Dr. Felkin:

> "Go on with Steiner, which is not the ultimate end of search, and we will come in contact with many serious students who will lead us to the real Master of the Order, who will be so overpoweringly impressive as to leave no room for doubt."

This time he was told by the German adepts that they were preparing for the reappearance of Christian Rosencreutz in either 1926, or 1933, or 1935. With historical hindsight, nothing could have been further from the truth. In 1926, Hitler had overcome any remaining rivals within the Nazi Party and assumed the title of supreme leader. In 1933, he was appointed Chancellor of Germany and in 1935 he announced German rearmament in violation of the Versailles Treaty. They were not good years for occultists, or Europe. Felkin was told that when CRC returned, 12 people would be selected from the different temples to be his disciples.

On this trip, the German Rosicrucians were little more forthcoming. The Felkins were told to buy a train ticket to a certain place on a certain day and they would be taken to the "Old Vault," where they would meet with various secret chiefs. The Old Vault would, of course, be the actual place where Christian Rosencreutz was buried.

Felkin clearly believed what he was told. He bought the ticket and stayed in Germany even as war was declared, trying to make this vital meeting. We will never know who Felkin found, or if this "Old Vault" or its secret chiefs were valid or not. Later Felkin told Waite that he could have taken him there, which could indicate that it was either a physical or an astral experience.

A while ago, I was contacted by a German Golden Dawn person who had been told a similar story by some very sincere German Rosicrucians who offered to take him there. I never heard back from him, so maybe he found it and was sworn to secrecy, or it was all a myth that he wanted to forget.

Fortunately Felkin's masonic contacts paid off. They managed to sneak him back to the UK, via Amsterdam. Felkin later spread an unlikely rumour that he had stayed in Germany to give the British some important intelligence about German troop movements. He may have done so, but that was certainly not the reason he remained.

Before he left Germany, Felkin had obtained from Steiner a ritual called the Link and some spiritual exercises called the Processes. The Processes were breathing and visualisation exercises designed to speed up psychic development. They were similar to the Middle Pillar used by Israel Regardie, or the Armour of Light[30] which was used by the later Society of the Inner Light. It is unclear how effective they were. They were half-heartedly incorporated into the Stella Matutina curriculum work and then more or less abandoned. Steiner himself also forgot them. The Whare Ra people I have spoken to were not impressed with the Processes or the results they gave. They also did not seem to have copies of any of them, and could only remember vague descriptions.

We will be looking at the Link in more detail later.

When she was in her most paranoid state five years later, the chief of the London Temple of the Stella Matutina, Christina Stoddard, claimed that:

> "They brought back notes of these ceremonies 6=5 to 8=3, and elaborated them, using for this purpose the Egyptian *Book of the Dead*,[31] some extracts from Mabel Collins'[32] writings, also the "Hymn of Hermes" and a mantra a compelling force – given to them by the Arab of "The Temple in the Desert," and these became the Higher Grades of the RR et AC! These, as they advanced in grade, are more and more given on the astral plane by the hidden chiefs, while the adept is in a trance or semi-trance condition, brought on by the preparation and opening ceremony, or by these hidden chiefs themselves."

---

30   Pixley, O. (1969). *The Armour of Light*. Cheltenham, England: Helios Book Service.
31   Budge, E. and Budge, E. (n.d.). *The Book of the Dead*.
32   Mabel Collins (9 September 1851-31 March 1927) was a theosophist and author of over 46 occult novels and theosophical books.

When we see the rituals later in this book, you can see what she means, but actually, it is not as bad as she makes out. Tony Fuller suspects that elements of these rituals might also have been inspired by Waite's 6=5[33] and also Felkin's membership of Florence Farr's Egyptian Order (G.O.T.S.). In Florence Farr's short-lived order we find the coloured cords, the coloured stars of certain rays, and Fomalhaut, Antares etc. similar to the 7=4. Having seen some of the evidence that Fuller has suggested it is somewhat compelling, and would suggest that Steiner was only a partial influence on the later rituals and Farr and Waite were a little more important.

Stoddard also said that the contact was fleshing out the traditional Golden Dawn teachings. For example in 1915 he said the following:

> "Before any ceremony, either in temple or private, fire must be banished and earth invoked and the [lesser] invoking ritual of Saturn performed to bring peace and calmness."[34]

If you believe Francis King's *Ritual Magic in England* (King, 1970), Felkin returned to his Christian mystical roots in January 1915 and started the Guild of St Raphael under the orders of his Arab teacher on January 9. It was to be called the Healers or Therapeuts, and Rev. J.C. Fitzgerald was to be made the head of it. It was expected that those who wished to follow that training should be taken from all the different Temples and keep in touch with one another.

There is little evidence to suggest that Felkin was involved with the order, although he might have been a founder member. According to the Guild's own newsletter the driving personalities behind the foundation of the Guild was Caroline Biggs, who was recorded as Secretary of the newly formed Guild, with the Reverend Canon R. P. Roseveare, of St Paul's Deptford, recorded as its first Warden. To be fair to King, those who cite this version of the creation of the Order claim that it was proved by minutes of the founding of the meeting

---

33 This ritual can be found in Regardie, I. (1984). *The Complete Golden Dawn System of Magic.* Phoenix, Ariz., U.S.A.: Falcon Press.
34 To many modern Golden Dawn people this would not make any sense, particularly those who have been trained always to start their rituals with the Lesser Banishing Ritual of the Pentagram. In fact, banishing fire would remove all existing energy from the room; the invoking earth is similar to the Lesser invoking pentagram for adepts and the invoking Saturn would create a feeling of calm. It is all a bit complex, and would probably be nicely covered by a lesser invoking ritual of the pentagram followed by a lesser banishing ritual of the Hexagram.

which were published in the Guild's Newsletter *Chrism*, in spring of 2002.[35] However, this issue of the magazine has no mention of any early meetings.[36]

At the end of 1915, Felkin gave a lecture where he proposed a different structure to the order given by Mathers. Instead of three orders, Felkin claimed there were six. The 6=5 and 7=4 were the third order, the 8=3 was the fourth, the 9=2 the fifth and the 10=1 was the sixth. Beyond the 9=2 were the Secret Chiefs who Felkin, like Mathers, believed existed in physical bodies. In Felkin's case that was easier to believe, because he thought he had met them.

He came up with quite an elaborate scheme of governance for the Stella Matutina, including a "Veiled Tribunal", and behind the whole structure was a mysterious much higher person called the 'Epopt'. The Epopt, whose name comes from the Highest Grade of the Eleusinian Mysteries, was remote and only to be consulted in dire emergency. Tony Fuller discovered that the person who filled the role was none other than Wynn Westcott.

In 1916 Felkin founded new temples in England. The first was the Hermes Temple at Bristol, which was headed by Miss C.E. Hughes. The second, The Merlin Temple, was in London, which was to be formed by Steiner's followers and 50 or 60 refugees from Waite's temple. Felkin apparently did not want them to mix with the others at his London Amoun temple because they had worked on different lines.

Merlin was never properly established, but did not completely die out. It was resurrected by John Brodie-Innes' successor John Carnegie Dickson and his wife after the AO shut down in 1939. Its approach was a lot closer to that of Dion Fortune's own Fraternity of the Inner Light, and it attracted star pupils from that school including Christine Hartley[37] who was a member between 1940 and 1942. However, its impact was insignificant and it swiftly faded into obscurity.

The third temple was restricted to members of the Societas Rosicruciana in Anglia and was known as the Secret College. It was active in 1921 but did not last long.

---

35   Wikipedia, (2015). *Guild of St Raphael*. [online] Available at: http://en.wikipedia.org/wiki/Guild_of_St_Raphael [Accessed 22 Mar. 2015].
36   Anon, (2015). [online] Available at: http://www.guild-of-st-raphael.org.uk/Publications/Chrism/2006-May.pdf [Accessed 22 Mar. 2015].
37   Richardson, A. and Hughes, G. (1989). *Ancient magicks for a new age*. St. Paul, Minn.: Llewellyn Publications.

There was some evidence that Felkin's health was failing and it was felt that moving to New Zealand would help. He was suffering from recurrent bouts of malaria, a scar from his African adventures. By now the New Zealand operation was ready for him to take over. In 1916, Felkin was offered life tenancy of "Whare Ra" and he and his family returned to New Zealand for good.

Felkin declared that the Mother Temple of the Stella Matutina was now in New Zealand. He left his daughter behind to liaise with Steiner and to run the English temples. Returning permanently to New Zealand would have been a culture shock to the Felkin family. Hawkes Bay was, and still is, a beautiful place, but it was incredibly isolated.

There are those who have suggested that Felkin had moved because he wanted to set up a global empire for the Golden Dawn. If that were the case, he picked the wrong place. Although communications were as good as anywhere else in the world, it was still a long ship journey, even to Australia.

New Zealand at that point in its history was also starting to find itself. WW1 was seen as a turning point where the nation fought for the British, but with a sense of national identity. Māori had been allowed to form their own battalion, despite concerns that they might use that training to rise up. (The last Māori uprising had been 50 years before.)

Mrs Felkin noticed that the capital city, Wellington, with its wooden buildings with corrugated iron roofs "made us feel at home immediately." Although the city "looked an odd ramshackle place to us, with its dingy houses, but the harbour and the circling hills were beautiful."

The railway journey to Hawkes Bay that followed seemed a joke. The train was painfully slow compared with English express trains, and cups of tea were bought to the Felkins constantly in unbreakable tea-cups.

"The stop for midday dinner while the whole trainload of passengers filed into a big barn of a dining room, bolted their dinner, drank scalding cups of tea, and filed solemnly back to the train, each one paying at a little ticket booth at the door as they passed," she wrote. "Later on, we became accustomed to this procedure, but the first time it struck us as comical. It also seemed to me a direct route to dyspepsia for we were only allowed 25 minutes to consume a three-course meal plus the inevitable tea. I should think New Zealand must use more tea per head of this small population than any other country in the world."

In her *A Wayfaring Man*, Havelock North is referred to as "Awatea" which in Māori means "bright pathway" but it is more likely a pun about the kiwi obsession with tea.

Mrs Felkin was surprised that people would just "drop in" and volunteer to all kinds of jobs for them. One man used to come and clean all the knives and boots, another attended to the oil lamps as there was neither gas nor electricity. People were continually calling with offerings of cakes and scones, or baskets of fruit and flowers.

According to Robert Ellwood in his *Islands of the Dawn*[38] book, Felkin was the first medical doctor resident in Havelock North, except for one or two temporary practitioners in the nineteenth century, and this gave him an immediate position of community prominence. This was confirmed after the influenza epidemic of 1918 (which ironically killed Samuel Mathers) passed the area by mid-December without anyone dying. The town board formally expressed its thanks to Felkin, who had headed a committee to combat the disease and had been completely successful. This was somewhat of a feat, as more than 8600 New Zealanders died of the illness. In Hastings 73 people died while Napier had 94 deaths.[39]

"Seeing him in this role leads one to appreciate that Felkin, clearly a man of many parts, was by no means always the unworldly being indicated by Golden Dawn historians," Ellwood wrote. He added that it was time to question occult historians who, generally writing from the London perspective and in total ignorance of the New Zealand phase of his career, portray Felkin as little more than a dreamer given to delusional visions and quixotic quests, as in his search for the true Rosicrucians in Germany.

"Whether this was ever entirely the case, or whether his character underwent a remarkable sea change with the 1916 move, is perhaps an open question. But there is no doubt that, after arriving in Havelock North as (for the first time in his personal Golden Dawn history) the occultist indisputably in charge, he came into his own and proved equal to a challenging task," Ellwood said.

---

38 Ellwood, Robert S. *Islands of the Dawn: The Story of Alternative Spirituality in New Zealand*. Honolulu: University of Hawaii, 1993. Print.
39 Nzhistory.net.nz, (2015). *North Island influenza death rates - The 1918 influenza pandemic | NZHistory, New Zealand history online*. [online] Available at: http://www.nzhistory.net.nz/culture/influenza-pandemic/north-island-death-rates#eastcape [Accessed 26 Mar. 2015].

It is my belief that the missionary who hacked his way through the African jungle was not a flake and was practical enough to cope with the occult scene in London, or any rougher aspect of New Zealand life.

Even with his daughter on site in the UK, Felkin was unable to stop the breakup of the Stella Matutina under the increasingly deranged Amoun chief Christina Stoddard. Stoddard became unhinged by one of her visions, which convinced her that the Stella Matutina was all part of a conspiracy lead by Black Rosicrucians.

She published her paranoid fears and ramblings in a book called *Light-Bearers of Darkness* under the pseudonym Inquire Within.[40] It sold quite well in 1930, appealing to those who see conspiracies in everything. In fact it was still in print in 2001 and is still quoted by those who like to see the Golden Dawn as being run by lizards. In its time, the book was part of the body of anti-Semitic Jewish conspiracy paranoia which was starting to grip Europe and would be used to cement Hitler's rise to power. Stoddard also capitalised on the fact that after WW1 the Germans were hated in Britain, so Felkin's German links were not going to win him many friends.

What is interesting about Stoddard is that she frequently gets her history of events right, even if her conclusions are incorrect. For example, she correctly explains why Westcott quit the Golden Dawn, which was not, as was claimed by Crowley, because magical documents with his name and address on them were left in a London cab. Instead, she implies that someone phoned Westcott's boss, something which appeared to be a plan to discredit Westcott by Edward Berridge.

Felkin tried his best to hold the temples together, often using astral projection techniques. This made matters worse. Stoddard was convinced that these astral connections were part of a web of evil which was designed to unite the world for a Jewish inspired communist plot. She undermined Felkin at every turn and eventually caused the London temple to collapse.

The Arab Master, speaking to Dr. Felkin of the dissensions in the London Temple, said in December 1918: "They must pass through a time of conflict before they enter the House of Peace." Unfortunately for the Arab and Dr Felkin they never got out of the time of conflict and never found any peaceful houses. Stoddard said that before

---

40   Inquire Within, (1930). *Light Bearers of Darkness*. London: Boswell Print. & Pub. Co.

Felkin had left England, and up to the closing of the Temple in 1919, the Order was rent by dissensions, jealousies, underground whisperings and open strife and rebellion. She said that the peace that the Arab wanted was the unconditional and willing surrender to the masters and their work, which she was determined they were not going to get.

It is not difficult to see what the problem was, and if Felkin had been interested enough in resolving it he would have just expelled Stoddard. Instead, he was patiently trying to take her through it.

"I think it would be better if, instead of fearing imaginary black Rosicrucians in Germany or elsewhere, you could consciously endeavour to co-operate with the true Rosicrucians who do undoubtedly exist and are seeking to guide Central European thought into the Light; you would then belong to the Great Work for the world," he wrote to her.

Looking at his letters, either Felkin did not understand how deranged she was, or wanted to help but did not know what to do. He was giving good advice, but he was assuming that the person he was dealing with was rational and was not taking each of his letters as proof of a reality which did not exist. It is a common problem for a teacher trying to help a student who has given loyal service but has just snapped under the burden of his or her own "stuff." You want to help, but a voice in your head warns you not to get too close or to turn your back on this person, as a knife will be put in your back.

Felkin kept nominal control over Bristol, but due to the distance the temple could do anything it liked, and did.

Felkin was clearly happy with what he had achieved. On September 19 1917 he wrote to Westcott:

> Care M.W. Supreme Magus,
> Yours of Aug.: 2nd: to hand 3 days ago. I am so sorry to hear your sad news & send you and Mrs. Wynn Westcott my very sincere sympathy.
> Thank you very much for sending on the Coloured Tablets, it is very good of you.
> I have had a long letter from Hammond saying he cannot get in touch with [Dr.] Dickson, otherwise he would start. Mrs Dickson writes me that her husband is frantically busy & now only gets home for Sundays sometimes. They have taken his best assistant too & given him an untrained man. I fear it must wait until after the War is over which I hope may be soon. The stars look like it anyway.

Great Conjunction Mars with Saturn October 1st – most evil for Germany, Austria & Kaiser. Also terrible earthquake in S & SE Europe. The grave affliction of 7th House = heaviest calamities to German Emperor. Jupiter in Gemini could aid Belgium. May it be so indeed. We have also had some very strange Communications from the Spiritual plane indicating the same kind of thing. I wish I could tell you of all we have got but it is too long to write.

Thanks for the papers promised – C. Jones says he is sending some not to hand as yet. You will have heard from my letters to you & C. Jones that some of the Australian Fratres are not too pleased with my appointment. They say they have no letter from you & that you promised to appoint who Drew wished. I hope soon to start a Branch in Hastings *[Felkin is referring to the SRIA]* but am waiting for Bingham & Andrews to come from Ch.Ch *[Christchurch]*: they are overdue.

YOU ARE NOT GETTING OLD. Cheer up please. My Companions join me in all good wishes.

With very kind regards

Robert Felkin

P.S. My OTR is going strong – 18 Pages already including a Bishop. SM: 20 Inner *[members]* & 34 Outer & 10 waiting to join. Not bad is it? House and Temple cost 2,500 pounds. Land three and a half acres 1350 pounds. Furniture for 364 pounds."[41]

One thing that did happen at that time was that Felkin lost his contact with the Arab. In September 1918 he was told that his work with the Arab was finished and neither he nor the London temple were to call him. A change of contact usually happens when there is a momentous event in the lives of a group, or that its work becomes more important. Some groups have more than one contact, but the Arab had been with Felkin for some time and was seen as being instrumental in getting the group to New Zealand.

What had changed was that the Felkins were no longer interested in Europe and were instead focused on providing serious training within the Golden Dawn system. Felkin mentioned to Stoddard he felt strange. Having seen such a change of contacts take place, I know what he meant. What is felt to be certain turns out to be fluid, and

---

[41] Thanks to Tony Fuller for this important letter, which I have included verbatim because it reveals much about the relationship between the two. It addresses Westcott as the Supreme Magus of the SRIA.

this feels confusing. Your normal astral haunts for information no longer provide teaching and you wake up in the morning exhausted because you have spent all night looking. Felkin said that around the Equinox he had some difficulty keeping a dark entity out of the temple. Magically this is also another side effect of a change of contact, a dweller on the threshold as a group crosses over into new ground.

Neville Meakin's Order of the Table Round had been established as a men-only side order to Whare Ra. To be a member you had to be 5=6 in Whare Ra, as it was designed to provide the community with a magical service. It did not remain a male-only ritual for long. Harriet Felkin was not having any of that. She insisted that a part be written for her so that she could take part in the meetings. Felkin obliged and she was the only female member at least until the 1960s.

By comparison to the main order, OTR membership was as tiny as it was elite – presumably because of the high grade required to join. It was also possibly an attempt to develop a third or higher level order for the Golden Dawn structure. Nothing ever came of it, but Felkin seems to have had a soft spot for the group and was particularly proud of his title of Grand-Master. Arthurian myth was an influence on Felkin and he tinkered with the Tarot card symbolism of the Golden Dawn to include some Arthurian symbolism. OTR was more heavily Christian than the religiously ambiguous Golden Dawn.

Until his death ten years later, Felkin worked hard in New Zealand to create a magical order that would last. Whare Ra may have been secret, but it managed to attract some of New Zealand's most important people. In modern times, they would find questions being asked about their membership by the sort of shady tabloids I used to work for.

It was not surprising; Whare Ra was the sort of occult school that many people dream of belonging to. Not only was there an impressive temple but the level of training was exceptional. Students were drilled in magical techniques and above all, ritual. Students with potential were spotted, usually by Mrs Felkin, and placed under the care of a senior magician who would train them in specifics.

During the day, Felkin developed his medical practice and a considerable reputation as a healer. In his obituary, the local paper noted that people travelled from Australia to receive his cures. During the week, there were regular outer order classes where the basics were drilled into the student. The weekend was reserved for second order teaching. Once a month there was meeting of the Order of the Table Round.

Unlike a modern Golden Dawn order where officers change positions, normally at Equinox, a Whare Ra officer was usually an adept who took the job for many years. Jack Taylor was a senior hierophant in the 1950s and early 1960s. Frank Salt and John von Dadelszen also took the role. Women held this important role too, including Taylor's wife Catherine[42] and Viv Thompson.

An officer came to understand their role particularly well. They would have an assistant who would stand in for them if they could not make it. Assistants had to be instructed so that they were not a weak link for the rite.

The rituals were only the starting point for a Whare Ra student. After someone was initiated, he or she would be informally spoken to by an adept, who would teach them the oral traditions and introduce them to their theories. This lead to an interesting development of the magical side of the order, with different adepts seeing the same ritual from different viewpoints.

Golden Dawn expert Pat Zalewski found some elderly people who knew Felkin, who said that he was a perfectionist who would not let the slightest thing go wrong. He considered that ritual had to be done perfectly and if an accident happened, it would be a sign that something would go wrong with the candidate's life or health.

Felkin did bring in grades above 7=4, which is something that many modern occultists mock. As part of the magical and mystical process, a magician works to "cross the abyss"[43] and merge with the Divine. Only people with rampant egos, megalomaniacal personalities or teenage boys publicly make any claims to have

---

42 Jack Taylor's wife, Catherine Violet Taylor was one of the unsung magicians of Whare Ra whose name merits recording as a brilliant magician. She attained all the Grades achieved by her husband and also served as Hierophant. She died of cancer some years before Jack, but received fulsome praise from those who knew her highly skilled and effective ritual. Her progress through the Grades was not rapid and although the intervention of the Second World War was undoubtedly a factor, she seemed to have a steady and patient commitment to the Great Work. Tony Fuller found the records of her Whare Ra career and it reads thus: 0=0 October 1935, 1=10 May 1940, 2=9 1942, 3=8 November 1944, 4=7 8 October 1945, Portal 1947, 5=6 June 1949, 6=5 22 April 1958 and 7=4 July 1962. She died in the mid-70s.

43 For a fictional account about how this is supposed to work see Ericson, E. (1983). *Master of the Temple*. London: New English Library.

managed this feat. So the idea of someone actually having an 8=3 grade was just silly. It is commonly believed that you cannot cross the abyss until you are dead.

The fact that Felkin's order went even higher, to 9=2, which was supposed to mean that the person had seen the face of God and lived, was even more laughable. Yet Whare Ra did have these grades. The 8=3 has never been found to have been published. Tony Fuller said that it was held in a three sided black tent structure. He also pointed out to me that the description (which can be found in this book) for the Whare Ra "preparation for the 8=3 grade" is taken word for word from Waite's Holy Order 8=3 ritual. Pat Zalewski also found that candidates were supposed to have a fish dinner before their initiation.

Zalewski thought that the grades were for administration purposes only, and were mostly for chiefs. That was not quite true as there were people with high grades who were never chiefs and some chiefs never received the higher grades. Euan (Hugh) Campbell was 9=2 and never a chief, while chiefs Betty Jones and David Osborne never made 9=2 and neither did Christina Stoddard. Father Charles Fitzgerald was 8=3.

So what was in these grades that made them possible for mere mortals? Firstly it was not that you had to *be* anything – simply that you had to have had an experience of it which transformed your life. I have spoken to someone who was an 8=3 who told me that she had been able to catch a glimmer of what that Binah state was like. It was something she could not articulate, but against which the mundane world could not compare and her physical life suffered for many years as a result of it. You catch the hem of a reality which you are too small to understand and it is just enough to open something within you. The personality has to be strong to take such an experience, and when you return it takes a long time to integrate. There are no great powers, as the myths and legends claim, but a greater Understanding and Wisdom about the true nature of reality.

Felkin himself said that he once, and only once, felt a state which he considered equitant to the 10=1, but as far as I am aware he never claimed this grade or bothered constructing such a ritual for the order – perhaps he was aware that few would manage it.

Whare Ra was more than just an occult group. It was a secret society; most of its members were high members of the local community and who controlled that local community. Not only did

Whare Ra have control of the Havelock North council, it also had members on the Napier and Hastings councils. If needs be, there were a few Members of Parliament, senior clergymen and a couple of governor-generals who could be called upon as loyal members.

In paranoid conspiracy terms, Whare Ra was the sort of nightmare which would give tin foil hat wearers a wet dream. Yet curiously, nothing in the New Zealand press was ever reported about it. The fact that Gardiner owned the local press might have had something to do with it, but the rival newspaper the *Napier Daily Telegraph* (which I worked for) would have loved to have run a story like that. It was more likely that Whare Ra was a secret and none of the local press thought of reporting it. This state of affairs continued long after Whare Ra was shut.

For example, when I was a senior reporter for the *Napier Daily Telegraph* I just happened to write the obituary for the last Whare Ra chief, John Herman von Dadelszen.

I wrote a very dull piece about how he was a Mayor of Havelock North. I was given names of local people whom I should interview, which I did. It was not until I spoke to Percy Wilkinson, who had seen my obituary, that I realised. He told me that not only was von Dadelszen a chief of Whare Ra but the people I had interviewed were all senior Whare Ra people. You'd think a secret like that would have managed to leak somehow over such a long period.

Indeed, there was a story of a Whare Ra member's wife who was a born-again Christian who was worried about the order's influence. She arranged a meeting with the local Mayor and Town Clerk to attempt to get the order shut down. Little did she know that the Mayor and Town Clerk were senior members of Whare Ra. If it were a conspiracy film, the woman would have suffered from "an accident." These sorts of things did not happen either.

Keeping its activities secret in a small village like Havelock North was a major achievement – particularly when some decisions were not clearly thought out. For example, Frank Salt recounted to Tony Fuller that women in the order had to wear red stockings, and many of them would troop through the village to the Temple wearing them. Something like that will get you noticed and be a source of comment – but somehow it did not expose the Order. Other cases included that of the Chief Betty Jones' mother, who was also a member and suffered from dementia. She would stop complete strangers in the street and say: "There's a holy ceremony tonight."

In the early days of the telephone in New Zealand, to make a call you had to go through telephone operators who knew everything going on in town. They would often tell callers "there is no point ringing her, she is out visiting her sister." Whare Ra people used the old currency as a code. In the days of pounds, shillings and pence people would speak of something costing "two and six" (two shillings and sixpence). Thus telephone calls would refer to "I'll see you tonight and give you that 3 and 8 I owe you" (or 4 and 7).[44]

If there was any conspiracy it was to keep the Order secret, and that was managed because it was benign and Christian. Most New Zealand towns had a Masonic lodge, with Masonic pubs and clubs. Pillars of the community who could not get into Masonic Lodges were often members of Rotary. The fact that it was Christian and its members obviously attended Church meant that whatever was happening it must be respectable, and not worth worrying about.

It is difficult for many modern people to understand how this level of secrecy could be maintained. Percy Wilkinson said that people who were your best friends in Whare Ra would ignore you if you met in the street. This prevented people having to ask difficult questions such as "how do you know him?"[45] As I describe later, this attitude to secrecy remained with Whare Ra members long after the temple closed.

---

[44] i.e. See you at the 3=8 Grade initiation ceremony.
[45] Tony Fuller was told the same thing.

Towards the end of his life, Felkin suffered from chronic ill health. According to his wife he was told to drink a glass of whiskey a night to relieve his symptoms. Since he was an alcoholic, this cure cannot have helped at all. He also became more interested in the Order of the Table Round, seeing within it an important formula for understanding his Christianity. It was telling that on his deathbed he insisted that he was buried wearing the regalia and sword of the Grandmaster of OTR rather than a Chief Adept of the Golden Dawn. He also was buried facing towards Whare Ra (where both orders met).

When Felkin died, aged 76, there were 100 active members in the second order of his temple. For a modern Golden Dawn person, the idea of having that many second order members is a dream. The biggest modern order I know of has initiated only 60 people into its second order over its entire 20-year history, out of a few thousand members. When you consider that the population of New Zealand was only 1,128,100, and Havelock North had 600 when Felkin died, you start to realise the importance of Whare Ra to New Zealand and Hawkes Bay's religious and esoteric life.

◀ III ▶ THE TWILIGHT OF THE DAWN

"If we will go forward without fear, trusting to what we have received, C.R.C. will stand even as he has hitherto stood, behind us, using us as instruments in the work which he has undertaken. If we are to be instruments, we must put aside the thought of self and think only of the message."
Harriet Felkin in a letter to Stoddard.

UPON THE death of her husband, Harriet Felkin began her own spiritual influence in New Zealand. By that time, she was nearly deaf and suffered from chronic ill health. Her successor John von Dadelszen told Robert Ellwood that she was a woman "of indomitable spirit and unusually wide interests." Although she maintained the order and her role in it as leader to her life's end, she was probably less interested in it than her husband. She was one of the world's great letter writers, sending letters of opinion and support to politicians and religious leaders around the world.

Harriet was an influence on the Radiant Health movement which was formally founded in New Zealand by Dr Herbert Sutcliffe, a Freemason from Lincolnshire in England, who had become interested in the new psychologies of Freud and Jung. Sutcliffe established the first School of Radiant Living. The schools taught a mixture of religion and psychology and believed that good eating and exercise affected the brain. There was an emphasis on fruit and vegetables and a belief that positive thoughts would make you happier and healthier, all of which found a receptive audience in New Zealand. One of its most famous converts was a youthful Sir Edmund Hillary.

Around 1940, Sutcliffe travelled to Havelock North and stayed with Mrs Felkin and it was she who inspired him to stay in the area and set up a health school, which thrived for more than 20 years.

Initially Harriet Felkin appears to have existed somewhat under the shadow of her dead husband, or looking at it in another way, was receiving instructions from him. Christine Zalewski[46] has a collection of channelled addresses by Dr. Robert Felkin received a year after his death. The addresses are dated from July 1927 to August 1927. These extracts are from scrapbooks which contain typed and hand-written addresses, given to members of Dr. Felkin's Golden Dawn Temple that ran from 1916 to late 1978 in a large basement under the house called Whare Ra, Havelock North, New Zealand. Either Harriet or Felkin's daughter Ethelwyn were the medium, and Felkin was the contact named The Chief. Here is an example:

The Chief: 2/7/27

The Higher Genius is like a child with a soap bubble, but unlike the child it can project upon its bubble those images which it selects. This Auric bubble forms the outermost tenuous sphere in a man's Aura, and the images and Symbols implanted within it may take a lifetime to penetrate to the coarser Sphere within. To the Genius time is of little account, even now I only reckon time as a convenience in dealing with you, for myself it is of little import, so that the Genius is quite content to watch the gradual growth and development of a Symbol even though it takes many lives before the physical brain receives the reflection and the body conforms to it. A whole lifetime may be spent in developing one Symbol, the Genius meantime implanting fresh Symbols which may not penetrate for a life or two lives ahead. But as the Human Soul advances, it learns to assimilate these symbols more and more quickly, until towards its culmination it is enabled, so to speak, to catch up, and not only to work out the Symbols of the past, but also the most recent. The physical brain becomes extraordinarily sensitive and receptive.

This did not last. Indeed Harriet told Jack Taylor if anyone tried something similar when she died, she would not show up. "If anyone says they are getting messages from me after I have died, don't believe them – it is a bad contact," she said.

Between 1936 and 1949 Harriet published her magazine *The Lantern* (monthly until July 1944, thereafter bimonthly), and apart from a lead article by Reginald Gardiner she wrote the lot. It was in this that she wrote *A Wayfaring Man*, not just about her husband but also biblical topics, including Jesus and His Friends, Joseph of

---

46   These important channellings were first published in the Winter Solstice edition of the Hermetic Tablet. *The Hermetic Tablet Vol. One Winter Solstice*. Rome: The Hermetic Tablet, 2014. Print.

Arimathea, and Paul the Apostle. Articles also appeared on lighter occult subjects such as the Church and the Sacraments, Living Rhythmically, and Civilisation and History, as well as poetry and epigrams.

Harriet Felkin was less interested in some of the more trivial details of training which bogged down the English Golden Dawn. While the training was leagues ahead of what was on offer in the United Kingdom, the concept of intellectual exams was less important to her. Pat Zalewski said that Harriet Felkin almost did away with exams before she died. Instead she favoured a more intuitive approach for when a student was ready to enter the next grade. One day she approached Barbara and Ian Nairn and asked them when they were going for the 5=6. Barbara said they had not sat their Portal exams yet and Mrs Felkin replied "Exams! Exams!" and arranged their 5=6 nearly immediately. Percy Wilkinson reported something similar. Mrs Felkin favoured passing a psychic test, something which was in line with what was happening in the United Kingdom with Dion Fortune's Inner Light order. The rationalisation was that while the outer order was for stuffing your head with intellectual information, the Second Order was all about doing, and the forces behind the order would mark you for elevation when you were ready.

According to Zalewski, testing was stricter after Mrs Felkin died and by the late 1950s it was advancement by abilities which had to be demonstrated.

While the order continued under her guidance and influence, she was the touchstone that the other adepts turned to when they had their questions. Being the chief adept over a group like Whare Ra was a tricky business because although you had absolute power, you were not supposed to use it. Each senior adept had their own contact, their own approach to doing things, and training method. It was rare that this caused conflict, but in cases where it did Mrs Felkin was called to mediate.

One such conflict was developing between the talented ritualist, clairvoyant and healer Jack Taylor and the able administrator and lawyer John von Dadelszen. The history of Whare Ra might have been different had these two managed to get on, but they had wildly different approaches to life. Taylor was a wild card and unpredictable; von Dadelszen was the conservative pillar of the community. Both benefited under Harriet: Taylor to be the best Hierophant the order had ever seen (so good at it that no-one could consider letting anyone else do the job for 15 years). Von Dadelszen was given increasingly important administrative roles, culminating in him ending up as the Order's chief. Under Harriet, whatever von Dadelszen lacked, Taylor provided – something that would fall apart at her death.

Harriet Felkin had a vision which claimed that a great occult teacher was going to arrive in New Zealand, who would teach. She started writing to Charles McDowell, an Australian Anthroposophist, who had an especial concern for Steiner's biodynamic system. As it turned out he had shared the same vision about a spiritual teacher and the need for a spiritual centre to be built in New Zealand for him. In October 1938 Harriet found a tract of nearly sixty acres of land in Taupo to be used as its site. It was purchased in the name of three trustees, John von Dadelszen, Ethelwyn Felkin and Reginald Gardiner.

This formed the basis of the Tauhara project in Taupo, which was supposed to be a venue for international esoteric teachers. The idea was that the teacher would have a place to teach when they showed up. While they were waiting, the trust was to be a centre for propagating organic and biodynamic horticulture and agriculture.

On January 7, 1939, with McDowell present, the site was dedicated and declared a "zoekaiphos" (a place of life and light). Harriet spoke of it as having grown out of her work in Havelock North, but implied that this was something different and separate.

"Preconceived ideas must not be allowed to constrict growth; The old must indeed act as a foundation, but when the foundation is laid then it must be built upon, and though the foundations do, to some extent, indicate the plan of a house, they must never be regarded as the house itself," she wrote about the project.

The Second World War intervened, and the project was suspended. Even after the return of peace, Tauhara had some problems owing to rising rates and expenses. Part of the land had to be sold off piecemeal to meet obligations. Then in 1970 the Taupo borough council sought to acquire the most valuable part of the land for a reservoir. In 1971 the trustees sold what was left of the original property and purchased a site overlooking Acacia Bay. This land has subsequently been developed to fulfil the original purpose, providing meeting and conference sites for spiritual groups of all sorts.

However, this particular centre would later play a key part in the death of Whare Ra, so it is not clear whether Harriet would have allowed it to happen if she had known.

Harriet Felkin's death in 1959, close to that of the founder Reginald Gardiner (1872-1959) put the order into shock. Felkin's daughter Ethelwyn carried on for three years before she too died. This did not leave a vacuum of skill, as everyone in the second order was highly trained, but it did end the sort of teaching leadership that the Felkins had provided.

Magicians are not the easiest people to manage and the more talented the magician, the more problems they can cause. Whare Ra was also factionalised. The system encouraged senior adepts to take students and train them, but that created cliques which were loyal to different people. Taylor controlled one of the largest cliques and was deeply upset that he did not get control of the Order when Ethelwyn died.

Taylor did not suffer fools gladly or believe in following all the rules. He was a 7=4 grade and had been given the link which would have given him the authority to set up any order he liked. However, he became fascinated with the Order of the Table Round and its system.

This put him at odds with other important leaders of the time, Frank Salt and John von Dadelszen. Taylor thought they were fools not to be suffered. John von Dadelszen and his wife were strict Christians and had difficulty with the more magical aspects of Whare Ra. They attempted to Christianise the order and replace some of the curriculum with bible studies. In the 1960s Taylor became furious with them, particularly as he noted that teaching previously given out at the 5=6 level was being redistributed to higher grades because teachers did not understand them anymore.

In the worst case, a paper which had been 5=6 was allocated to the 8=3, which was an administrative grade and meant that the paper would only be seen by the chiefs.

Like many people a little out of their depth magically, and with fundamentalist leanings, the von Dadelszens tended to be autocratic and jackbooted when it came to ritual.

Around this time, one the chiefs, Archie Shaw, decided he had had enough and decided to quit. His role was offered to Frank Salt but he turned it down, preferring his role as Demonstrator. Jack Taylor was the next obvious candidate. But von Dadelszen was unable to work with him and appointed Betty Jones instead. This angered Taylor and caused a split within the group. Taylor still had his base which was centred on the much smaller Order of the Table Round, which met in Whare Ra itself.

This led to a showdown, which resulted in the Order of the Table Round being evicted from Whare Ra and setting up in an large wooden army hut elsewhere in Havelock North. It was not quite high noon at Whare Ra and there was little in the way of actual conflict. In fact all the people in Taylor's faction, including Taylor, remained members. John von Dadelszen found an old ritual for some senior positions in OTR which were equal to the Golden Dawn 5=6. The rituals had not been used, but it was clear that they would give OTR the equivalent of the GD's higher degrees. Von Dadelszen gave Taylor the rituals on the condition that he cleared off.

With these new rituals, Taylor and Wilkinson and a few others of that group rewrote the OTR rituals so that they encompassed many of the inner ritual formats of the Golden Dawn, but with an Arthurian theme. Taylor remained adamant that OTR was not a teaching order like Whare Ra, and the two orders effectively existed side by side in Havelock North, with many members belonging to both groups. Another important change that Taylor made to OTR was to admit men and women, and allowed people to join the order without being a Whare Ra 5=6. But it also had clear Golden Dawn features which would only have been seen by a 5=6 in Whare Ra. It is also my theory that Taylor and Wilkinson built an inner structure for the ritual which was similar to the Golden Dawn's. In this way, although he was not made a Golden Dawn chief, Taylor became one.

With OTR out of the building, one particular crisis was averted. But it was starting to become clear that Whare Ra had lost its way and the chiefs were trying to cover it up with a degree of autocracy which had not been seen before.

In 1962, after the closure of the Hermes Temple in Bristol, Charles Renn wanted to complete his 7=4. At that time Mrs Carnegie Dickson was the senior chief at Hermes and the head or "Metatron" of the Cromlech temple. She sent him to New Zealand to get the grade, but he was so impressed with Whare Ra he decided to emigrate. Mrs Carnegie Dickson agreed that he should take Cromlech to NZ, as it had also closed in the UK at the same time as Hermes.

Cromlech then was based in Richmond, near London. Charles was given the Warrant signed by Mrs Carnegie Dickson as a 9=2. She gave him vast quantities of papers and Temple furniture.

At Whare Ra there was considerable interest in Cromlech material, which had been mentioned in its course material. In fact a few Cromlech papers had been included for study at Whare Ra, sometimes attributed to Felkin's Arab contact. In one case he wrote "Sun Temple Teaching from A.B.S.: Short Chapters from a very ancient book called the *Book of the Wisdom of the Sun*," which is almost a complete steal from the preface of the Cromlech/Sun Order "Three Veils of Negative Existence" paper.

The consecration of the Cromlech Temple Ark (essential for Temple work) in NZ was held at 8pm on Saturday 12 December 1964. The NZ Temple was called "Io-Ana" which apparently means "God's Cave." Most of the 'names' of Whare Ra were there, including Jack Taylor, Euan Campbell, the Reids and others.

Taylor later told Pat Zalewski that he was only there to help out and Io-Ana failed to get properly established. But there was more to it than that. It was popular amongst Whare Ra people and more than 14 senior Whare Ra people joined.

Unfortunately Charles Renn died a year later from a sudden heart attack, which left the order without a senior initiator. Many of the Whare Ra people felt that they themselves should replace Charles as Metatron rather than Beryl Renn, who was "a mere 5=6 woman".[47] Renn said later that Taylor was one of those who wanted to take it over.

In 1966 she wrote to Mrs Carnegie Dickson for advice. Carnegie Dickson advised putting the Order into abeyance, which she did until 1991 when she reactivated the order by initiating its current head.[48]

Soon after Charles' death, von Dadelszen visited to collect any of his Whare Ra material, but he missed a large metal box containing huge quantities of Cromlech, AO and GD material which Carnegie Dickson had given to Charles.

That was not the only new influence on the Havelock North Whare Ra. In 1964, the person who was responsible for popularising modern alchemy, Dr. Albert Richard Riedel (1911-1984), who was better known as Frater Albertus, arrived in New Zealand and set up his alchemy training system.

Taylor famously said "Frater Albertus seems to think a lot of himself," something which was echoed by the Builders of the Adytum's chief Joyce Chesterman, who had some dealings with him.

---

47 It was entirely unfair. Beryl Renn was psychic, tall, no shrinking violet, and an excellent healer.
48 Beryl died in November 2016 aged 95.

She described him as a trouble maker, who caused some considerable problems.[49]

Albertus himself shifted his attentions to Australia after that, where most of his alchemy work is still practiced. However, there was a thriving alchemy community in Hawkes Bay which was based on his teachings.

In 1963, an AO offshoot started by Paul Foster Case was starting to make some headway under the New Zealand organiser Alistair Wallace. Wallace was a member of Whare Ra but felt that Builders of the Adytum (BOTA) had a fresher, more open attitude to the teaching, particularly when it came to Tarot.

BOTA's involvement in New Zealand had started in the early 1960s. Frank Goodie, an Auckland bookshop owner, played a recording that Ann Davies had made of a Kabbalistic Healing Service to Alistair Wallace.

According to Felkin researcher Roel van Leeuwen,[50] Wallace believed that there was a hidden code in the BOTA chants and started writing to Davies. It is hard to see what he was looking for; the BOTA chants were the same as those used in Whare Ra, set to music. However it was the beginning of a friendship between the two. As a result, she visited New Zealand in 1963, 1964 and 1969 with a view to establishing the BOTA here.

Well that was the theory at least. Davies saw a lot of value in Wallace's order, Whare Ra. She claimed that her enthusiasm for visiting New Zealand was because she had been receiving communication from the inner planes that she was to bring some "lost sheep of British descent from somewhere south into the fold." There was a little more to it than that. She was romantically enamoured with Wallace, who was by all accounts a charmer (or as others less politely described him, a womanizer or aging Lothario). Later they would become engaged, although apparently that was about as serious as Wallace's other 'complicated' relationships. Wallace was a 5=6 at Whare Ra and reasonably respected, but it was a moot point if his personal life was going to stand in the way of him progressing further.

BOTA's founder Paul Foster Case was a 5=6 in the AO in the United States, but the quality of teaching he had received from Moina

---

49 Will and Joyce Chesterman were very supportive of Albertus but he did treat them badly as a "hotel and a taxi service". When BOTA's head Ann Davies died he attempted to claim he was her successor. He was ignored in BOTA.
50 "Nzoccult." *Nzoccult*. N.p., n.d. Web. 23 Mar. 2014.

Mathers was limited. He had completed the grades too fast, even for one who should have been seen as a rising star. He also had none of the grade work above ZAM. Much of BOTA's material was nothing to do with the Golden Dawn and was based on his own ideas, and not AO teachings. This was not to say that these were slight, in many ways they were better than anything Moina Mathers provided, but they did have certain quirks which would sink the group in the eyes of Whare Ra people.

The first was his obsession with the New Thought movement which was popular in the US occult scene. The idea is that you visualise something you desire happening and suggest to your unconscious mind that it should. To any of Whare Ra's adepts this would have been regarded as a dumbed down version of magic. The other thing was that Case was against the Golden Dawn's use of Enochian.

Case objected that the Enochian Magic system was corrupted because it came through a skryer who was not a clear channel – Edward Kelly. His reason for believing this was less rational; he thought it had killed his friend.

Case's AO initiator was Michael James Whitty, who was the editor of the magazine *Azoth*. Case and Whitty were close – Whitty republished Case's attribution of the Tarot keys in *Azoth* and collaborated with him in the development of the text which would later be published as *The Book of Tokens*.[51]

In December 1920, Michael Whitty died of a heart attack after a long bout of Bright's Disease.[52] His death, though sudden, had been long predicted, as Bright's Disease was slow and considered uniformly fatal. Case was deep in shock and believed Whitty's health problems were attributable to the dangers of Enochian magic. Bright's Disease was hereditary, so unless Whitty's family were also practising it, the Enochian angels had an alibi and were off the hook. BOTA did use the famous Enochian tablets within its order, but it insisted that they were translated into Hebrew. There were some changes in the lettering, which made the system incoherent. Some

---

51   Case, P. (1989). *The Book of Tokens*. Los Angeles, Calif., U.S.A.: Builders of the Adytum.
52   Whitty's death certificate lists the cause of death as chronic Bright's disease, which was the same kidney ailment which killed Golden Dawn founder Wynn Westcott. Contributory was a lesion of the heart valve. He died in the vicinity of Exposition Park, near the campus of U.S.C. at 3950 Hill.

of BOTA's brightest minds have tried without success to make Case's tablets intellectually work on the same rational basis as the Golden Dawn's Enochian system.

To be fair to Case, he never wanted BOTA to be a magical order that replaced the Golden Dawn. He wanted the order to be a correspondence course, which was fairly lucrative and did not require meetings to be organised. He practically had to be forced at gunpoint to develop a ritual component to BOTA.

There was a BOTA myth that Case was such a superb AO magician that he was able to recreate the rituals from memory. In fact, the ritual component was mostly built using Aleister Crowley's *Equinox* with some adaptations of his own. He did not want a Second Order but while he was out of town, his members built a Golden Dawn vault for him using ping-pong tables and he felt obliged to set one up.

Ann Davies had been close to Case, at one point having a difficult sexual relationship in his house in front of his wife (until she was finally asked to leave).[53] She really had little to teach and her own attempts to add to material written by Paul Foster Case were less original efforts and more extrapolating and re-enforcing what he had already suggested. Still she had nothing to give students who wanted practical information. Davies had marketed herself as the head of the Golden Dawn and needed access to all the Whare Ra teaching material and resources, which were considerable. Having all that paperwork would have given some credibility to Davies' claims that BOTA was the true successor of the Golden Dawn. All she needed was for the last surviving Golden Dawn temple to acknowledge her Order and merge with it.

While it may be surprising, there was some support for the idea of jump-starting Whare Ra and giving it some new life. Certainly Wallace did a brilliant job of championing Davies. In 1963 Taylor wrote to her.

Letter from Jack Taylor to Ann Davies, March 21 1963:

---

[53] This story was well known at the time and was even the subject of a letter between Regardie and Ithell Colquhoun. The facts appeared to confuse her which was why she claimed Ann Davies was Paul Case's wife in her book *Sword of Wisdom*.

40 Tainui Drive	The Rev. Ann Davies
Havelock North	Prolocutor General
H.B.	B.O.T.A.
New Zealand	California

G.H. Soror,

Mr. Alistair Wallace has suggested that I should write to you.

This I am very happy to do, as the information you have been generous enough to supply interests me very much.

First, about myself. I am 60 years of age, married, and my wife and I belonged to the Felkin group for approx. 30 years.

This last fact I am always rather diffident about admitting as I feel that after all the sacrifice and work done by Mrs. Felkin and Miss Felkin and their friends, to assist us, one should be very much further advanced than one is.

Be that as it may, my wife and I have been and still are intensely interested in this line of study.

I have known Alistair ever since he joined the Group: and have had some small part in his training. Hence he discussed with me the suggestion of writing to you before doing so.

I have also known W.G. Gilmore of Taradale (N.Z.) for a number of years, though not as intimately as Alistair.

In Gilmore's case our ideas and his differ more frequently than they agree. But, in spite of this we are able to maintain a friendly and benevolent relationship and are happy to be able to call them our friends.

Neither my wife nor I hold any position of authority in the Felkin group at present, though we are regarded as Senior Members; and have frequently been assured that our "opinions are valued" even if not always agreed with.

Turning to your letter to Alistair, our information on the History of the Order agrees with yours, with the rather minor difference that Regardie was a member of an English Temple (his name appears on their Roll) and received his teaching from there and not from Crowley.

The English Temples have now ceased to exist, and we knew of no others until hearing from you.

We are also interested in your remarks about the Enochian Tablets, and can quite conceive that they might have caused trouble. As to their merits or demerits as a subject for study, with respect, I think that there might be room for discussion, but this does not seem necessary at the moment.

The Twilight of the Dawn

Unfortunately, most unfortunately, your remarks about personality clashes and inability to distinguish between psychic awareness and Spiritual perception apply rather severely to our own Group at the present time.

Indeed it is just these factors that have given rise to a search amongst some of our members for a possible source from which authoritative guidance might be obtained (on the physical plane).

We were told by Mrs. Felkin before she died (about five years ago) that "Someone" would come to take her place as our Leader. But, so far none of us are aware that that has happened.

I had several discussions with her and found that she agreed with certain intuitive impressions I had had on the matter.

As to the rest of the Group, I cannot speak, except to say that I feel sure that one and all hope that her words will prove true.

For ourselves, we are quite sure that they will, because of our knowledge of her ability in the past and the number of times on which her prophecies proved correct.

And because of certain intuitive messages received: and which, judged as well as we are able, in the light of our personal experience seem to us to be true.

As to what the general reaction will be when that happy day comes …… well I guess we shall each have to make our own individual decisions.

Alistair has evidently mentioned the Tauhara Estate to you. This is a Major Work and will, I believe, become one of the Great World Centres at the right time. But I have always understood that it would not interfere with the work of the Order itself.

Started by Mrs. Felkin and an advanced member of the Steiner Group in Australia (now dead) it aroused considerable enthusiasm before the war, but later dwindled: with the advancing age of Mrs. and Miss Felkin.

The younger people left in charge lost interest: and it was about to be sold a few months ago.

Then (unfortunately I sometimes think) I had the idea that I had been told, whilst asleep, that I must try to do something about it.

I contested the idea very thoroughly, feeling that I already had more than I could manage, but since the feeling persisted I finally gave in and looked around for help. The result has astonished everyone (myself included) and the project (albeit a long one) is well under way.

In spite of this I feel that I shall have little more to do with it other than to see it started.

I feel quite sure that my own work lies here. At some future date; with the Felkin Group. And both now and then, with another Order which Dr.

Felkin brought to N.Z. (O.T.R.) and which is the descendent of a very old Chivalric Order.

By a chain of unforeseen circumstances, I find myself, ably assisted by my wife, now having to lead this Chivalric Order.

This, also, almost passed out of existence a few years ago, but now shows considerable Life and Vitality: and will I believe have a major part to play in the coming years.

It may be significant that all three activities, the Order, the Tauhara Group, and the Chivalric Order, have one after another drifted to a point of near extinction whilst under the control of those now in charge of the Order.

The fact that the Order has now reached such a state of crisis distresses us more than I can say (those in charge seem blissfully unaware of this). We hope and pray that "Someone" will come who is of sufficient calibre to revivify that also. We feel that they will, but the "waiting" is trying indeed.

At present we ourselves can do nothing to help, beyond praying for it: as our ideas of how it should be run and the ideas of those in charge differ too widely.

I trust that this information will be of some interest to you: and should you feel that you can let me have more information about the B.O.A.T. *[Sic]* and/or the Pronaos I shall be most interested and grateful.

Yours fraternally,

S.S.
W.H. Taylor.
S.U.A.T.

The Whare Ra chiefs also talked about forming a BOTA outer order in Hawkes Bay and there was some support for the idea.

When Wallace invited Davies to visit New Zealand later that year, she arranged a lecture at the Napier Hotel. He prepared the ground extremely well using Mrs Felkin's vision of a spiritual teacher coming from abroad. This was the vision that had founded the Tauhara Centre, and Wallace realised that if he could convince enough people that Ann Davies was this teacher, he could take over Whare Ra and turn over the Tauhara centre to BOTA.

Wallace started embellishing Mrs Felkin's vision by saying that the world teacher predicted to appear was a woman with red hair, so that Davies could claim to be the one. Until that point, Felkin's world teacher had not been identified as a man or a woman, and certainly did not have red hair. The prophecy was far enough in the past for most people to have forgotten such details. Wallace's rumour was accepted by those in BOTA at least until the 1980s. As far as I am aware this book is the first to call it what it really was – an asset grab by Davies and Wallace.

Most past and present members of Whare Ra attended the BOTA meeting, but the result was not what Wallace and Davies had hoped.

Most of the problem was one of presentation. Davies was flamboyant and outspoken at the best of times, and was playing the part of the great teacher. She talked up Paul Foster Case, BOTA and herself in messianic terms. This came across to some of the members as being a hard sell – something you expect from American snake-oil salespeople rather than serious occult teachers. Taylor felt that she was selling herself as the adept of the world and her order as the replacement for the Golden Dawn. Talk of New Zealanders being her "lost British sheep" did not go down well.

Another problem was that Wallace, who was an alcoholic, had prescribed Davies some 'Dutch courage' to calm her nerves before giving her talk. She was visibly drunk, which did not really fit in with the desired image of the ginger-headed messianic saviour of the age.

Particularly unimpressed was a young Ron Raison. Raison was a gardener at Whare Ra and was later to be a key player in Order of the Table Round in the 1990s. Raison thought Davies was so funny he had to leave the room. He was found by Jack Taylor outside the pub, bent double over a car, laughing. He later said that he had never seen such a comedy performance.

The Enochian question was also something which caused amusement. Whare Ra people did not consider the Enochian system that powerful. It was never really developed that much in Whare Ra and according to Percy Wilkinson, his feeling was that if BOTA thought it was that dangerous, they were clearly doing it wrong.

Davies was later to complain that the Chiefs of Whare Ra had treated her very badly and would not even let her see the temple. She also complained that the Whare Ra people asked her "intellectual questions" which was something she was not used to in the US, where her followers tended to be all-adoring.

However, Davies and Wallace did come close. Under a deal she brokered, Whare Ra members' grades would be acknowledged as their BOTA equivalents. But if Davies thought that Whare Ra and its assets would transfer over to BOTA she was sadly mistaken.

Joyce Chesterman, who along with her husband Will, took over BOTA New Zealand from Wallace in 1969, said the relationship with Whare Ra was problematic. "Those Whare Ra people were always causing such trouble," she said. "We had done our best for them, by acknowledging their grades, but that was never enough."

Once Whare Ra members had joined BOTA they soon discovered that in comparison it was completely lightweight. While the Order had a good correspondence course, its ritual and practical teaching showed nothing of its Golden Dawn roots. It had no grades beyond 5=6 and it used BOTA chapter rituals in a way that many Whare Ra people felt was pointless. Many of them stayed for the Tarot teachings but did not find much within the order which was better than Whare Ra. Some remained as members of both organisations, but most just drifted back. When I joined BOTA in 1984 the remaining few Whare Ra members were treated with fear. I remember I was invited around to the Hastings house of a rather nice elderly woman whose name I have completely forgotten, but I was briefed by the BOTA leadership that she was "Whare Ra, but don't mention it."

Whare Ra and BOTA formally swapped their rituals and some material, and Davies realised that by comparison she had nothing, and Whare Ra had little reason to follow her. The BOTA correspondence course was her strongest card and it was not enough. She started to worry that her own members would start to defect to Whare Ra instead. Now it was her turn to put the blocks on the developing relationship before they found out. Notes between her and von Dadelszen show her resisting moves between the two organisations with "dog ate my homework" type excuses.

The last straw for Whare Ra was when a sycophantic piece about Davies was published in the US newsletter by Wallace. It attacked Whare Ra and described it as having "run out of steam." The article was circulated amongst the Whare Ra people, and any plans to work closely with BOTA were indignantly shelved.

Davies and Wallace split up; not over the Whare Ra matter, but because Will Chesterman caught Wallace in bed with another woman. Chesterman ended up taking over BOTA in New Zealand and put all his money into establishing the organisation in that country. However, the relationship between them and Whare Ra was always problematic. Will and Joyce always felt slighted that they had applied for membership to Whare Ra and were turned down. It was further compounded by Chesterman's overwhelming love, bordering on deification, of Davies. BOTA members did belong to both orders, but kept their involvement in Whare Ra secret.

Even as late as the 1980s it was not a good idea to mention the name Whare Ra or Order of the Table Round at BOTA headquarters in Naenae.

However, in the early 1970s, Whare Ra really was rotting from the inside; in some ways the problem was literal. Firstly the building was badly in need of renovation. Betty Jones and her husband Ray had moved in to start the restoration work. Ray did a splendid job, but unfortunately Betty started to show symptoms of the Alzheimer's that had killed her mother and also started to cause a problem for the Order. Recruitment slowed down and teaching calcified. Some, mostly based around Taylor, felt that under von Dadelszen the life had gone out of it. Unofficial training continued, but the feeling was that the order itself was not doing much.

Percy Wilkinson never bothered collecting his 7=4, even though he was encouraged to do so by von Dadelszen while the order was running (and by Taylor after the order closed). "There is little point," he told me. "That grade is mystical and I have no use for it."

In the mid 1970s something happened which confirmed things for von Dadelszen He lost the contact with the inner beings behind the order. Since the days of Felkin, the chiefs had picked up teaching and instructions from the same sets of contacts, but suddenly, without an explanation, they disappeared. As we have said earlier, this happens when there is a change in the group which makes it no longer viable for the work of one particular contact. Another teaching about the secret chiefs was that they were also responsible for bringing in new recruits, so this lack of interest from the wider world was also seen as proof the secret chiefs had abandoned Whare Ra. Normally, depending on the work of a group, another contact can often be found, but in this case von Dadelszen couldn't. The Order was of little use to any secret chief.

By 1978, von Dadelszen made the difficult decision to close Whare Ra, sell the property and to put the money into the Tauhara project. The decision was made unilaterally and without any consultation from others within Whare Ra. The senior members I spoke to were still furious about it years later. There were rumours of someone gaining financial advantage, but no one ever said whom. On 24 August 1978, a letter was circulated to members announcing the closure:

> "Dear Fratres and Sorores,
>
> This letter is addressed to all members of the Order of S.T., including members of the Second Order. It is with great great regret that we write to inform you that the temple is closing and there will be no Vernal Equinox ceremony.
>
> Those of you who have been present at recent Equinox ceremonies will surely have been aware, not only of the lack of numbers, but also the lack of power in the temple. Those who have read their annual reports can scarcely have failed to notice that no new members have been admitted since 1975. Indeed, there have been no grade ceremonies at all for the last two years or more."

While the members knew that Whare Ra was in trouble, it still had members, and with the right leadership it could have drawn a second breath. In fact, if it had managed to survive a couple of years longer, it would have been the star performer in the Golden Dawn renaissance which began in 1978 with the founding of Chic Cicero's temple and continues to the current day.

Had von Dadelszen predicted this, he would have seen that Whare Ra would have had a premier place as the source of a real Golden Dawn lineage and training. The temple could have been an international centre for occult training in the Golden Dawn tradition, something that even Felkin would never have seen.

But von Dadelszen did not have the luxury of that hindsight, and in fact what he might have been witnessing was the beginnings of a change in New Zealand and Havelock North which made the existence of such an Order a relic of the past.

New Zealand's post-war socialism was also decaying. Its last gasp under the ultra-conservative Prime Minister Robert Muldoon was unpopular and based more on the weaknesses of the Labour Party. The country's identity was also changing, with a greater divide between the four main cities and the rest of the country. This would lead to a clash between the old and the new which was symbolised by the violent protests over the Springbok rugby tour in 1981 and the final replacing of old New Zealand in 1984 under the more right wing Labour government of David Lange. This lead to a collapse of the farming industry which had long been propped up by subsidies and had kept Hawkes Bay artificially wealthy. The restructuring of the country took years and the result was a much more advanced and sophisticated nation.

However, while New Zealand is and will always be a supporter of New Age groups, it is unlikely that they will ever have the financial and political power which was mustered by Whare Ra. The problem was the same in the United Kingdom. Large groups such as the Society of the Inner Light and the Theosophical Society, which had property, started to retrench as their membership changed. Oddly this coincided with the occult renaissance of the 1980s where more occult material was available than ever before, but it did not favour big autocratic orders. Instead it supported the development of much smaller, short lived groups with more democratic structures, or groups based around the skills of single teachers.

Big orders still exist; in fact the most successful was Chic Cicero's modern incarnation of the Hermetic Order of the Golden Dawn, which at last count had more than 20 groups distributed worldwide. But even this order is small and its financial resources insignificant in comparison to Inner Light and Whare Ra in their heyday.

In short, the writing was on the wall for Orders like Whare Ra – and any secret chiefs were going to invest their time in something different.

Von Dadelszen told all the members that they could keep their grade material, and burnt the group's regalia, temple furnishings and records.

Some things were rescued. The temple's pillars, the two sphinxes which flanked either side of the dais steps, and many copies of the rituals and lectures were passed on and preserved. But, according to one person who was in Whare Ra at the time, the amount of paper which was destroyed was extensive. "The bonfires took all weekend," she said.

While it is easy to be hard on von Dadelszen for the holocaust of Golden Dawn history, he was obeying his oath. Papers that were destroyed were not Whare Ra teachings, but the personal information of members who were key parts of New Zealand history. These are names that would have surprised the New Zealand press including Andrew Hamilton Russell (23 February 1868 - 29 November 1960) who is one of New Zealand's great military heroes and commanded the New Zealand forces during World War One; New Zealand's Governor

General and the Admiral of the British Fleet John Rushworth Jellicoe, and numerous important business people and local politicians. Sadly, what also was destroyed were missing papers and correspondence between the early Golden Dawn members and Felkin, and much of his dealings with continental Rosicrucian groups.

There was also the matter of what to do with the vault and the temple. This was no small thing, as after 60 years the temple was a dynamo of power. Some of this was due to the fact that no-one ever performed a banishing ritual on the temple or the vault during those 60 years. Unlike many modern Golden Dawn orders, which perform a banishing ritual before and after a ritual, Whare Ra didn't.

A quote from Frank Salt: "As the Temple was never used for any but ceremonial purposes, no banishing was ever used before a ceremony. We invoked the Elementals before the appropriate Grade, and banished them at the closing. Members performing private ceremonial there did as they saw fit, though each proposed ceremony was vetted by Mrs Felkin first. I cannot recall two ceremonies being performed on the same day, though in an emergency this could be done."[54]

It was so solidly built that when Whare Ra closed its doors von Dadelszen tried to scrape off the colours and found it too difficult. Instead he ripped up the carpet and the light from the roof, sealed it up and pretended it was not there.[55]

The Whare Ra vault had a fairly sinister reputation. Part of the problem was that it was always wrong and it is not clear why. The colours were not based on anything that Whare Ra had written down. Even allowing for paint to lose its colour over the years, the vault was too dark. Some of the colours which had been selected were muddy and brown, and you would think that someone over the course of 60 years would have done something about it. But they didn't.

---

54   In a letter to Tony Fuller.
55   It was later discovered by the new owners, who thought they had bought a house designed by the famous Kiwi architect Chapman-Taylor, and discovered the secret panel with the vault in it by accident.

After Mrs Felkin died, some people started doing experiments that she would not have approved of. One elderly Whare Ra member, Barbara Nairn, told me that the 6=5 room was being used by a group of adepts carrying out experiments using Mathers' Goetia. The adepts involved in this circle were not named, but it is clear that they knew enough to get something, but not enough to control it.

What happened was never talked about, but suddenly that room was only being used for the 6=5 initiation and nothing else. To make sure that no-one used it easily (6=5 initiations were rare) the chiefs ordered that it filled with old boxes and used as a storage room.

Life at Whare Ra went on, but it appeared that there was something rotten in the vault. Several of the later people who went through the 5=6 started to complain of odd feelings. It is difficult to say if some of those were from the initiation itself or something else. For example, one person I spoke to who was one of the last few 5=6s told me this:

> "After my initiation I stood in the door of the vault with my crook and staff. There was such a strong feeling that "this is all an abomination" that I had the urge to destroy the entire vault. I never went back to that vault ever again."

After Whare Ra was closed, Betty and her husband were moved out and the house was offered to members of the Order and then sympathetic associates. The head of BOTA, Will Chesterman, told me that he had been offered it and gave serious consideration to buying it.

He went up there and looked around, but said that there was something really horrible about the place and he realised that it would "take too much effort to clear." That might have been a dig at the Whare Ra people. There was very little love lost between Chesterman and the elders of Whare Ra anyway. However, that was one of the few times I ever heard Chesterman describe something psychically.

Pat and Chris Zalewski's teacher Jack Taylor told them not to go to the vault because it had been contaminated. When Chris Zalewski attempted an astral visit she found the astral form of Taylor barring her way.

The old Whare Ra adepts used to meet at the Chivalric Hall, and it was there I heard some other interesting stories. The first was that the first owners of the house left because they found it haunted, and it was scaring the children who were using the old temple and its vault as playroom. I was not able to confirm this at all. However, one story was recurring.

Von Dadelszen was a stickler for ritual in the masonic way. Everything had to be done perfectly right. A lawyer and Mayor of Havelock North, he carried himself with perfect authority and conviction. The only problem was that he did not realise that the vault had more than one level. He thought it was just the physical vault and any astral stuff which was contained within it. To be fair he did do a good banishing, but he did not know how to dissolve the higher levels of the vault. It was a moot point if he even knew they existed. What he effectively did, according to Barbara and Percy Wilkinson, was push the "inner vault" outside the physical structure. Percy told one of his students that it had been attached to a tree in the garden, which promptly died.

Several of Jack's students visited Whare Ra at the invitation of the owners, and they were walking around the garden when they found a tree stump. One of the students was incredibly psychic and told me that the energy which came off it was like nothing she had ever felt before. She was not sure if it was good or bad, but it was certainly powerful and in the wrong place.

I know exactly what she means. MOAA's vault is portable and assembled in my living room. We have to set it up and consecrate it every time. Shut it down and disassemble it. The first day after our first 5=6 initiation, I was sitting at the computer and had the feeling I was being watched. I saw quite clearly a vortex about three feet from the ground hovering above the floor exactly where the centre of the vault had been. I shifted that energy to the correct level, but I had not realised before that I needed to do that. The Golden Dawn's *Book of the Tomb* did not contain instructions for a portable vault, nor did it give von Dadelszen instructions for demolishing one which had been in place for 60 years.

I don't believe that the soul of the vault would have caused much in the way of problems (other than killing the tree) and the connection might even fade with time.

The closure of Whare Ra was not the end of the Order in New Zealand. Many of the adepts were furious at von Dadelszen for closing it. While some maintained their token membership of BOTA, others remained friends, met, and trained people.

The largest group was that which was centred on the still functioning Order of the Table Round. It was led by Jack Taylor and Percy Wilkinson. Taylor was carrying out experiments in colour healing and had some significant breakthroughs. Wilkinson had been Whare Ra's astrologer and continued to train people in that.

Taylor also trained and initiated people within the Whare Ra system. Mrs Felkin had given him the Link (see later) long before the troubles, and he felt he had a right to pass it on. He gave it to Pat and Christine Zalewski along with the 6=5 and 7=4 grades of the Order. They then used it to form their own Thoth-Hermes Temple in Wellington. This group continued to train people until the middle of the 1980s.

Von Dadelszen himself had some regrets about closing Whare Ra. In addition to helping to train interested people himself, he also authorised Frank Salt to train others and perhaps re-establish the order. Salt trained several aspiring magicians to carry on the tradition, but he was too old to start anything himself. One of his notable students was Tony Fuller, along with a couple of others who also hold high enough grades to carry on the Whare Ra tradition.

Percy Wilkinson attempted to assist the development of a temple in Hawkes Bay in the 1980s. Despite his support, however, it folded. Instead he focused on the Order of the Table Round.

What is interesting is that few of them are attempting to re-enact Whare Ra but are seeking to take it in new directions. Felkin showed that for a tradition to survive it has to adapt and transform.

Percy Wilkinson once said to me: "Whare Ra is gone, it had done what it was supposed to do and it ended. It should not have ended the way it did, but there is not much we can do about that. But there was a lot in it which is still relevant to today, which can be passed on."

IV WHARE RA & ME

MY MAGICAL life started out in 1984 with Builders of the Adytum in New Zealand. At that point, it was being run by Will Chesterman. In the middle of the 1980s Chesterman made it clear that I was going nowhere in BOTA because I was a journalist and he was worried that I would write all its secrets in a book (that book has never been written). I moved to Napier to work on the *Napier Daily Telegraph* and met up with Mike Burden through a BOTA study group we had formed under the protection of a woman called Ros Geddes. Geddes' job, as Chesterman's appointment, was to keep Mike and me in line and prevent us from doing any serious magic.

Fortunately Mike and I got on well with Geddes, who was well aware of the problems which were developing in BOTA at the time. We felt that they were similar to those problems which blighted Whare Ra a decade earlier. The Havelock North study group worked well and may have eventually gone somewhere if it had had support from the old Whare Ra people and if Ros had not died in a car accident.

The BOTA group had set up in the Plunket Rooms in Havelock North but never attracted the attention of the Whare Ra members who were lifelong members of BOTA. It was an indication to me and to Will and Joyce Chesterman that the old Whare Ra people were not interested in BOTA any more.

Mike had joined the Order of the Table Round (OTR) and was being trained in astrology by Percy Wilkinson, who was then the highest-ranking person in OTR. Wilkinson loved to talk about Whare Ra, but it was clear that it was something he'd done in his past, rather than his main interest.

Mike introduced me to Pat Zalewski and took me along to Percy's house where the game of finding out things would begin. At the time I was uninterested in joining the Golden Dawn, but I had read about it. Percy and I used to talk about magic, something that I never heard from BOTA and the Chestermans. Well, I used to ask carefully framed questions and get carefully framed answers back.

However, meetings at Percy's house became more than just Mike and me. People used to appear (Barbara Nairn was one) for the chats, and such was the secrecy it was only by guesswork that I worked out that they were former Whare Ra people. I mentioned before that the method that Whare Ra used for training was for senior adepts to adopt people, and to make sure they knew what was going on. I met several people who were adopted by this group and they all went on to do important things, either with OTR or occultism generally. Pat Zalewski said that the same thing happened to him when he visited (while Jack Taylor was still alive).

The method of training was based on asking the right question at the right time. They were never going to sit down and give you a complete picture of anything, you had to show that you knew what you were talking about and then they would give you the missing piece. Even then, there were no guarantees. When you talked to Percy, there was sometimes a pause as he thought whether his answer was going to break his Whare Ra oath.

Sometimes students picked up whole techniques, although it was hard to say if this was a Whare Ra technique or something that was part of the adepts' own experiments. For example, I learnt a lot about the magical use of banners which I have never seen written down, or even expressed outside that small circle. We were given one example involving the Banner of the West and were expected to extrapolate a range of ideas from that one suggestion. Then, in the next meeting, someone would tell you if your ideas would work. What would then happen was that these techniques would be distributed amongst the group's circle.

There were some stories about a Whare Ra character called Hugh (Euan) Campbell. Campbell was one of the most experienced and knowledgeable magicians in Whare Ra and held the 8=3 grade. He had a deep psychological scar which made him prone to binge drinking – he would disappear for a few weeks at a time. However, Campbell was famous for being the person that Dion Fortune claimed was badly affected by the Abramelin ritual.[56]

---

56 Abraham ben Simeon, and Mathers, S. (1975). *The book of the sacred magic of Abramelin the mage, as delivered by Abraham the Jew unto his son Lamech, A.D. 1458*. New York: Dover Publications.

In her book *Psychic Self Defence*,[57] Fortune repeated a story written by "H Cambell" which she had read in *Occult Review* in December 1929.[58]

"Desiring some information which I could not get in any ordinary way, I resorted to the System of Abramelin, and to this end prepared a copy of the necessary talisman, perfecting it to the best of my ability with my little stock of knowledge. The ritual performed, I proceeded to clear my 'place of working.' A little knowledge is a dangerous thing; my ritual was imperfect and I only rendered the talisman useless without in any way impairing the activities of the entity invoked. This looks like nothing else than gross carelessness on my part; and to a certain extent this is true – but the point I wish to make is this; that my knowledge of this particular system, and therefore my ritual, were imperfect and in any case, I had been shown no method of combating this particular entity when once aroused. Now note the results.

"Unfortunately I have no account of the date when these occurrences began, but the first hint of trouble must have come on or about March 3, 1927. I can guess the date with fair accuracy because, as I was to learn, the manifestations were always strongest about the new moon and after I had gone to sleep. Upon this occasion, I can remember waking up suddenly with a vague feeling of terror oppressing me; yet it was no ordinary nightmare terror, but an imposed emotion that could be thrown off by an effort of the will. This passed almost as soon as I stood up, and I thought no more about it.

"Again on April 2, or thereabouts, I was troubled by the same feeling, but regarded it as nothing more than a severe nightmare, though the fact that my sleep was distorted towards the time of the new moon had occurred to me; while as full moon drew on, the nights were peaceful again.

"The new moon of May 1 brought a recurrence of the trouble. This time very much more powerful, and necessitating an almost intolerable effort of will to cast if off. Also it was about this time that I first saw the entity which was rapidly obsessing me. It was not altogether unlovely to look at. Its eyes were closed and it was bearded, with long flowing hair. It seemed a blind force slowly waking to activity.

---

57   Fortune, D. (1957). *Psychic Self-Defence*. Wellingborough, Northamptonshire: Aquarian Press.
58   Fortune, D. (1929). *Occult Review*, December.

"Now there are three points which I must make quite clear before I proceed. In the first place, I was never attacked twice in the same night. Secondly, when I speak of physical happenings, the smashing of glass and voices, they were never, with one absolutely inexplicable exception, actual, but pure obsessions; and this leads to the third point. Not one of these incidents happened while I was asleep. Always I found myself awake with the terror upon me and struggling violently to cast off the spell. I have had nightmares before, but no nightmare that I have ever had could hold my mind in its grip for minutes at a time as this thing did, or send me plunging through a ten-foot-high window to the ground below.

"The first indication I had that these visitations were absolutely out of the ordinary course of events came on May 30. About midnight I was suddenly awakened by a voice calling loudly, 'Look out,' and at once I became aware of a red serpent coiling and uncoiling itself under my bed, and reaching out onto the floor with its head. Just as it was about to attack me I jumped through my window, and came to Earth among the rose bushes below, fortunately with no more damage done than a badly bruised arm.

"After this there was absolute peace until June 30, when the real climax came. I had seen the thing again on the night of the new moon, and had noticed considerable changes in its appearance. Especially it seemed far more active, while its long hair had changed into serpent heads. The night after I was awakened by a violent noise and jumped out of bed. I then saw the noise was caused by a great red obelisk which crashed through the west wall of my room and leaned against the wall at the east end, smashing both that and the window to pieces but missing my bed, which was in an alcove to the left of its path. In its transit it had smashed all the mirrors, and the floor and top of my bed were strewn with broken glass and fragments of wood. This time the obsession must have lasted some minutes, I dared not move for fear of cutting myself, and to reach the matches – wherein, I knew, lay safety – I had to lean across the bed and again risk the glass. Yet in my heart, I knew that all this was false, but had no power to move. I could only stand there, incapable, looking at the shattered room in a state of hopeless terror.

"And now comes the most extraordinary part of the whole business. When I had finally mastered the obsession, I went to bed again dead tired, and I know that the only sound I made that night was jumping to the floor; also my room is at least a hundred yards from the rest of my family, yet next morning at breakfast I was asked what was the terrible noise in my room during the night.

"After that I realised that the game was up. I had not taken these occurrences lying down, but I knew that it was impossible for me to try to control the force which I had set in motion. In desperation, I turned to a good friend, who, I was aware, knew much of these things. She did not hesitate, but came at once to my assistance, and from that day to the present, the trouble has absolutely gone from me.

"Such is the case; and I only hope it may warn those who are contemplating my folly to treat with the greatest of care any printed systems of magic, and not to use them at all unless they have the fullest control over the entities invoked."

In this case, the good friend who healed him was Harriet Felkin, but it was she who told him that he had to be very careful working too much with a group. Jack Taylor once said of Campbell that he was an example of an overactive brow chakra and the alcohol was to dampen the pain of what he had experienced.

Fortune said that it was a typical case of dabblers who had no experience playing with things. If she had any sense, she would have realised that Campbell was not a novice, as a novice would have had no chance of getting those results from the Abramelin system.

Because of what happened to Campbell, Whare Ra adepts had a respect for the Abramelin system which bordered on fear. One of them told me that he kept his copy of Abramelin in a locked box away from the rest of his collection. "Those magic squares are dangerous," he told me.

Campbell was a tragedy. Had he managed to conquer his alcohol problem, he would certainly have been a great Whare Ra chief. Golden Dawn researcher Tony Fuller has seen some of Campbell's diaries in which were included beautiful artwork of each of the Enochian Aethers.

In 1934 Campbell had visited the UK to read the Dee diaries in the British Library. He came back with extensive photographs of the diaries, having realised that Whare Ra and the Golden Dawn had been using the system incorrectly. It was Campbell who encouraged Whare Ra to use Dee's missing Heptarchic magical system which had been overlooked by Mathers and Westcott.

Coming from BOTA, we were taught of the perils of Enochian magic and were told that it was too powerful for many people to control. Case's warning made Enochian seem a lot more powerful than it was. Percy said there were much more powerful things in the Golden Dawn system than Enochian. Campbell would have killed himself much earlier in life if it had done any damage. If Enochian was going to drive Campbell mad, it would have had to drive some distance towards madness and meet Campbell halfway there.

That is not to say that this group was the only collection of Whare Ra adepts who were teaching, and in some cases, initiating. Another similar group had formed around the former Whare Ra teacher Frank Salt.

After a while Percy suggested I join OTR, and I have to say it was the most magical initiation I have ever had. I think that it was from that initiation that my magical path really began.

When my blindfold came off there were many adepts in the room who I later discovered were Whare Ra or had been trained by them. At the time, I felt that Whare Ra had not died, but had continued in the form of OTR.

To this day, I am kicking myself that I did not ask more about the inner techniques that the GD used. There were questions that were answered that I only really understood when I became involved with the Golden Dawn.

The magical processes that were being used in OTR were a variant of what was being used in Whare Ra. That is not to say they were the same, but the effects were what was supposed to happen in an initiation. Percy gave me a lot of helpful tips and techniques which proved vital when I formed the Nottingham temple of the Hermetic Order of the Golden Dawn and later the Magical Order of the Aurora Aurea.

I moved to the UK with the aim of finding more about magic, and it was there that I worked exclusively with the Inner Light tradition in the form of Servants of the Light. It was about that time that Pat's books about the Inner Aspects of the Whare Ra rituals came out and I got the link between what was happening in the Whare Ra and what I was doing with the British groups.

After five or six years, I returned to New Zealand and conducted a workshop at OTR. I was pleased when the old Whare Ra members turned up. Percy had died by then and had handed his tools and book collection on to Mike. Mike inherited all Percy's astrology, Enochian, side order and other papers. Some ended up with others. I thought my workshop would be like teaching your grandmother how to suck eggs, but I got on very well with Barbara Nairn, who thought that it was good to hear practical magic being talked about again. I picked up a lot from her. She was an incredibly regal woman who had considerable power, even though she was ill.

Other Whare Ra members would fill me in on the gossip of the order and it was from them that I got some of the stories of the old days which have found their way into *Gathering the Magic* and various blogs.

The phrase "getting blood out of a stone" was an apt way to describe getting Whare Ra-specific information, other than stories. I once saw on Percy's desk a clipping of the obituary I had written when the former Mayor of Havelock North had died. I asked him if he knew him, in a disinterested journalist sort of way – it was just a dead mayor obit and I had not been that interested in writing it. Percy laughed and said, "You know he was the chief of Whare Ra, don't you?" What was even funnier was some of the people I quoted in the article were also Whare Ra but I had not known it. Such was the secrecy of the group. I did later meet a lot of them.

There are a couple of Whare Ra adepts still around, although they are very elderly. When Paola and I went to Hawkes Bay in 2011, we met up with Mike and the members of the Table Round again. We were married on TeMata Peak, which is the place where Whare Ra met and OTR still meets.

One of our wedding presents was Percy's 5=6 nemyss. Mike, who was the best man at the little ceremony, felt Percy would have wanted us to have it. Certainly, it felt incredibly symbolic when he gave it to us. In hindsight, I have been incredibly lucky with the people I have met and the teachers I have had. When I wrote *Mathers' Last Secret* I dedicated it to Percy, who I felt was the unsung Magus of Whare Ra and had done a lot to protect its traditions.

During that trip, Paola and I met up with a senior member who was initiated by Taylor. A person who we jokingly refer to as our "secret chief" and who helped connect our work with the Magical Order of the Aurora Aurea to that of Whare Ra.

SECOND ORDER RITUALS
& COMMENTARIES

◆ V ◆   6=5 RITUAL

REQUIRED FOR THE 6=5 RITUAL[59]

SHEKINAH or MATRONA:
Rose-coloured tunic, long black veil, alabaster lamp with oil, spray of acacia.

CHIEF ADEPT: KING OF SALEM:
Blue and purple nemyss and robe, ankh, winged sphere wand and lamen.

SECOND ADEPT: EXCELLENT PRINCE OF THE HORIZON:
Red and orange nemyss and robe, ankh, phoenix wand and lamen.

POSTULANT:
(in 1st point) black cowl; (in 2nd point) purple cloak, red slippers.

THIRD ADEPT: NOBLE LORD OF EVENTIDE:
Yellow and rose robe and nemyss, ankh, lotus wand and lamen.

THE VAULT is entirely draped in red. The pastos in black stands uncovered, with the head to the north. Pedestal at the head. Light veiled.

In **PORTAL:** two pillars, red ankh holding brazier at south. Blue tat holding bowl of water at north. Outer side of the vault door covered with blue curtain on which is orange Sol on cross. Strip of emerald-green cloth up the centre of the floor. White and gold altar divided middle. Thirty-three lights, 2 extinguishers.

---

[59] This version of the ritual was Percy Wilkinson's own copy. It differed slightly from a Stella Matutina version that I have seen from a US collection in which the candle sequence and speech, which can be found in the teaching section, was included. It also differs slightly from another Australian version which has some more crossings out. That speech and the diagram was included at that point. All I can assume was that Whare Ra did not see the need for it.

The three adepti sit in triangle facing the vault.
The postulant must receive full instructions as to silence, knocks and gestures beforehand.
Bell (used in opening, but location and who rings it not mentioned), candle for Chief Adept to take into vault.
Censer.
Tarot keys of Justice and the Hanged Man for 2nd point.
Strip of linen to bind postulant in 2nd point.
Hierophant's lamen for 1st point. Scales with heart and feather for 2nd point.

Preparation of the "Light" by Shekinah:

She pours the olive oil into the alabaster lamp and says:
"The oil is the life of the Tree, let the Tree give its life."

She mingles her blood with the oil and says:
"The blood is the life of the man, let the man give his life."

As she kindles the light in the oil, she says:
"The light is the life of the world, let all the living rejoice."

OPENING

Chief Adept: *(rises)* (!)
2nd Adept: (!!)
3rd Adept: (!!)

Chief Adept: Avete Fratres et Sorores *(all rise)*

Ch. + 2nd Adepti: *(in unison)* Benedictus Dominus Deus Noster.

All present, led by 3rd: Que dedit nobis Hoc Signum.

(All touch rose cross on breast)

Chief Adept: Very honoured Adepti Majores, assist me to open the vault of the adepti in the exalted grade of Geburah.

Chief Adept: Excellent Prince of the Horizon, see that all present have been admitted to the mystery.

6=5 Ritual

2nd Adept: Very Honoured Fratres et Sorores, give the sign *(done)*.

Chief Adept: Noble Lord of Eventide, what is the word?

3rd Adept: Elohim Gibor.

Chief Adept: Grant us thy strength, oh Lord! Excellent Prince of the Horizon, what is the mystic number formed therefrom?

2nd Adept: The number is 20.

Chief Adept: Noble Lord of Eventide, what is the signification thereof?

3rd Adept: It is the union of the Enochian tablets and the Kerubic emblems.

Chief Adept: The Lord is my strength and my song.

2nd Adept: He is also become my salvation.

Chief Adept: In the strength of Elohim Gibor, let us with tranquil minds and recollected hearts enter into the Valley of the Shadow.

2nd Adept: Thou wilt keep him in perfect peace whose mind is stayed on thee.

3rd Adept: The Night cometh and also the day; if ye will return, return ye. *(Turn down the light in the vault.)*[60]

Chief and 2nd Adepti open the door of the vault and enter.
Chief adept passes to east (and takes candle).[61]
2nd adept remains at west.
3rd Adept remains without. (1 bell)

Chief Adept: Oh death, where is thy sting?

2nd Adept: Oh grave, where is thy victory?

---
[60] Line crossed out by hand.
[61] "And takes candle" was added by hand.

Ch. & 2nd Adepti: Thanks be to God which gives us the victory!

They place their wands with the ends resting within the pastos and raise their ankhs, joining them above wands.

Chief Adept: Say then, my brother, what is the emblem which we raise above the grave?

2nd Adept: It is the symbol of life; the union of the girdle of the Great Mother with the Tau cross of death; it is the emblem of that eternal life of spirit which the Divine Ones pour forth among men, delivering him from the body of Death.

Chief Adept: Verily thou hast answered well, my brother. Let us then entreat the Great Mother thus to raise us all from the death of the soul to life in the spirit.

They turn to the north east, still keeping their wands in the pastos but separating their ankhs, which they raise in invocation. They sink on one knee.

3rd Adept also kneels and rises without ankh.

Chief Adept: Mother of life, hidden home of the Fire of the Spirit, grant to us thy life. Mother of all, Matrona, we would be even as the burning bush, which was not consumed — a sign to those who may have eyes to see. Star of the Sea, in thy hands is the lamp of understanding, show us, if but[62] for an instant, a ray of that light divine. Rose of the world, vouchsafe to us breath of thine ineffable fragrance. Tower of ivory, enclose us in thy protecting purity. Give us, we beseech thee, this day and hour, thine aid in the high purpose for which we are here assembled. Strengthen the postulant, who seeketh enlightenment through the gates of darkness; that passing through the valley of bitterness, he may therein find the wells of living water. Reflect upon his soul those visions of the Spirit which will[63] awaken the understanding and beckon us to the Pisgah heights of holiness. There may he find the Pearl of Great Price which is also[64] the lodestone of the wise.

---

62 "but" inserted by hand.
63 "will" is crossed out by hand.
64 "also" is inserted by hand.

SHEKINAH

(Turn up the Light in the Vault.)[65]

2nd Adept: Shekinah!

3rd Adept: Shekinah!

All 3 adepti: Shekinah!

(Handwritten) 3rd adept turns up the light in the vault.

The vault, which was in darkness at first, gradually becomes lighter, revealing the figure of Shekinah, holding a lamp under her veil. At the last word, she holds forth the lamp in silence, letting the light shine on the adepti in turn. They bow their heads a moment. Shekinah withdraws silently. The adepti rise and quit the vault in silence.

POINT 1

Vault light out. Vault door is closed. Adepti seated in triangle — postulant has been previously instructed in knocks &c. He is robed in white, with black cord round waist, black cowl overhead, black slippers. He carries Hierophant's lamen. 3rd adept goes out and sees that he is duly prepared, then returns, leaving door slightly ajar. Postulant knocks once, hesitatingly. Inside a bell sounds twice.

2nd Adept: The hour of night approaches; the shades of evening close in; he who hath wandered far, travelling through the heat and burden of the day, seeketh rest.

Chief Adept: Let us then redeem the time. Excellent Prince of the Horizon, where is the place of rest?

2nd Adept: East of the Sun and west of the Moon. *(Postulant knocks more firmly.)* Rest after toil doth greatly please.

Chief Adept: How then hath he who seeketh for entrance prepared for that rest?

---

65 This line was crossed out.

2nd Adept: By a faithful obedience to the rules of our order; by that bodily purification which reflects the purity for which we strive; by the observation of abstinence and silence for a period of 20 hours; in token whereof we impose upon him the final test before admitting him within the portal.

(He turns to 3rd adept and says)

Noble Lord of Eventide, before admitting the postulant ascertain that his pledge is duly maintained.

Postulant knocks thrice urgently. 3rd adept opens door but bars the way saying:

3rd Adept: "By what right seekest thou entrance to these sacred precincts?

Postulant in silence offers Heiro's lamen. 3rd adept takes the lamen and stands aside to let postulant in and then the 3rd adept says:

3rd Adept: Merciful King of Salem, I have tested the postulant and silence is maintained.

(3 bells sound) (Moves postulant to the end of the carpet.)
3rd adept moves postulant forward a few paces at each "Who then is it?" until at the last "what then is this?" they are at the top of the steps facing the door of vault.

Chief Adept: The hour cometh and even now is when the Son of Man shall appear. Art thou therefore prepared to discard the vestments of the flesh that the soul unfettered may go forth to meet Him in the Air?

Postulant gives Sign of Osiris Slain. 3rd adept removes the black cowl standing behind postulant.

Chief and 2nd adepti rise & turn towards him. Chief adept raises wand and ankh on high.

Chief Adept: Oh ye divine ones, who are in the presence of the supreme, grant me your arms, for I am he who shall come into being among you.

6=5 Ritual

3rd Adept: Who, then, is this?

2nd Adept: I am the divine soul, which dwelleth in the Seven Spheres.

3rd Adept: Who, then, is this?

2nd Adept: I am he who is not driven back among the gods.

3rd Adept: Who, then, is this?

2nd Adept: I am yesterday; I know tomorrow.

Chief Adept: Yesterday is Osiris and tomorrow is Ra; I am the Only One, the Ruler of That Which is Made.
Who, then, is this?

2nd Adept: I am the Phoenix, the living present, arising from the ashes of the dead past; I am the Keeper of the Volume of the Book of Things which shall Be. Eternity is the day and everlastingness is the night.

3rd Adept: Who, then, is this?

2nd Adept: I am Thoth, the scribe of the holy offerings; I am he who riseth in his place, who cometh into the holy city. I have made an end of my shortcomings and I have put away my faults.

3rd adept loosens cord from postulant's waist.

3rd Adept: What, then, is this?

2nd Adept: It is the loosening of the corruptible in the body of Osiris, victorious before all the Gods; all his faults are driven out; it is the purification of Osiris on the day of his birth.

Chief Adept: I pass over the way; I know the head of the pool of truth, even the pool of Siloam, which is the pool of healing.

3rd Adept: What, then, is this? *(He points to door of vault)*

Chief Adept: It is the northern gate of the underworld, even the door of the tomb whereon thou mayest behold the Sun in his nadir, crucified between the pillars of the Tree of Life.

(All face east.)

Chief Adept: Homage unto Thee, oh Thou Lord of Light and Truth, oh sovereign prince who doest away with sin. Destroy Thou the faults that are within me, that with a clean heart I may approach when Thou dost say "Come therefore hither."

(A pause. Chief adept turns to postulant, who has been led slowly forward during the forth going and now stands close to the door of the vault.)

Already, Frater ✱✱✱, a triple obligation rests upon thy soul; in Malkuth were thy feet bound, that they might keep in the path of judgment and equity; on the path of the arrow thy loins were girt by the bonds of purity and self-restraint; in Tiphareth was thy heart bound by the threefold cord of love, service and sacrifice. Keep, therefore, the commandments of the Lord; bind them about thy neck; when thou goest they shall lead thee; when thou sleepest they shall wake[66] thee; when thou wakest they shall talk with thee. Art thou then prepared having thus bound thy body with the spoken word, so now to bind thy soul with the silence from which thou art not yet loosed? If thou dost with thy mind assent, signify the same with the sign of light.

(Postulant makes LVX signs in silence; 2nd and & 3rd adepti place him back against door of vault with arms outstretched, supporting arms.)

Chief Adept: He that findeth his soul shall lose it; and he that loseth his soul for my sake shall find it.

2nd Adept: He that taketh not his cross and followeth after me, is not worthy of me.

(4 bells sound)

---

66 Word crossed out and the word "keep" written above by hand.

THE OBLIGATION

(Chief Adept recites[67] the words and at the end of each clause the postulant bows his head in silence.)

1. I, Frater ✳✳✳, Associate Adeptus Minor of the 5=6 grade of the ancient Rosicrucian fraternity of the Rose of Ruby and the Cross of Gold, standing here before the door of the vault of the adepti, do solemnly affirm and testify to the faith which I hold in my heart in those greater mysteries, to which the lesser mysteries are the door; I believe that they are implanted within the soul in silence and that through the veils of silence only can they be beheld. Standing thus in the sign of Osiris slain, with all sincerity and singleness of heart, do I affirm that I will ever maintain the most perfect silence in respect thereof. I promise that I will never reveal them to the profane, nor will I hint of them to those in the order who are below the rank of Theorici Adepti Majores.

2. I will henceforth endeavour to close my ears to the call of the evil and impure, whether around me or in my own heart, being well assured that he who gazes upon evil things or listens to the lure thereof – save only with the firm intention and will to stem its progress and transmute its power into the good, the true and the beautiful – can but increase that evil. As it is written, "who is blind but my servant, or deaf as my messenger, whom I have sent?"

3. Also will I be blind to the sins and weakness of others, save only when it is my high privilege to aid and raise them[68] who seek for help. And may I be granted true humility and charity of spirit for such work.

4. I will henceforth pray continually that my own footsteps may not stumble, nor stray from that straight and narrow path of which it is said "few there be that find it." May I be guided therein by the word, which is a lamp to those who seek; that laying aside every weight I may reach forth to that which is before us.

5. And finally, I will remember that the attainment of spiritual vision, or striving therefore, does in no wise lessen, but increases my obligations

---

67 I placed the word "recites" in place of the word "repeats" as it did not make any sense.
68 Word "them" crossed out and the world "those" written in by hand.

on the material plane; and in token thereof I will earnestly seek to live a pure and honourable life, to comfort those who mourn, to bind up the broken hearted, to proclaim liberty to the captives and the opening of prison to those who are bound and to bring light to those who sit in darkness. And may Elohim Gibor give me strength to fulfil this vow.

(3rd Adept brings censor to chief adept, who censes postulant in the form of a pentagram. Head, right foot, left hand, right hand, left foot and up to head again. 2nd and 3rd Adept lead him from the portal in silence.)

POINT 2

The white altar is placed midway between the entrance and the door to the vault. Upon it are arranged the coloured candles, unlit. West of this is an aisle supporting the Tarot keys of Justice and the Hanged Man, concealing the candles from the postulant.

Chief and 2nd adepti are seated on either side of the altar: the door of the vault is open. 3rd adept remains in the west. Postulant now has bare feet except for scarlet slippers, and a purple cloak is thrown around him. The admission badge is a pair of scales with a heart in one scale and a feather on the other. 3rd adept goes to fetch the postulant: As they enter, 5 bells sound (5 bells.) 3rd adept puts aside the scales.

Chief Adept: Who is this, who cometh from Edom with dyed garments from Bozrah?

2nd Adept: I have trodden the winepress alone and of all the people there was none with me; and I looked and there was none to help and I wondered why there was none to uphold.

Chief Adept: It is good that a man should both hope and quietly wait for the salvation of the Lord, for he will not cast off for ever, for though he cause grief, yet he will have compassion according to the multitude of His mercies. Wherefore let us now pray to Him that thy footsteps fail not in thy passage through the Valley of Death.

All kneel, facing east.

Chief Adept: Oh Lord of Strength, Elohim Gibor, in all humility of spirit we invoke Thy blessing. Look down, we implore Thee, upon this postulant, who now kneeleth before thee and knocketh at the gates of the grave.

Grant him Thine aid, oh God of Israel, who givest power unto Thy people. Pour forth Thy benediction, we beseech Thee. Oh thou fire-hearted one, who dost send death that we may attain unto life everlasting; Thou at whose Word the thunders roll and the darting lightning flashes forth, grant that in the midst of storm we may find peace. Master of the diadems of Fire, crown him with light, that, emerging from the darkness of the tomb, he may enter upon the dawn of endless day! AMEN.

A pause. All rise and chief adept points to the tat pillar from which 3rd adept takes bowl of water to place in postulant's hands.

Chief Adept: Thus far, oh postulant, hast thou climbed the Mountain of Abiegnus, even the sacred mountain of initiation. Thy feet have trodden paths, steep indeed and narrow, yet clearly marked by those who have gone before thee. At every step, friendly hands have been stretched out, ready to aid thee; friendly voices have spoken encouragement in thine ear. Now must thou step forward alone into the darkness of the grave, remembering that it hath been said, "I have trodden the winepress alone." To each one who seeketh the Light cometh the period of darkness – that Dark night of the Soul of which the saints have warned us. To each cometh a time when the soul must receive the purification of absolute negation before she can hear the command "Enter thou into the joy of Thy Lord;" that purification of which the piscina of our earlier ceremonies is the foreshadowing.

Noble Lord of Eventide, place the bowl of water in the hands of the postulant, that he may behold his face as in a glass darkly.

3rd adept does so, instructing postulant to bend his face and look steadily at the reflection.

Chief Adept: Behold then, my frater, thyself submerged, even as of old the postulant was held beneath the waters of baptism until he entered the gates of death, emerging then, and then only, purified from the stains of Earth. Thus must thou also purify thyself, body and soul, in darkness and in silence before thou canst pass along the path of purgatorial fire, of which the southern pillar is the emblem, to that resurrection which we in patience hope for. No man liveth to himself and no man dieth to himself; rather each gathereth in the life of his fellows, even as a mirror gathereth images of all around it. The still mirror reflects truly and the living mirror perfects the unequal image. No troubled image finds therein its rest; for it restores that which was broken, and that which it sends forth again is peace.

But to send forth peace, first we must overcome, and herein lieth the mystery of the double letters, as thou wast told that one letter and one planet denote opposites. For in the path of Mars indeed is found war and destruction, but in the palace of Mars, which is Geburah, thou mayest find peace.

3rd Adept replaces bowl and indicates Tarot key of Hanged Man.

2nd Adept: Herein, my frater, you may perceive somewhat of the same symbolism, under another similitude. In our system of correspondences the Tarot key of the Hanged Man is attributed to the path of Mem, and in the teaching concerning the Tarot which you have already received, you have learned that the signification of this key is sacrifice. But there are other and deeper significations than this, since the Hanged Man (under which title we may remember that our Lord was "hanged upon a Tree") is also entitled the Drowned Giant, and in this likeness may be said to refer to the Adam Kadmon of the Kabbalists — the ideal man who reflects the image of God, even as thy face was but now reflected in the bowl of water. And herein is a great mystery, for in each of us is submerged that image, but oftentimes so distorted by the waves of tempestuous passion that it is unrecognisable save to the discerning eye of the adept, whose vocation it is to utter the word of power, "Peace, be still."

In the act of creation, it may be said that the Supreme sacrificed Himself by imposing certain limits, whereby He was thenceforward bound in manifestation, even as the Word conformed to the limitations of humanity in His incarnation.

Therefore must we also offer ourselves as a living sacrifice, holy, acceptable unto God, which is our reasonable service.

6=5 Ritual

> The 23rd path of Mem is called the Stable Intelligence, and it is so called because it has the virtue of consistency among all numerations.

2nd adept returns to his seat and chief adept comes forward and points to the key of Justice.

Chief Adept: The path of Lamed, you have already learnt, is attributed to the Tarot key of Justice, which leads from the Beauty of Tiphareth to the Severity of Geburah, and it may thus be said to denote the equilibrium between emotion and will. It represents, as you see, a queen seated upon her throne, her foot resting upon a fox, her hands grasping a sword and a pair of scales. Thus shall the soul, upheld by the firm will, tread underfoot the desires of the flesh, and rule her kingdom by the light of the spirit. "Mercy and Truth have met together, righteousness and peace have kissed each other," and in that embrace shall spring the Perfected Man, ready to face with tranquil mien whatsoever the day may bring forth, life or death, joy or sorrow.

> The 22nd path of the Sepher Yetzirah is known as the Faithful Intelligence, and it is so called because by it, spiritual virtues are increased and all dwellers on Earth are nearly under its shadow.

The chief adept moves to east of altar. 2nd adept hands him the censer.

3rd adept slips cowl over postulant's eyes and lights the 33 candles. Remove Tarot keys.

2nd and 3rd adepti take their places south and north of altar, each with an extinguisher.

The temple is in darkness save for the candles.

3rd adept removes cowl and cloak (from postulant).

Chief Adept: I am the Great One, Son of the Great One; I am the Fire, the Son of Fire: I have knit myself together, I have made myself whole and complete; I have renewed my youth: I am Osiris, the Lord of Eternity. Thirty-three are the centres of Life in my body, thirty-three were the years of my life upon Earth; at the end thereof did I relinquish my material life upon the Cross of Tiphareth. I am the word spoken in silence. I am the Anointed of the Lord. Nine are the letters of my Name.

2nd Adept: Homage unto Thee, oh Lord of the Starry Skies: and of the Aeons of the Bornless beyond. Thou art more glorious than the Sun in its rising, Thou who didst sacrifice the life of the flesh.

3rd Adept: Oh grant unto me a path whereon I may pass in peace, for I am just and true. I have not spoken lies wittingly, nor have I done aught with deceit.

2nd and 3rd adepti put out four brown candles.

Chief Adept: He that believeth in Me believeth not in Me but in Him that sent Me. And he that seeth Me seeth Him that sent Me.

2nd Adept: Homage unto Thee, oh Soul of Everlastingness; Thou Soul Who dwellest in eternal light. Thou art Lord of life and death, for Thou hast died unto the passions.

3rd Adept: Oh grant unto me a path whereon I may pass in peace, for I am just and true. I have not spoken lies wittingly, nor have I done aught with deceit.

2nd and 3rd adepti put out four red candles.

Chief Adept: I am come a light unto the world, that whosoever believeth in Me should not abide in darkness.

2nd Adept: Homage unto Thee in Thy dominion over the luminaries; the diadem of fire encircleth Thy brows; Thou art the One who maketh the strength which protecteth us, and Thou dwellest in peace above all, for Thou hast died unto the Body of the Stars.

3rd Adept: Oh grant unto me a path whereon I may pass in peace,[69] for I am just and true. I have not spoken lies wittingly, nor have I done aught with deceit.

2nd and 3rd adepti put out four green candles.

---

69 Line was crossed out.

Chief Adept: I am the vine, ye are the branches. He that abideth in Me and I in Him, the same bringeth forth much fruit; for without Me ye can do nothing.

2nd Adept: Homage unto Thee, oh Lord of the Vineyard; Thou turnest back the worker in evil and causest the vine to bear fruit: for Thou hast shed the blood of Thy desires.

3rd Adept: Oh grant unto me a path whereon I may pass in peace, for I am just and true. I have not spoken lies wittingly, nor have I done aught with deceit.

2nd adept puts out red light in centre.

Chief Adept: I have glorified Thee on Earth, I have finished the work which Thou gavest me to do: the glory which Thou gavest me I have given them, that they may be one.

2nd Adept: Homage unto Thee, who art beautiful at morn and at eve: the never resting stars sing hymns of praise unto Thee; the stars which never fail glorify Thee, for Thou art dead unto sin.

3rd Adept: Oh grant unto me a path whereon I may pass in peace, for I am just and true. I have not spoken lies wittingly, nor have I done aught with deceit.

2nd and 3rd adepti put out 7 violet candles.

Chief Adept: I have declared unto them Thy name and will declare it, that the love wherewith Thou hast loved me may be in them, and I in them.

2nd Adept: Homage unto Thee who art crowned King of Kings, oh the divine substance. Thou sendest forth the word and the Earth is flooded with silence at Thy renunciation.

3rd Adept: Oh grant unto me a path whereon I may pass in peace, for I am just and true. I have not spoken lies wittingly, nor have I done aught with deceit.

2nd and 3rd adepti put out 6 yellow candles.

Chief Adept: These things have I spoken unto you that in me ye might have peace. In the world, ye shall have tribulation, but be of good cheer. I have overcome the world.

2nd Adept: Homage, unto Thee, Thou Prince of Peace; the souls of the east pay homage unto Thee, and when they meet Thy Majesty they say "Come, come in Peace."

3rd Adept: Oh grant unto me a path whereon I may pass in peace, for I am just and true. I have not spoken lies wittingly, nor have I done aught with deceit.

2nd adept puts out 4 green candles (above this was done by 2nd and 3rd together)

Three candles now remain alight. <u>Chief adept takes the white one</u> and faces east, still swinging the censer; one blue one at each side remain.

2nd and 3rd adepti lift aside all the rest, leaving space for postulant to pass through.

Chief adept leads the way into vault, places light on pedestal and gives censer to 3rd adept and cloak.[70]

Chief adept passes to south.

Postulant stands west of the pastos.

2nd adept stands beside him, takes strip of linen and winds it slowly round him as chief adept recites sentences, binding brow, lips, heart, solar plexus and hips.

Six bells sound.

Chief Adept: *(for brow)* Be not curious in unnecessary matters, for more things are shown thee than thou canst understand.

(For lips) Be silent, oh man, before the Lord, for He is raised up out of His holy habitation.

---

70   "and cloak" was crossed out by hand.

(For heart) Woe be to the fearful heart and faint hands, and to him that goeth two ways.

(For solar plexus) The greater thou art, the more humble thyself, and thou shalt find favour before the Lord.

(For hips) To know the Lord is perfect righteousness; yea, to know His power is the root of immortality.

The bandage being now on, chief and 2nd adepti assist postulant into the pastos and lay him down, head to north, hands crossed at wrists, palms up, above his head. They sprinkle salt over him.

2nd Adept: So shalt thou rest in peace.

Chief Adept: Until the day break and the shadows flee away.

PRAYER OF COMMITMENT

Chief Adept: Oh Thou who makest perfected souls to enter into the everlasting glory, cause now, we beseech Thee, the perfected soul of this our frater to be victorious over death. Having ears, may he hear with understanding; having eyes, may he perceive the spirit; having lips, may he speak the truth; having a heart, may he love righteousness. Quicken in him, oh divine creator, the life divine, draw him with cords that he may run after Thee, bind him to the altar that he may evermore serve Thee. Amen.

They withdraw from the vault, leaving the door slightly ajar. The vault is in darkness, save for the candle. The hours are sounded and sentences for the 36 hours are read outside.

1. I will both lay me down in peace and sleep; for Thou, Lord, makest me to dwell in safety.
2. Thou wilt keep him in perfect peace, whose mind is stayed on Thee, for he trusteth in Thee.
3. He giveth his beloved sleep.
4. When thou liest down, thou shalt not be afraid, yea thou shalt lie down and thy sleep shall be sweet.
5. Though a man shut his eyes to the last, still cometh death, the Render of the Veil.

6. If thou hadst known how to suffer, thou wouldst have had the power not to suffer.
7. The place of rest, the home of peace, is in truth the very cross itself, the firm foundation, on which the whole creation rests.
8. I have torn myself asunder, I have brought unto them the mysteries of light to purify them, for they are the purgation of all matter.
9. Blessed is the man who crucifieth Malkuth and doth not allow Malkuth to crucify him.
10. Blessed is the man who knoweth the Word, for he hath brought down heaven and bound the Earth and raised it heavenwards; and he becometh the midst.
11. Watchman, what of the night?
12. The morning cometh and also the Night. If ye will enquire, enquire ye.
13. I sleep, but my heart waketh.
14. The heart sleepeth; who shall wake it? The wind of dawn hath stirred the night, day is near.
15. The morning is my messenger; rise thou up and greet me; the night is also from me, bless me and rest.
16. Of the universal aeons there are two growths, without beginning or end, springing from one root, which is the power of silence, invisible, inapprehensible.
17. The mystery which is beyond the world, whereby all things exist, because of it all mysteries exist and all their regions.
18. Cease not to seek, day and night, until thou hast found the purifying mysteries.
19. Before the eyes can see, they must be incapable of tears.
20. Before the ears can hear, they must have lost their sensitiveness.
21. Before the voice can speak in the presence of the masters, it must have lost its power to wound.
22. Before the feet can stand in the presence of the masters, they must be bathed in the heart's blood.
23. One is the nature below, which is subject to death; and one is the race without a king which is born above.
24. And he cried "a lion". Behold I stand continually upon the watchtower in the daytime, and I am in my ward whole nights.
25. And He said, I am thou and thou art I, and wheresoever thou art, I am there I am, in ALL am I sown.
26. Wheresoever thou willest thou gatherest me, and gathering me, thou gatherest thyself.

27. I shall be merciful to thee in the cross of light.
28. Rejoicing, I come to Thee, Thou cross, the life-giver, Cross whom I know now to be mine; I know Thy mystery, for Thou hast been planted in the world to make fast things unstable.
29. Until the day break and the shadows flee away, I will get me to the Mountain of Myrrh and the Hill of Frankincense.
30. The people that walked in darkness have seen a great light; they that dwell in the Land of the Shadow of Death, upon them hath the light shined.
31. For on this mountain shall the hand of the Lord rest.
32. He will swallow up death in victory, and the Lord will wipe away tears from all faces.
33. Who is this that leadeth them but she that dwelt in darkness and in silence? Whose coming is as the beauty of the beloved when the Sun shineth out from the[71] clouds.
34. Pilgrim of the day, go forth and meet in every face the Risen One. If He wake, He will greet thee, and thy portion shall be double; if He slumber, hail Him in silence; wake Him not. He knoweth His own hour and God is over all:
35. Thy dead men shall live; together with my dead body shall they arise. Awake and sing, ye that dwell in dust; for thy dew is as the dew of herbs.
36. Hold no longer silence, cry ye aloud for the beauty of the Divine Mother; for in her is peace.

There is a pause. Shekinah appears from behind the curtain in the northeast with the alabaster lamp and spray of acacia. She bends over postulant and kisses him on the brow, saying:

Shekinah: Arise, shine, for thy light is come, and the glory of the Lord is risen upon thee.

3rd adept turns up lights.[72]

Shekinah lays acacia on postulant's breast, then anoints him on his feet, solar plexus, lips, brow, and palms of hands, saying:

Shekinah: *(for feet)* The Life of the Tree is thine – arise and walk.

---

71 "the" was crossed out by hand.
72 This line was written in by hand.

(For solar-plexus) The Life of the Man is thine – receive and give.
(For lips) The Life of the Word is thine – utter and love.
(For brow) The Life of the World is thine – receive the spirit.
(For palms) The Life of the Stars is thine – be filled with joy.

There is a pause, then Shekinah removes acacia, moves to the foot of the pastos and says:

Shekinah: The place of hiding is opened, thy place of hiding is revealed. Behold, thy soul hath dwelt in darkness; let her now return unto light.

Thy spirit withdrew unto the stars, which never diminish, return to bring power to thy soul. Thy brow is like unto the king's, thy lips are opened, and thy heart is upon its throne. Thou hast knowledge, yea movement is restored unto thy hands and feet. Thy father dwelleth in thee, oh son of the most high. Thou art the Son of the Great One and thou hast seen the hidden things. Thou shalt not die a second time, for thou hast gained the mastery. Arise, then, and come forth, that in the power of silence thou mayest save mankind. I send thee forth, fail not, nor falter, but remember that which thou hast received.

Turn up light in vault. Shekinah withdraws.

Chief and 2nd adepti enter vault. Chief goes to the east, 2nd stands at west. They bend down and take postulant's hands, placing their free hands behind his shoulders and thus assist him out of the pastos.

2nd adept removes the bandages, while the chief adept says:

Chief Adept: Hail, hail unto thee who hast died; rise up …… thou hast embraced thy bones, thou hast gathered together thy flesh and blood; Elohim Gibor guardeth thee; Elohim Gibor strengthened thy hands; yea He guideth thy feet; thy lips are open,[73] thou hast received thy head; thou hast received thy soul, and thy spirit hath returned to thee from the stars which never diminish.

They lead postulant out of the vault so that he stands just outside door, chief adept at south, 2nd adept at north. Shekinah comes to door behind him. Water drops from her raised hands onto his head.

---

73 "ed" has been added by hand.

2nd Adept: Happy is he who hath looked upon the place of rest; the waters shall not overwhelm him. _____[74]=Server of Silence, shall be his name.

Chief Adept: I am the Lord of those who are raised up, who came forth, out darkness.

Postulant: *(as prompted by the 2nd adept)* I have entered in as one who hath no understanding. I have come forth as lord of life through the beautiful law.

Chief and 2nd adepti turn and face postulant. 2nd adept shows two signs.

2nd Adept: Behold, thou shalt turn away nine eyes from evil, even as Nephthys turned away her face from the destroyer of Osiris; and thus shalt thou withdraw thy soul from temptation, even as Isis withdrew from darkness.

Chief Adept: *(shows the grip)* Herein is reflected the five powers which have been restored to thee. It is the sign of the Mighty One – Blessed be He – even of Elohim Gibor, the Lord of Strength. Twenty is the number of his name.

They turn to the postulant, facing east, and all kneel at the door of the vault.

Shekinah stands within the door holding the butter, honey and milk. As she offers butter and honey, they all make the sign of Nephthys; as she offers milk the officers make the sign of Isis.

Shekinah: Butter and honey shall ye eat, that ye may know to refuse the evil and choose the good. Desire ye the sincere milk of the word that ye may grow thereby.

They remain kneeling in silence. Shekinah withdraws to the east.

Long pause.

Turn out the vault light. Light fades.

---

[74] "Δοῦλος Σιγῆς Doulos Siges, Parademos Che Vallis" has been written by hand.

Chief adept rises and closes the door of the vault and then turns and says:

Chief Adept: In the name of Elohim Gibor, depart in peace, for the Shekinah hath withdrawn herself.

(He faces east and exclaims):

Shekinah, thou Queen of the east, forget not thy sons. Tabanu, Taboons, dwell in our souls.

Queen of the Dawn land, Bath Qol, speak to our spirits that we might go with thy blessing.

Oh thou, beautiful daughter of Light!

After a long pause, chief adept stoops and raises the postulant in silence and the 2nd adept leads him out.

THE END

VI
6=5 RITUAL COMMENTARY

THE 6=5 is broadly a continuation of the 5=6. In the 5=6 you were expected to understand magic and work mostly on refining yourself. In the 6=5, you were expected to carry out more Macrocosmic magic for the good of humanity. This often required you to deal with the abstract forces that many consider as evil. The idea was that you would end up being a warrior in the dualistic battle between good and evil.

However, the ritual itself has many hints which if taken to its logical conclusion could have led an initiate into a different place magically, where many ended up. There is an absence of any evil-smiting and there are hints that the 6=5 was more about dealing with the Underworld than any Christian ghostbusting. A knowledge about this style of Underworld magic was never really understood within the Golden Dawn system, although it is hinted at. The 6=5 grade was a logical point to bring in Goetic magic.

One of the most common books on Goetic magic was Mathers and Crowley's *Lesser Key of Solomon*. Recent research has indicated that this Christianised text was later than many Golden Dawn people believed. Further research carried out by modern researchers such as Jake Stratton-Kent[75] suggest that true Goetia was a return to the pagan underworld magic of ancient times which had been literally demonised by later Christian users.

New generations of magicians are finding that Goetia, though still unpredictable, is less about dealing with demons as working with the dead, the Underworld Gods and those shadow sides of forgotten Ghosts.

When you look at the 6=5 ritual with that in mind, you can see that it predicted that discovery, and works well with that concept.

Take for example the preparation of the olive oil by Shekinah which is possibly the only account of blood magic being used in the

---

75   Stratton-Kent, Jake. *Geosophia*. [Dover]: Scarlet Imprint/Bibliothèque Rouge, 2010. Print.

Golden Dawn. In this, she pours the olive oil into an alabaster bowl and puts her blood into it. She then places a wick into the oil and burns the candle. This magical technique cannot be found outside older pagan magic and is unchristian in its approach. As she pricks her finger, she says "the blood is the life of man, let the man give his life." The lighting of the wick turns the ritual into a sacrifice. The room would have been filled with the sacrificed energy of Shekinah's blood. The phrases are wrong for a Christian approach. It is the blood of Jesus which needed to be sacrificed and not that of a man. It is no good to argue that Shekinah is the female side of God either and that therefore this sacrifice is that of Jesus. "The man" in this case is clearly the candidate who is being called by divine destiny to give up his life as a sacrifice.

This idea of a sacrifice being needed to enter the Underworld, or to talk to the beings within it, comes from the earliest period of human history. To enter the world of the dead, this ritual is saying, you have to be sacrificed.

I should point out that there are other ways to see the same symbol. In Exodus 27:20 it was seen as the fuel for spirituality: "You shall charge the sons of Israel, that they bring you clear oil of beaten olives for the light, to make a lamp burn continually."

The Roman Goddess of Wisdom, Minerva, taught the art of cultivation of the olive tree and extraction of its oil and the ancient Greeks had a legend of a contest between Poseidon, the god of the sea, and Athena, goddess of peace and wisdom. The victor would be the one who produced the most useful gift for the people of the newly built city of Athens.

Poseidon struck a rock with his trident and a spring emerged from which a horse appeared, which would be a symbol of strength and power and an invaluable aid in war. Athena threw her spear into the ground, and it turned into the olive tree – a symbol of peace and a provider of food and fuel. The people declared that Athena's gift was considered the greater, and the new city, Athens, was named after her.

Pat Zalewski in his commentary on the ritual points out that Athena represented voyages. This makes her symbol ideal for the journey into the Underworld which is about to start. By adding blood to the mix, the 6=5 was creating a mythical fairy called Melusine. Melusine was serpent from the waist down but this could only be seen when she was having a magical bath. She was famous for protecting and healing. Her stories start to appear in the 15th century. Zalewski thinks that this legend means that the postulant has to make a series of transformations as part of their journey.

During the opening, this theme of entering the realm of death is reinforced with the Christian references to the Valley of the Shadow and 1 Corinthians 15:55.

It would be easy to see these simply as Christian bible verses, but they were also a feature of the Christian funeral ritual. To an Anglican you would be subconsciously carrying out a funeral ritual for the candidate. This is an interesting technique to send the candidate into the Underworld by means of a mini-funeral service.

The ritual's focus is that of the grave. Unlike the 5=6, where the tomb is supposed to be filled with Christian Rosencreutz, this one is empty, and curiously it is not the Christian Cross which is called to resurrect the soul from the grave but the pagan Egyptian Ankh Cross, with its allusions to the Girdle of Venus or Isis.

In the outer order, this taking of an astral shell of the candidate and placing it between the pillars is a common magical technique. Between the pillars the astral form is instructed by the godforms of the grade so that when it is reconnected to the candidate during the final part of each ritual, the candidate's sphere of sensation and unconscious knowledge changes and is transformed.

In the 5=6 and 6=5, this astral form is placed in the pastos. In the 6=5 another form of astral body is required. It has to be strongly influenced by the three higher cabbalistic bodies – the Yechidah, the Chiah and the Neshamah. These bodies are attributed to the highest stations on the Tree of Life. They are fused with the candidate's astral form when the officers, who represent these bodies, place their wands to the pastos. The base of the wand is in the coffin where it connects to the candidate's astral body. They are being held by the white bands. The Ankh crosses are linked above the pastos to create a channel for the higher forces of these spheres. This impregnates the astral fragment of the candidate and mimics the Ancient Egyptian image of a Ka which was an astral and spiritual fusion.

This Ka, which was shown in Hieroglyphic as two outstretched arms, was part of the name of the God of magic, Heka. Heka literally means "activating the Ka," because the Ancient Egyptians thought that magic was performed by activating the power of the soul. This part of the ritual is providing the postulant with a Ka which can be easily activated. This advanced astral body is also tuned to Mars thanks to the fact that the walls of the vault have been draped with red. This means that all the colours of the wall are reflected into this astral body through that colour. Although the colours of the vault wall cannot be seen, they radiate into the back of the curtain creating a solid mixed wall of force. This strongly influences the simulacrum/Ka in the vault. This is literally being flavoured throughout the opening, and until the postulant sits into it in the last section.

The Chief Adept does not invoke any Christian god, but instead the Great Mother Matrona. Matrona was a Latin name for a Celtic Mother goddess. She was venerated in regions of Germania, Eastern Gaul, and upper Italy between the first to the fifth century AD. The Celts seem to have used the name to represent many different Goddesses, but many of them had an Underworld connection (the most obvious is Larunda who was a Roman Queen of the Underworld and silence). The ritual equates her to Shekinah which is doubly odd as there are few similarities.

Shekinah wears black and hides the light under her veil. This represents the spark of light contained within matter. When the temple is opened she reveals the light. This symbolically means that the candidate has died and the spark of life is freed for its journey to the Underworld.

In this ritual, the door of the vault was said to be that which led to the underworld. The pillars were special blue and red pillars about 2 metres high. Ankh pillar in portal in north, facing inwards and Tat in south. The Tat was tapered, having four horizontal shelves painted in the elemental colours. On the bottom shelf stood a bowl of water (with circular mirror at bottom). On the top shelf was a burning brazier (or spirit lamp).

The vault itself was entirely draped in Red and the pastos in black.

Part one begins with the candidate knocking on the door holding the Hierophant's lamen, which is a symbol of the 5=6. He is wearing his adept's white robe, but has a black belt, shoes and black cloak. This has similarities to the robes worn by a Goetic magician described in Reginald Scot's *Discoverie of Witchcraft* (1584)[76] which was familiar to both Felkin and John Brodie-Innes:

> "Let the Exorcist, being cloathed with a black Garment, reaching to his knee, and under that a white Robe of fine Linnen that falls unto

---

76   Scot, R. (1972). *The discoverie of witchcraft*. New York: Dover Publications.

his ankles, fix himself in the midst of that place where he intends to perform his Conjurations: And throwing his old Shooes about ten yards from the place, let him put on his consecrated shooes of russet Leather with a Cross cut on the top of each shooe."

The candidate is dressed with the darkness of the Underworld over the robe of glory, mimicking the Shekinah with her light underneath darkness. But unlike other rituals he is not at all passive. He is approaching the Vault, or the gate of the underworld under his own steam.

Crucially he has made a vow of silence for 20 hours, and will remain so as he enters the ritual. It is a mistake here to equate silence with secrecy. I have been told that the reason that the candidate is able to enter the ritual is because he has kept his vow of secrecy. In fact, it is a reference to the 0=0 initiation, which is also an invocation to the Underworld.

"Hiero: The voice of my higher soul said unto me, Let me enter the Path of Darkness, peradventure thus shall I obtain the Light. I am the only being in an abyss of darkness. From the darkness came I forth ere my birth, from the silence of a primal sleep, and the Voice of Ages answered unto my soul, I am he that formulates in darkness. Child of Earth; the Light shineth in the darkness, but the darkness comprehendeth it not."

The idea in the 6=5 is that the candidate is preparing to enter the silence of the primal sleep, the darkness of death and the underworld. Larunda was incapable of keeping secrets and told Juno of Jupiter's affair with Juturna, the wife of Janus. Jupiter cut out Larunda's tongue and ordered Mercury to conduct her to Avernus, the gateway to the Underworld and realm of Pluto. Mercury, however, fell in love with Larunda and together they created two children, referred to as the Lares. The Lares were Underworld beings who lived in the real world and became spirits of places, particularly houses.

Larunda was worshipped as the "silent one" and has clear connections to Matrona and Shekinah. In the legend, she is the exposer of Jupiter and his opposite. On the Tree of Life, Mars is the opposite of Jupiter.

In addition to his normal title, the Chief Adept is called the King of Salem. This is a reference to Melchizedek, whose name can be translated as "my king is righteous."

Melchizedek was a king and priest mentioned during the Abram narrative in the 14th chapter of the Book of Genesis and was seen as a prototype of Jesus. In Genesis he is described as a king of Salem, which means "Peace" and priest of El Elyon. He brings bread and wine and blesses Abram in what Christians see as the first communion. The Letter to the Hebrews calls Jesus Christ a priest forever in the order of Melchizedek. The Chief is using the Godform of the High Priest with symbolism that connects him to Christ. He wears Blue and Purple robes which symbolise the powers of Chesed or Mercy. He carries the same implements that he did during the 5=6.

The robes are a lot simpler. Gone are the Egyptian nemes and each officer wears a square of coloured material tied with a cord. What is interesting is that nemes are still mentioned in the requirements. It appears that the change to the square cloth was made after the Felkins printed the rituals.

The 2nd Adept is the Excellent Prince of the Horizon and he wears the Red and Orange of Geburah. The title suggests the Dawn and it is interesting that it is this grade that is literally dawning on the candidate.

The 3rd Adept is the Lord of the Eventide, and he wears the Yellow and Rose of Tiphareth. The title suggests sunset and the fact that the grade of Tiphareth is past.

What is telling about the second and third adepts is that they are connected to the beginning and end of the night, with the Chief taking the role of Priest between them. In the Golden Dawn we are always told that two forces create a third, so therefore the actions of the Night represented by the 6=5 are controlled by, and give birth to, the 7=4.

On his first encounter with the Chief Adept, the candidate is told that the "hour cometh and even now the son of man shall appear." He is asked if he is ready to discard his body of flesh and meet him "in the air."

On the face of it this is a reference to the Second Coming: 1 Thessalonians 4:17.

> "Then we which are alive and remain shall be caught up together with them in the clouds, to meet the Lord in the air: and so shall we ever be with the Lord."

However, it is hardly being used to mean the same thing as the "rapture" concept, dear to so many born-again Christians. It is saying that if you want to meet the Son of Man, you have to drop your body and meet him in the Air.

The location "in the Air" is not the same thing as sky. The air refers to anything which is below the rule of the moon. Sub-lunar beings are the astral creatures, elementals, dead, and gods which Christians believed were demonic.

The chief is telling the candidate that to meet his higher spiritual self he has to drop his body and enter into the astral underworld. Stratton-Kent has pointed out that the Underworld had different locations in various points in history. Initially it was considered as being under the earth and then later it was projected onto the sky. The 6=5 places the Underworld in a sub-lunar state. You have to drop your body, but you can go up or down.

The candidate silently gives the sign of silence to indicate that he is ready to make that sacrifice. The next section comes from Book Three (plate 17 of the Papyrus of Ani) of the Ancient Egyptian Book of the Dead. As each challenge is spoken, the candidate is pushed closer to the vault.

Again, this sequence could be written off as copying the 5=6 where some of these phrases appear. If you look at the source, you can see that something deeper is intended.

That book begins with the sentence: "Here begin the praises and glorifyings of coming out from and of going into the glorious Khert-neter, which is in the beautiful Amentet, of coming forth by day in all the forms of existence which it may please the deceased to take, of playing at draughts, of sitting in the Seh hall, and of appearing as a living soul."

The purpose of this spell in the Book of the Dead was to enable a dead person's Ba to re-join its corpse in the Underworld. If the spell was recited, it would enable the dead person to live on in the Underworld as if it were this world. It also enabled the Ba to travel between this world and the next. This chapter is supposed to allow free movement beyond his tomb.

This becomes explained when the candidate's girdle is removed and it is described as the loosening of the corruptible in the Body of Osiris. It is a preparation for a form of astral projection.

Here also the door of the vault is clearly identified as the door to the Underworld. It is only in the Underworld, says the Chief Adept, that you can see the Sun in his Nadir, crucified between the Pillars of the Tree of Life.

So there has to be an oath in the grade and that is a five pointed affair connected to Geburah. The oath is an important sacrifice, which allows you to enter the grade. For this reason, it is done while standing as if you were bound to a cross. The candidate is saying his oath at the door of the Underworld, which in this situation is also the door of the Judgement Hall of Maat.

The first clause is to silence – not secrecy. The candidate agrees that Greater Mysteries, to which the Lesser Mysteries are the Door, are implanted within the Soul in Silence, and that through the Veils of Silence only can they be beheld. This is not a secrecy oath; it is acknowledgement that you can only see the Greater Mysteries when you are silent. The only thing you agree is that you will not reveal them to the profane, nor hint of them to those in the Order who are below the rank of Theorici Adepti Majores, but that clause of the oath is largely redundant because you really cannot.

The second clause is a little trickier. The candidate says that they will close their ears to the call of the evil and impure, whether around them or in their own heart. "He who gazes upon evil things or listens to the lure thereof – save only with the firm intention and will to stem its progress and transmute its power into the good, the true and the beautiful."

If taken literally this rules out anything to do with evil, especially the summoning of demons at all. It is difficult to do any of the sorts of demon summoning suggested by Crowley's Lesser Key if you are not willing to give evil a hearing. In addition, if you are about to head into the Underworld, you are almost certain to see things which many good Christians would consider evil. However, the oath implies that you have to stem the progress of evil and transmute its power into "the good, the true and the beautiful." Then there is this cryptic comment: "As it is written, 'Who is blind but my Servant, or deaf as my Messenger whom I have sent.'" This is a reference to the bible verse Isaiah 42:19. Looking at it in context, that particular verse is a moan about Israel.

> "Hear, you deaf! And look, you blind, that you may see. Who is blind but My servant, Or so deaf as My messenger whom I send? Who is so blind as he that is at peace with Me, Or so blind as the servant of

the LORD? You have seen many things, but you do not observe them; your ears are open, but none hears."

By quoting this particular verse, this section of the oath is apparently contradictory to the first. On the one hand you are supposed to close your ears and eyes to evil, but then it gives you an example from Israel where they were doing just that, and in the eyes of Isaiah were doing evil. This would be missed by modern Golden Dawn people who generally do not know their bibles, but for Whare Ra adepts it would have been obvious: Isaiah never said that the Israelites were good because they were deaf and blind. Normally in occult writings you see the phrase from Revelation "let he who has ears to hear" being used as a precursor to something which needs to be read deeply to be properly understood.

The message here is that you are not supposed to listen to the call of evil. Since the oath fails to define what evil actually is, it is probably talking about objective rather than subjective evil. In the 0=0, the candidate is told that evil is about going to extremes and nothing to do with entities who others might consider evil.

The third clause talks about being blind to the sins of others unless it is your job to teach them something. The idea is that by ignoring what others are doing you will somehow become more humble yourself. This is a call to Christian ideals, but is surprisingly incompatible with the concepts of Geburah. It is also directly contradictory to the 0=0 where people who ignore evil are dubbed "permitters of evil" through their inaction.

However, this clause is similar to the one above. It implies that you deal with evil by ignoring it and concentrating on the good. However, the get out clause is "if you have to teach." If you wanted to do a ritual to overthrow a corrupt government, or politician, you could not do that if you "ignored evil." You could do that ritual if it was your job to teach the politician or government a lesson and only then if you had responsibility for that particular act. Since we get the governments we deserve, we equally have a duty to teach a corrupt government a lesson, either through magic or the ballot box.

The fourth clause is to "pray continually that my own footsteps may not stumble, nor stray from that straight and narrow path" and to be guided therein by the word which is a lamp to those who seek. Taken literally this is a Christian creed, to read your bible every day and pray that you are not tempted to drift to extremes. Like the other clauses, this is not what it seems to be either. The oath is a reminder of the 1=10 where the candidate is shown the dangers of going to extremes. The Word here is the more of an invocation to the first chapter of John's Gospel.

"In the beginning was the word [logos] and the word was before God and the word was God." Following the Word then is to listen to your Higher Self, which was before the throne of God during creation and was actually God itself. There is a big difference between following your true divine self and the words written in a book and approved by a Roman politician 1700 years ago. In the Magical Order of the Aurora Aurea, we tend to equate the Logos with the Egyptian God Thoth, who is a representative of the Mind of the One Thing.

The last clause is interesting because it reminds the 6=5 that he cannot run away from matter. This is a point often forgotten by mystics and Gnostics who see matter as evil. The Adeptus Major has to seek to live a pure and honourable life, to comfort those who mourn, to bind up the broken hearted, to proclaim liberty to the captives and the opening of prison to those who are bound and to bring light to those who sit in darkness.

This again is almost opposite to the previous clauses, where inaction is called for. This is a rallying call for an esoteric revolutionary.

The clauses of the oath are sealed into the candidate's sphere of sensation using a pentagram of Earth. This is the only time, other than the 1=10, where an elemental force is not controlled by a Spirit pentagram. In my opinion, both were in error and the oath should be sealed with an active and passive Spirit pentagram followed by the Earth pentagram. Personally, I would also favour using a Fire pentagram, as the grade is to do with the Martian, fiery Geburah. The candidate is then led out to allow this particular piece of psychic surgery to take effect.

In Point Two, a white altar is placed midway between the entrance and the door to the vault. Upon it are arranged the coloured candles, unlit. West of this is an aisle supporting the Tarot Keys of Justice and the Hanged Man, concealing the candles from the postulant. I have been unable to find someone who could tell me about the size of the tarot cards in any of the Whare Ra rituals. In the outer order, the cards were not coloured, because the colour scales were supposed to have been revealed. In the 6=5 there is no point hiding the colours. To do what is specified here, the card would have to be quite large.

Pat Zalewski has released his versions of these cards and so they do not need to be gone into here.

The postulant enters the temple holding scales and a feather. This is because he has entered the Underworld and the temple of Maat from the Book of the Dead. It is for this reason that the Book of the Dead cartouches were painted on the Whare Ra pillars in reverse.

The cartouche for the white pillar on nearly every Golden Dawn temple has been placed on the black pillar and the black pillar on the white. This is because the white pillar is supposed to contain all the Second Order mysteries and the black one the First Order.

It is obvious that the First Order is all about the Judgement Hall of Maat and this is shown on the black pillar. Much is made of this in the Whare Ra portal ceremony. If Whare Ra was going to use the Judgement Hall for the 6=5 as part of its Underworld initiation then the pillars would have to be flipped.

Pat Zalewski pointed out on his web group that the cartouches work either way.

> "Felkin solved the problem and switched it back to match what was being taught. You can also see this from an alchemical colour perspective as well, the Blackening to the Whitening… The pillar plates to match aspects of the 0=0. I am firmly siding with Felkin here, regardless of what Brodie or Mathers had on their pillars. I am told some temples never had any plates on them at all."

Based on the idea that the Judgement Hall happens quite late in the Book of the Dead, it does make sense that it is connected to the 6=5. After all, another meaning of Geburah is Judgement and the Justice card is a way to enter this sphere.

The scales and feather indicate that he has been judged and is allowed to enter the temple. On the face, this judgement did not ever actually happen, but it was alluded to during the oath.

The scales are put to one side and the Chief Adept says "Who is this who cometh from Edom with dyed garments from Bozrah?" The Second Adept replies: "I have trodden the winepress alone and of all the people there was none with me; and I looked and there was none to help and I wondered why there was none to uphold."

This sticks out like a sore thumb and is complete rubbish if you do not understand your Old Testament and realise it is a hacked-about bible verse. It comes from Isaiah 63:1-3:

1 Who is this that cometh from Edom, with dyed garments from Bozrah? this that is glorious in his apparel, travelling in the greatness of his strength? I that speak in righteousness, mighty to save.

2 Wherefore art thou red in thine apparel, and thy garments like him that treadeth in the wine vat?

3 I have trodden the winepress alone; and of the people there was none with me: for I will tread them in mine anger, and trample them in my fury; and their blood shall be sprinkled upon my garments, and I will stain all my raiment.

Edom, besides being a place, is the word for 'red' in Hebrew. The same word is used in the next verse "Why are your clothes 'red?'" Bozrah means a 'sheepfold.' It was one of the verses which was used to link the Old Testament with Christianity. The chapter is about the reconciliation brought about by the Messiah. The reconciliation involves retribution and vengeance against sin.

This statement links the postulant to Christ who is in a position to judge the wicked.

Then there is another statement which is a paraphrase taken from an obscure bible verse from Lamentations 3 v26-32:

26 [Teth] It is good that a man should both hope and quietly wait for the salvation of the LORD.

27 [Teth] It is good for a man that he bear the yoke in his youth.

28 [Yod] He sitteth alone and keepeth silence, because he hath borne it upon him.

29 [Yod] He putteth his mouth in the dust; if so be there may be hope.

30 [Kaph] He giveth his cheek to him that smiteth him: he is filled full with reproach.

31 [Kaph] For the Lord will not cast off for ever:

32 But though he cause grief, yet will he have compassion according to the multitude of his mercies.

These verses were prefixed by a Hebrew letter, although that does not appear to be the mystery of the use of this particular chapter.

As the name suggests, Lamentations is all about how miserable experiences can be useful. In fact it suggests the concept of a Dark Night of the Soul. So rather than bringing in the powers of Geburah onto others, the forces of Judgment are being turned onto the candidate and create an effective dark night of the soul where the postulant has to lean on his unseen higher self to survive.

One thing which is common with this grade is a tremendous feeling of despair and misery. Dr. Pullen Burry (1854-1926), who abandoned his family and the Golden Dawn to seek his fortune in the gold rush, attempted to push himself into the 6=5 state without any assistance from an esoteric group. He complained to Paul Foster Case that his dark night of the soul was a direct result of his 6=5 attempts.

To curtail these problems for the postulant, there is an invocation to the "Fire-hearted One" who "sends Death" in the hope that in the midst of storm "we may find Peace." This prayer was inspired by the Leontica or Lion Grade so called Mithraic Ritual which was available in translation published in the Echoes from the Gnosis Series, by G. R. S. Mead.

> "Hear me ... o Lord, Who with Thy Breath hast closed the Fiery Bars of Heaven; Twin-bodied; Ruler of the Fire; Creator of the Light; o Holder of the Keys; In-breather of the Fire; Fire-hearted One, Whose Breath gives Light; Thou Who dost joy in Fire; Beauteous of Light; o Lord of Light, Whose Body is of Fire; Light-giver, Fire-sower; Fire-loosener, Whose Life is in the Light; Fire-whirler, Who sett'st the Light in motion; Thou Thunder-rouser; o Thou Light Glory, Light-increaser; Controller of the Light Empyrean; o Thou Star-tamer!"

Next the Chief Adept creates a mini-pathworking which shows the postulant climbing the Abiegnus, the Sacred Mountain of Initiation. The candidate is told that everyone needs the purification of absolute negation before they can hear the command "Enter thou into the joy of Thy Lord", again reinforcing the need for some form of dark night of the soul.

Now the postulant is shown his face reflected in water, and recreates the Hanged Man tarot card. There is a lot in this simple ritual act. Firstly, he is recreating the One Thing as it moved on the face of the waters, and thus created the universe. Although he is not actually baptised in a Christian sense he is seeing the principle. The universe is a mirror in which his divine self is reflecting itself.

The candidate is assured that by sacrificing himself he too will learn.

After a lecture on the tarot cards and the path, which follow the same templates as the outer order, the postulant is blinded by having the cowl put over his eyes. The candles are lit and the black robe is taken off. The temple is in darkness other than the candles which put out a lot of heat and light. The ritual returns to the Book of the Dead [Chapter XLIII] and a spell which was supposed to prevent your head being cut off in the Underworld.

> Saith Osiris Ani: "I am the great One, son of the great One; I am Fire, the son of Fire, to whom was given his head after it had been cut off. The head of Osiris was not carried away from him; let not the head of Osiris Ani be carried away from him. I have knit together my bones, I have made myself whole and sound; I have become young once more; I am Osiris, the Lord of eternity."

The ritual has removed the concept of losing the head at all, and has concentrated on the part of the ritual which knits together Osiris's bones. Having looked into the waters, the candidate has entered into death and needs to be reassembled.

To this spell has been added that: "Thirty-three are the centres of Life in my Body, thirty-three were the years of my life upon earth; at the end thereof did I relinquish my material life upon the Cross of Tiphareth. I am the Word spoken in Silence. I am the Anointed of the Lord. Nine are the letters of my Name."

There is a lot in this passage which is difficult to place within a Golden Dawn context. Obviously, 33 years was the life of Christ, but the repeating of the number 33 might be a connection to the 33-year cycle which was mooted by Steiner. Steiner had presented his Calendar of the Soul in Cologne on May 7th 1912, and it was certainly current thinking when Meakin was visiting much earlier. Steiner thought that important events took place in a 33 year-cycle. This worked from Easter to Easter and was based on Christ's life.

I should point out that I think that the impact of Steiner on the life of Whare Ra was minimal. I asked one senior Whare Ra person if there was any point reading Steiner and she said "no." She was surprised at Steiner's link to Whare Ra and did not think it was ever mentioned to her.

Recently someone who should know better claimed on the internet that Whare Ra, like everything in Havelock North, was dominated by Steiner. While it is true that Havelock North is now famous for its Steiner schools, they are a recent edition to life in the area and only appeared about the time that Whare Ra went into terminal decline. Other than the conversation I had about Steiner, I never heard a single Whare Ra person mention him, or his teachings, at all.

Pat Zalewski thinks that the number 33 equates to the "oil vessel" and as each candle is extinguished that healing oil fills the candidate. Each candle extinguished is a shutting down of a part of a person to get something better, and it is a comprehensive 33-fold sacrifice. If Steiner is the inspiration then the number suggests the totality of history and all aspects of a human being. It is the total extinction of everything that it means to be a human so that something new can be born. This is a pagan idea of sacrifice to get the gods on your side – something appropriate for the Underworld theme of this ritual.

The colours, meaning and the position of the candles is difficult. Firstly you have to realise that the altar is rhomboid and is formed by creating a vesica between two circles. This creates an idea that the altar stands between two worlds, in this case the divine and the material.

The two pairs of brown candles are the four somatic divisions, while the two sets of four are the four Zoa and the "Four Archangels of the Revelation." This is a little problematic as Revelation mentions seven angels before the throne (which are assumed archangels).

The Zoa is a term which is not used much and they are easily confused with the Cherubim. The word is Greek and means Living One. They are the more animal expression of the Four Holy Creatures and they form the four sides of the throne of God. Each Zoa has one face and six wings. One is a Lion and is the divine idea of predators. Another has a face like a Calf and is the divine idea of herd animals. Another has the face of an ape and is a model for primates and the last has the face of a flying Eagle which is a model for flying creatures. To clear up the confusion, the Cherubim carry the Zoa. When these candles are extinguished it means that the higher animal nature in a person is snuffed out. They lose their animal side. I am assuming that what Felkin meant were the four-quarter archangels, which means that divine aspects of the elemental kingdom are removed.

The five lights in the centre are the five senses, and their red colour denotes the passions which in the past have been the vehicle which has carried the person, while their position signifies their purification through sacrifice.

The two pairs of three colours represent the six divisions of Ruach in the Kabbalistic divisions of the soul, the Logos or Microporous. Where you see seven colours, it represents the seven chakras and finally the three single lights are the three divisions of the Higher Soul or Spirit – Neshamah, Chiah and Yechidah.

First four red candles are extinguished. These represent the fact that the postulant has died to their passions. Then the four green lights are extinguished as the Chief adept talks about vines and branches bringing forth fruit. This is the sex drive and the natural forces.

The next thing removed is the single light in the centre. This represents the seed or Divine Idea of passions. The rest of the candles represent a gradual shutting down of a person's life, exactly like in death.

As in death, the soul returns to the source, where it can be united with the source and allowed to return with the divine mission more clearly encoded.

The only thing that is left are four blue candles which represent the highest form of the soul, which are kept burning to stop the person dying. This is small comfort for the postulant who is likely to feel dead, cold and disoriented.

As far as the postulant is concerned, they are dead. Indeed the next thing that the Chief Adept does is perform a sort of Extreme Unction. This Catholic ritual is sometimes called the Last Rites and is supposed to prepare the dying person for heaven. In the 6=5 ritual it is supposed to prepare the self for the Underworld Initiation. In the Roman Catholic rite the parts of the body anointed in Extreme Unction are the eyes, the ears, the nose or nostrils, the lips, the hands and the feet, because these represent our senses of sight, hearing, smell, taste and touch. This is because they are supposed to be the means through which people commit sins. Here it is the brow – for the mind, the lips – for speech, heart – emotions, solar plexus – lower self, thighs – the physical body. Unlike the Roman Catholic Last Rites the postulant is bound with bandages like an Egyptian mummy. Both things mean the same symbolically, even if all the invocations appear to be Christian in orientation.

The candidate is placed in the pastos with their head facing North, which is the direction of the Western Underworld. They sprinkle him with salt, which is a nod to the Egyptian mummification process and to Nephthys as the Death Goddess who preserves by removing watery corruption. If it truly were an Egyptian underworld initiation, at this point the body would be placed with their feet towards the West, which is the direction that Osiris was carried into the lands of the dead. However, the North is associated with the cold lands of the Underworld.

Remember that at this point the candidate has been united with their new astral body, which is linked to them during the Prayer.

There then begins the most interesting part of the ritual. The candidate's consciousness enters their new astral body and journeys through the 36 decans. Each decan is marked by a prayer and the ringing of a bell and a prayer of the hours. During the journey the person is met by a godform which represents that decan and gives the postulant its power. There are several ways of seeing this:

Firstly you can see the journey as a return to the source similar to the Archons of Gnostic teachings which were supposed to be met and defeated at death. If this were the case you would meet each of the Archons in their three-fold aspect. Otherwise you can see it as a journey on the boat of Ra through the hours of the day and night. The latter does not really work because there were 24 clearly marked divisions in this journey.

However, the temple to Hathor at Denderah (Late Period) has a list of decans on its ceiling and the gods and goddesses who rule over them. There were 37, and the first one was supposed to be the stepping off point and was like an ascendant in modern astrology. Work by Joanne Conman in her paper *The Egyptian Origins of Planetary Hypsomata* has identified which constellation is ruling in the Egyptian decans. I have added the gods of the decans and this should give plenty of scope for further research. Note that I have used Crowley's *777* Egyptian gods of the decans rather than the traditional ones because they are from the Golden Dawn.

Modern name of Star	Date rising	Zodiac Decan	Decan No.	God ruling the Decan
Arcturus	17 September	Mercury in Virgo	7	Pi-Osiris
Spica	25 September	Mercury in Virgo	8	Panotragus
Alphecca	7 October	Mercury in Libra	9	Zeuda
Zubeneschamali	17 October	Mercury in Libra	10	Omphta
Hadar	27 October	Saturn in Libra	11	Ophionius
Antares	7 November	Saturn in Scorpio	12	Arimanius
Ras Alhague	16 November	Saturn in Scorpio	13	Merota
Vega	25 November	Saturn in Scorpio	14	Panotragus
Kaus Australis	4 December	Saturn in Sagittarius	15	Tolmophta
Nunki	11 December	Saturn in Sagittarius	16	Tomras
Altair	20 December	Saturn in Sagittarius	17	Zeraph
Alpha Cygnii	29 December	Saturn in Capricorn	18	Soda
Dabih	7 January	Saturn in Capricorn	19	Riruphta
Enif	16 January	Mars in Capricorn	20	Monuphta
Sadalmelik	26 January	Mars in Aquarius	21	Brondeus
Markab Seheat	5 February	Mars in Aquarius	22	Vucula

Modern name of Star	Date rising	Zodiac Decan	Decan No.	God ruling the Decan
Schedar	15 February	Mars in Aquarius	23	Proteus
Fomalhaut	26 February	Mars in Pisces	24	Rephan
Mirach	7 March	Mars in Pisces	25	Sourut
Almach	17 March	Venus in Pisces	26	Phallophorus
Mirfak	28 March	Venus in Aries	27	Aroueris
Algol	9 April	Venus in Aries	28	Anubis
Epsilon Perseus	19 April	Sun in Aries	29	Horus
Capella	29 April	Moon in Taurus	30	Serapis
Menkalinan	12 May	Moon in Taurus	31	Helitomenos
Aldebaran	22 May	Moon in Taurus	32	Apophis
Zeta Taurus	2 June	Moon in Gemini	33	Taautus
Castor	13 June	Moon in Gemini	34	Cyclops
Rigel, Pollux	24 June	Moon in Gemini	35	Titan
Procyon	7 July	Moon in Cancer	36	Apoltun
Sirius	17 July	Jupiter in Cancer	1	Hecate
Regulus	28 July	Jupiter in Cancer	2	Mercophta

Modern name of Star	Date rising	Zodiac Decan	Decan No.	God ruling the Decan
Alphard	7 August	Jupiter in Leo	3	Typhon
Denebola	17 August	Jupiter in Leo	4	Perseus
Zavijava nu Hydra	27 August	Jupiter in Leo	5	Nephthe
Vindemiatrix Canopus	6 September	Jupiter in Virgo	6	Isis

There are a lot of misconceptions about the Prayer of the Hours in this ritual. There have been some American temples which have taken this particular idea literally and insisted that the candidate stay in the box for 36 hours. When I was last in Hawkes Bay I mentioned this to a high grade Whare Ra person who smiled and said: "There will be always people who attempt to give grades they have not got to people who do not deserve them."

When you realise that the time period being talked about is in connection to the decans, if you were going to be really literal about it, the candidate should be in the box for at least a year!

The confusion comes because the ritual calls the prayers spoken outside the vault "hours". These are not literal hours but a reference to the Liturgy of the Hours in the Christian Church. It is based on the idea of marking a passage of time with a prayer. This included Matins, during the night, Lauds or Dawn Prayer, Prime or Early Morning Prayer, Terce or Mid-Morning Prayer, Sext or Midday Prayer, None or Mid-Afternoon Prayer, Vespers or Evening Prayer, Compline or Night Prayer. To Felkin the idea of chanting the hours was to mark a passage of time and *not* a literal hour.

That said, there is some advantage in drawing out the experience of going through the decans. Whare Ra's practice of doing this in 30-60 seconds feels like you are being rushed around the universe at many times the speed of light. As soon as you meet a godform you are whisked off to meet another, much in the same way that the Queen is when she is introduced to workers at a Royal Variety performance.

The actual prayers do not seem connected to the meaning or influence of the decans or their godforms, but somehow open the doors at the right time and place. It is my belief that these keys were channelled, and were an arrangement between the Inner Planes and Felkin.

While the Hours are being chanted, Shekinah is in the Mars room watching the progress of the candidate astrally, and moving him on if he gets stuck. The Mars room was not that large but the Shekinah had an altar there, and it would make sense for her to do so. The symbol here being that as the postulant rises up, so then the divine feminine self sacrifices to meet him.

The Shekinah enters into the vault through the hidden Mars wall and the lights are turned up. The temple until now has been in darkness and the candidate has had his eyes shut. To someone watching the ritual, Shekinah would just appear out of nowhere in a blaze of light. Sadly, this bit of theatre is missed by the candidate who is literally still "out of it" at that point.

She has the alabaster lamp with the special oil and a sprig of acacia. The sprig of acacia is symbolically linked to the third degree of Freemasonry. It grew abundantly near Jerusalem, and Moses was told to make the tabernacle, the Ark of the Covenant, the table for the shewbread and the rest of the sacred furniture from it.

In chapter XXVIII of Albert Mackey's *The Symbolism of Freemasonry*[77] the author said that the acacia was the symbol of the immortality of the soul, initiation, and innocence.

> "In this one symbol, we are taught that in the initiation of life, of which the initiation in the third-degree is simply emblematic, innocence must for a time lie in the grave, at length, however, to be called, by the word of the Grand Master of the Universe, to a blissful immortality. Combine with this the recollection of the place where the sprig of acacia was planted, and which I have heretofore shown to be Mount Calvary, the place of sepulchre of Him who "brought life and immortality to light," and who, in Christian Masonry, is designated, as he is in Scripture, as "the lion of the tribe of Judah," and remember, too, that in the mystery of his death, the wood of the cross takes the place of the acacia, and in this little and apparently insignificant symbol, but which is really and truly the most important and significant one

---

[77] Mackey, Albert Gallatin, and Robert Ingham Clegg. *Mackey's Symbolism Of Freemasonry*. Chicago: The Masonic History Company, 1921. Print.

in masonic science, we have a beautiful suggestion of all the mysteries of life and death, of time and eternity, of the present and of the future.

Thus read (and thus all our symbols should be read), Masonry proves something more to its disciples than a mere social society or a charitable association. It becomes a "lamp to our feet," whose spiritual light shines on the darkness of the deathbed, and dissipates the gloomy shadows of the grave."

All this makes the acacia a perfect symbol for what Shekinah is doing next. She awakens him with a kiss to the brow, which seals the higher spiritual body into the candidate. She places the acacia onto the physical body of the candidate and seals the body completely. I know of several people who have gone through this experience, and you physically feel yourself coming alive.

The sealing prayer links him to the Divine Man, Adam Kadmon, and effectively resurrects him as a new being. She then disappears behind the Mars wall and the postulant has his bandages removed.

He is let to stand just before the door of the vault when another piece of theatre takes place. The candidate has seen that the vault was empty when he was rescued from the pastos. Now the Shekinah emerges from the secret Mars door, comes up behind the candidate, and sprinkles him with water.

The candidate is given a new mystical name: Doulos Siges, Parademos Che Vallis or Server of Silence. He is told that Doulos Siges is Ancient Greek. Doulos is literally a slave but in the bible it is metaphorically one who gives himself up to another's will or those whose service is used by Christ in extending and advancing his cause among men.

An Italian ancient languages expert Dr. Alfonso Ricca told me that both phrases are rubbish and are simply mock ancient Greek. *Siges* is not written as it should be pronounced in Greek, but the second sentence is correct.

Erasmus of Rotterdam in the 16th century created a different pronunciation from that spoken in Ancient Greece and this is the sort of Ancient Greek taught in schools. Dr. Ricca said that this does not use the Erasmian pronunciation. This could mean that either it is older than Erasmus, or it has been faked by someone who knew Ancient Greek pronunciation. However, this would not explain the corruption of the word "parademos", which can only be damaged in that way by being passed down orally by people who did not know Greek.

"This phrase could be really old and bring in itself a positive memory of Daemon and Baal, or be subsequent to Christianity and have a negative conception, perhaps linked to demons," he told me.

But there is also the problem of a correct translation of "para", which changes depending on the case of the name. In this case, *demos* is a genitive form and according to the dictionary, *para* with the genitive would mean: "it properly denotes motion from the side of, from beside, from."

I will take his word for it. Technically, it would appear that the mystery name stretches the rules of Ancient Greek, if not breaking them completely.

‹VII› EXPERIENCE OF 6=5 RITUAL

THIS CHAPTER PROVIDES THE RITUAL REPORTS OF WB YEATS INTO THE 6=5.

Impression of 6=5 Ceremony
Postulant Frater D.E.D.I.   October 16/1914.

The Vision of Shekinah was not at all clear. Apparently, the living figure should be enshrouded by a very large one; in this case, the figure appeared to be imperfectly materialised. The alteration of the usual physical appearance of the Postulant was very marked – he was of a more refined substance, more transparent, and a clearer (more distinct) body illuminated and permeated the physical one. He also had a much more beautiful appearance – one got a glimpse of what his Resurrection body might be. This alteration in appearance was obvious at once on his entrance, so must have been the result of his preparation. He had a surface of clear whiteness that could be written upon.

At first he appeared somewhat afraid. As he advanced slowly towards the Vault Door – before the Obligation – Great black Wings enshrouded him from behind, and seemed to make a Casket or Shrine for his Higher Self – who descended within them – the wings hovering above and behind him – (not touching him) during the Obligation. His Astral Feet appeared crossed as he stood at the Door during the Obligation, he also appeared divided in two. He gave himself a nasty jar by speaking (repeating the Obligation at first). His arms stretched out formed the solid centre of the wings of the Figure which enshrouded him, one of great strength and delicacy, dark and semi-transparent, with iridescent blue, green, and orange tints, like a Pheasant's neck. He became larger towards the end of the Obligation, and also again was – afraid.

During the Prayer – at the beginning of the 2nd Point, "Knocketh at the Gateway of the Grave", he appeared to think of Water. (Was he ever nearly drowned?)

Experience of 6=5 Ritual

As he gazed into the Bowl of Water, he seemed to see his Higher Self enshrouding him from behind – but vaguely.

At the extinction of the Brown Candles – there seemed to be a kind of Grill between them and the progress to the 4 Red Candles, difficult to get through. He felt the putting out of the Green Candles acutely, and sank down. He did not expect the extinction of the one Red Candle, it gave him a small shock. At the extinction of the seven violet Candles he rose up firmly again.

As he lay down in the Pastos – a great darkness fell over him – it began with the winding of the Bandage. There appeared to be great heavy pushing Powers trying to weigh him down.

The following occurred during the ringing of the 36 Bells, and the corresponding Sentences.

At the Fourth Bell Crossed Swords point downwards were held as a barrier before him.

At the Fifth Bell they were raised – and held straight across, level, before him, about the height of his thighs.

Between Six and Seven Bells his Arms went out in response, in the Form of a Cross and he passed through the Swords. Eighth Bell. He became separated (left part of himself behind) and passed up.

At the Tenth Bell, he was only half conscious on the physical plane.

At the Twelfth Bell, he became firmer just before it. At the Thirteenth Bell, he is faint.

At the Fourteenth Bell, he is very cold.

At the Sixteenth Bell, he again emerges into a further higher plane.

At the Seventeenth Bell, he is like a transparent Rainbow. The Colours of the Planets play upon him. They then merge into brilliant White Light and for the rest of the Bells he shone with it.

The sprinkling of the Salt appears to denote that Salt is the Purest form of Earth, for while ordinary Earth assists the decomposition of the Body, Salt preserves it.

The Rising from the Tomb, and the standing at the entrance to the Vault, and the Sprinkling appear to involve very great and serious effort on the part of both Postulant and Officers, in order that what has been obtained in the Tomb may be brought back to the physical man and incorporated with it, and retained.

⟨VIII⟩ 6=5 TEACHING MATERIAL

SYLLABUS 6=5 [78]

1. Study the obligation and plan how to carry out the twofold life literally. This is a mystical grade and has no lectures or examinations.
2. Copy four Trees in their appropriate colour scales.
3. Copy and practice 6=5 exercises.
4. Try to find your own path for the Inner Life.
5. Now is the time to fill in gaps of the 5=6 syllabus and to choose your special subject in which to qualify.
6. Study and work at the Auric Egg.
7. Climb the Tree, i.e. meditate on each Sephirah and path in order, beginning with Malkuth, clairvoyantly if possible.
8. Paint and consecrate Tarot pack.
9. Paint telesmatic figure of Rising Sign or Sign of Sol; see Schemhamephoresh.
10. Practice Prithivi Akasa Tatwas to find out your past lives so as to gain a sense of continuity.

DAILY RHYTHM FOR THOSE OF THE GRADE OF GEBURAH

On awakening, make this affirmation.

"I will arise and shine, for my Light has come, and the Glory of the Lord has risen upon me."

Before leaving the room in the morning, say:

"The Life of the Trees is mine, I will arise and walk, the Life of the Man is mine, I will receive and give, the Life of the Word is mine, I will

---

78 The bulk of these are from Percy Wilkinson's collection, although the SS letters come from Jack Taylor who was living in Napier at the time.

utter and love, the Life of the World is mine, I receive the spirit, the Life of the Stars is mine, I am filled with joy, ELOHIM GIBOR guards me, ELOHIM GIBOR strengthens my hands, yea He guards my feet."

About noon, as an intercession for the dying, especially those in zones of war or catastrophe, say:

"Oh Lord of strength, Elohim Gibor, in all humility of spirit I invoke Thy Blessing. Look down, I implore Thee, upon those dying in warfare or catastrophe, and knocking at the gate of the grave. Grant Thine aid, Oh God of Israel, who givest power unto Thy people. Pour forth Thy benediction, we beseech Thee. Oh Thou fire-hearted One who does send death that we attain unto Life everlasting: Thou at Whose Word the thunders roll and the lightning flashes forth, grant that in the midst of storm we may find peace. Master of the Diadems of Fire, crown them with Light that, emerging from the darkness of the tomb, they may enter upon the Dawn of Endless Day."

Alternative for those undergoing operations:

"Oh Thou who makest perfected souls to enter into everlasting glory, cause now we beseech Thee, the perfected soul of [insert name of person] to be victorious over death. Having ears, may s/he hear with understanding; having eyes, may s/he perceive with the spirit; having lips, may s/he speak the truth; having a heart, may s/he love righteousness. Quicken in him/her, oh Divine Creator, the Life Divine: draw him/her with cords that s/he may run after Thee: bind him/her to the altar that s/he may evermore serve Thee."

On going to bed, repeat:

"Mother of Life, Mother of all, Matrona, we would be even as the Burning Bush which was not consumed – a sign to those who have eyes to see. Star of the Sea, in Thy hands is the Lamp of Understanding; show us if for an instant Thine ineffable fragrance. Tower of Ivory enclose us in Thy protecting Purity. Strengthen me who seeks enlightenment, through the gates of darkness, that passing through the valley of bitterness I may find therein the Well of Living Water. Reflect upon my soul those visions of the Spirit which awaken the understanding and beckon us to the Pisgah Heights of Holiness. There may I find the Pearl of Great Price, which is also the Lodestone of the Wise."

SHEKINAH – THE FOUR SCALES OF COLOUR

Sephirah	ATZILUTH King	BRIAH Queen	YETZIRAH Prince	ASSIAH Princess
Kether	White	White	White	White rayed with gold
Chokmah	Pure soft-blue	Pearl grey	White flecked with red	Blue & yellow
Binah	Crimson	Black	Crimson with black edge and rays	Grey, flecked pink
Chesed	Deep violet	Blue	Deep purple	Deep azure, flecked yellow
Geburah	Orange	Scarlet	Bright scarlet	Red flecked black
Tiphareth	Clear rose pink	Daffodil yellow	Rich salmon (pink)	Golden amber
Netzach	Amber	Green	Bright yellow-green	Olive, flecked golden
Hod	Violet purple	Persimmon (tawny orange)	Red-russet	Yellow-brown, flecked white
Yesod	Indigo	Dark petunia	Very dark purple	Citrine, flecked azure
Malkuth	Yellow	Tertiaries	Tertiaries, flecked into glowing gold	Black, rayed with yellow

PLANETARY

Planet	ATZILUTH King	BRIAH Queen	YETZIRAH Prince	ASSIAH Princess
Saturn	Dark indigo	Black	Blue black	Black, rayed blue
Jupiter	Violet blue	Blue	Purple	Bright blue, rayed yellow
Mars	Poppy red	Red	Rich scarlet	Scarlet, rayed amber
Sun	Clear rose	Golden yellow	Rich amber	Amber, rayed red
Venus	Emerald green	Sky blue	Pale blue green	Cerise, rayed pale green
Mercury	Primrose yellow	Violet	Grey	Indigo, rayed violet
Moon	Pale silvery blue	Silvery white	Very cold pale blue	Silver, rayed sky-blue

NOTE:
The 6=5 Tree gives Sephiroth in the Queen scale and paths in the King scale.
The Prince scale is usually a blend of King and Queen.
The Princess scale is very often flecked or rayed.

LECTURE ON THE FOUR SCALES OF COLOUR
By G.H. Chief M.C.

You have in the order notes a list of the 7 rainbow colours and their corresponding notes in the scale, but I would like to suggest that, while the King scale of colour is cognate to the major scale of sound, the Queen scale is akin to the minor and the Prince to the chromatic. That leaves the Princess unaccounted for, unless we seek out the half or quarter tones of the East; are they not related to the flecked and rayed colours of the Princess, blurred let us say one imposed on the other.

In actually depicting this scale the colours are represented as sharply divided, but if you consider them clairvoyantly you will see that they waver and mingle as the colours of moving water shift and blend as you look at them, or as lights interplay with the movement of clouds. So on a windy day in spring have you seen colours interchange in a wood as the young leaves rustle, and the shadows play over a mass of wild hyacinths or primroses.

The Princess must always be taken as something changing, unstable and evanescent; the flecked and rayed colours should actually be so cunningly interwoven that they would change with each movement of the canvas like shot silk.

Now as you consider the four scales of colour, passing imperceptibly from one to another, so must you also learn to pass from one plane to another, gradually raising and transmuting that upon which thoughts and desires dwell.

As the colours of the Princess scale are mingled, and those of the Prince clear, the Queen Scale soft and negative, but those of the King deep and rich, so it is with other things. If, for instance, you concentrate on love, you will see how mixed and doubtful a thing earthly love is. But if you raise it up through the aspects of loyalty and devotion, you presently become aware that above all these lies the pure and selfless ardour of divine love.

Of the four Trees you must further consider that two are positive, two negative, two masculine, two feminine. Therefore it follows that two correspond to the waking consciousness, two to the sleeping. But while at the first glance that seems perfectly simple and clear, a little reflection will show you that it is less so than you thought.

We have already seen that the Princess scale, which belongs to the lowest of the four, is negative, and must therefore belong to the sleeping consciousness. Let us examine this statement more closely. The Princess in the Tarot is represented as a young person; but a young person from the occult standpoint is one who is yet unawakened, therefore the Princess scale and lowest Tree must correspond to one who is as yet immersed in the material.

From that it will follow that the scale of the Prince signifies one who has awakened. How are we to interpret the Queen scale? This takes us a step farther into psychology. An ordinary undeveloped man dreams very little, his dreams are fragmentary; they have no spiritual significance. But when a man awakens to the underlying realities of life, he becomes sensitised, his soul is set free and he begins to stretch out groping hands in search of guidance.

The response comes through dreams, and though he may be unable to bring through clear consecutive memories of his sleep experiences to the physical brain, yet he can and does receive as much teaching as he can assimilate. This is the vitalising of the Queen scale. Therefore, when you wish to receive teaching on a particular subject during sleep, it is a good plan to dwell upon the appropriate Sephirah or path in the Tree of the Queen.

Of the King scale it is more difficult to speak, for it belongs to the region of pure light, the source of all colour and music. To that region only the Initiate has access, and that which he receives is in the nature of light and life.

LECTURE ON MEDITATION AND CONTEMPLATION
6 = 5
By G.H. Chief M.C.

If you do not practise rising in the planes sufficiently, you should form the habit of doing this daily, until it becomes so natural as to be spontaneous. Learn to look, not only at daily life, but more especially at ceremonies, from this point of view.

But to do this you must fully understand that rising in the planes is not a kind of mental aeroplane; if you are in an aeroplane the higher you go the flatter the landscape appears, until it is veiled by clouds or becomes indistinguishable through the layer of atmosphere; your horizon widens, but to all intents and purposes your view becomes two dimensional.

But where you rise in the planes, you do not go up in the sense of looking down on things; you move into the midst and enter upon multi-dimensional consciousness. Remember that when Christ appeared to the disciples after His Resurrection, He was in their midst. From this viewpoint you perceive the interior life and meaning of all things; instead of becoming small and flat they gain an entirely new significance; and this is true not only in relation to space and life, but also to time, and what we are accustomed to calling inanimate objects.

FIRST EXERCISE

To begin with, polarise your own sphere of sensation; visualise as clearly as you can the four Trees, one within the other, but all with the axis coinciding with your own plummet line. Now gradually withdraw your consciousness into the centre of Tiphareth and hold it there while you breathe six times; then rise up into Da'ath (coincides with the pineal gland) and from there look out as from a watch tower through the rainbow network of your sphere as it revolves slowly round you. Do this each day until it ceases to demand effort. That is the first exercise.

SECOND EXERCISE

(Not to be attempted until you have attained to a degree of ease in the first):

Look at an inanimate object (table); seek for the inner force which holds it together and see with your inward eye the tremendous unceasing movement which is necessary to produce the apparent immobility of the outward form.

Stand in the garden and look at the house with the same inner vision. If that ordered activity should cease or no longer co-ordinate, the whole would crumble to dust before your eyes, as our bodies crumble when the governing soul withdraws.

Learn to look through the external form to the interior force. The true craftsman does this unconsciously, and uses this internal force to guide his hand in sympathy with it, so as to produce the harmonious expression; that is why the great craftsman select certain woods to work with. The activity of each wood is fitly expressed in certain lines and types.

THIRD EXERCISE

A natural sequence to the last.

Concentrate upon a series of living things one by one. A tree, a flowering shrub in bloom, an animal, an insect. In each case try to follow out the life processes, first from without then from within, so that you look at the world from their point of view.

When you have done this, say for one month, return to the first exercise of folding up into your own Tiphareth and rising into Da'ath, only now you must look out from Da'ath and reach out to all these other forms of existence until you fully realise the unity in diversity that exists in all around you; not to lose yourself in them but so that you are in perfect harmony with their rhythm, just as you instinctively keep in step with a passing band.

When you have caught the cadences of life immediately surrounding you then you can reach out further. The next step is more difficult, for now you have to reach out from the known to the unknown. Just as you begin by formulating the four Trees in your own sphere, so now you must formulate them in the sphere of the Earth. In doing this you should be conscious of other Trees beyond those with which you are familiar. You cannot see them for they belong to planes as yet beyond your knowledge and their range of colour is beyond your vision but you may be dimly aware of their presence.

Polarise your own central pillar with that of Earth; conceive Earth's Tiphareth to correspond to the equator, while Da'ath lies within that zone which we call temperate. When you have done this, then as before withdraw into Tiphareth and thence ascend to Da'ath and look out, not through your own personal sphere, but through the sphere of Earth, and gaze abroad until the inner sight penetrates to the depths of space; then turn to your text books and assure yourself of the direction in which the particular fixed star you seek lies. Be sure you have a clear general idea of the relative positions of Earth and star, at whatever time you propose to follow up this step in our series.

Find the position of Earth, sun and star in relation to each other from the point of view of Da'ath of Earth. Having this clear in your mind, then at the appointed time withdraw as I have described into Tiphareth of Earth, pause there breathing quietly and rhythmically while you count 36, then ascend to Da'ath, breathe quietly counting 12 and turn your vision toward that path which corresponds to the sign through which we must travel to reach the star.

Project your consciousness along that path, first in the Princess then the Prince, then the Queen, then the King scales. Then bid your consciousness pursue the same path through the successive scales beyond your vision but not altogether beyond your comprehension, since they exist also in your own finer sphere.

Do not attempt this all at once, go slowly step by step; practise Princess scale until you have mastered it, then going through that, attack the next, each day a little farther, until at last you can speed along swiftly and surely beyond Earth's sphere and cast your vision out to the star itself. Then reverse the process and penetrate further and further to the heart and essence of its life.

THE CROSS

0=0

Rejoicing I come to thee, thou Cross, the Life-Giver, Cross whom I now know to be mine. I know thy mystery, for thou hast been planted in this world to make fast things unstable.

Let us strive to understand the divine ideas underlying these ceremonies, and the use of the Cross as the master-symbol by which all transmutation is effected. Our Lord said: 'Ye must be born again of water and the spirit' and He referred, no doubt, to initiation and the great master-symbol of initiation is the Cross.

As a symbol it is as old as the planet, for it has been used in one form or another by almost every nation, in every civilisation. The Third Root Race formed it from the ash-tree, whence issued the men of bronze. They called it the Tzite Cross. There was also the Swastika, the most sacred symbol of India, sometimes called by the Masons the Jaina Cross, the Greeks the Tau Cross.

In our order in the 0=0 ceremony, we see the cross of the four elements in perfect balance. It is balanced because it holds at its centre the spiritual power of the Hegemon, the symbol of balance in the Piscean Age as shown by the fish-headed sceptre – in Egypt by the feather of truth head-dress, in the Aquarian Age no doubt, by the symbol of balance.

There are four lustrations, markings of the Cross upon the candidate; his bodies, physical and psychic, are consecrated simultaneously. Eventually, the lustrations flower upon the altar, for he himself handles the Cross of the Four Elements. There are four lustrations, and in the middle of the temple is the Cubical Cross: the candidate as yet unfolded for service – nevertheless he flowers in the mystic repast.

1=10

The order, by its drama, enacts the evolution of the race – from animal man to divine man and its magic is in the Tree – the Cross, by the Cross, which in a certain sense represents the personality of man, the slow emergence of the useful and proper faculties takes place.

After the first purification, we rise from our knees and seal our promises by the oblation of salt – the emblem of purified earth. We are beginning to grow the wood of the Cross – its upright beam; in the choice of the central pathway we know that the arms of the Cross are still beyond our ken.

The master symbol junctions in the 2=9 by means of the whirling Cross, the Swastika, the Hermetic Cross, which bears upon its arms 17 squares as the ritual explains; the Sun, the Four Elements and the 12 Signs of the Zodiac – all the powers requiring integration by the initiate on his long journey. Such a symbol, by its whirling, brings to life the latent powers within those who contemplate it. And so we start our journey. Therefore, with Jesus Christ, true God, ascend the Cross, the One and only Word.

2=9

The Word in truth is symbolled forth, by that straight stem on which I hang. Lo! The Central Cross, the cubical Cross is unfolded, it bears upon it all the signs and powers for thy redemption!

The candidate has within him a stirring, a budding of life, he has purified the soil where the tender roots of the Cross shall sojourn and grow. He can be trusted to contemplate a glyph of its perfected man, his powers unfolded, to which he is pledged to attain; his mind therefore must be purified before a further step on the journey can be attempted.

The Light-bearer, therefore, guides him to the abode of the Kerubim, the guardians of the arms of the Cross, with whose symbols he is sealed. He begins to hear the sweet voice of the Master as he chants the litany of the Cross:

'Thy head stretched forth and up into heaven that thou mayest symbol forth the Heavenly Logos, the Head of all things. Thy middle parts are stretched forth as it were hands to right and left, that thou mayest gather together into one those that are scattered abroad. Thy foot is set in the Earth, sunk in the deep, the abyss – that thou mayest draw up those that lie beneath the Earth, and mayest join them to those in heaven.'

Hear, therefore, my brothers, the Truth expounded; the path Tau is the Ladder of Jacob, and the sure testimony that man was made for the heights.

In the Cubical Cross the whole destiny of man is revealed, every path is indicated, every Sephirah named.

So by the path Tau does the candidate finally emerge from Malkuth and begins his outward and upward journey.

3=8

Our candidate has become the poet, the artist, discovers in himself hidden faculties; from the solid Greek Cross he gains balance, from one arm power, another vision, another strength, another energy, from the Sun in the midst he rises like Casmillos to the trumpet call of the Archangel; on the bitter Cross of his personality he may place the great symbol of the star of the grade, the planet Mercury – he must learn to hold his soul cup-like to receive the divine-love, that he may give of its fullness to others. From the portals of Shin, Tau and Qoph he gains balance in diversity, he begins to hear the voices of the elementals: the organ-like notes of the water, the flute-like notes of air, the sibilant sighing of air, the drum-like beat of the heart of the Mother of the Earth.

He has a great vista before him, for in this grade he can find power in perfect balance, but he must hold the Cross with both hands! 'For power in no way differs from thought, and yet are one; from the things above is discovered power, from those below thought.' We presume that the candidate can now be trusted with power, for he is given the first of the planetary symbols to contemplate, the planet Mercury – the Messenger of the Gods. Upon the Cross of his own weak personality is superimposed this mighty symbol. Dedicated power is of the armour of God.

Light looked down and beheld darkness; 'Thither shall I go', said Light! Peace looked down and beheld war; 'Thither shall I go', said Peace! Love looked down and beheld hate; 'Thither shall I go', said Love! So came Light and shone, so came Peace and gave ease, so came Love and brought life! And the Word was made flesh and dwelt among us.

4=7

The candidate has become the warrior, he is one of the great company of warriors; those who wrested from the Tree, the Cross, the Sword, to fight for righteousness. He aspires to be one with the warriors of the past.

Arthur and his gallant company, the Black Prince, Baldwin, first King of Jerusalem, whose body was buried near the Holy Sepulchre, Coeur-de-Lion, who is entrusted with the sword Excalibur, which he gave to Tancred, the Maiden-Knight Sir Galahad. ALL those who fought for the Cross, with divine fire.

The Calvary Cross of 12 squares, to my poor mind the symbolism is lost in the Waters of Nu! Perhaps the ancients juggled with the Zodiac and the symbol settled hap-hazard!

The Calvary Cross of 10 squares refers to the ten Sephiroth in balanced disposition as the ritual sets forth – therefore, we assume that the candidate's Sephiroth, those peaceful Chakras are in active motion – the candidate is ready for service because he has attained to a certain degree of equilibrium. There is much profound teaching hidden in this symbol, and the candidate has now access to their treasures, and it is a very beautiful Cross for contemplation.

I kneel at its feet and feel the stability of our Lord In Malkuth; in Yesod I see His exalted vision; in Hod I gather His tears for the purification of mankind; in Netzach I bathe in His purifying fire, in Tiphareth I feel the beat of His Heart, in Kether I am filled with the perfume of roses – therefore I say: 'Oh fairest Queen of Roses! Flower Bedew our parched ground from out Thy Heart whence soul-reviving waters flow increasing, until Mercy's dower makes each of us a part of Thy true Self – each soul a pure reflection of Love's red, flaming rose, its own perfection.'

The Calvary Cross of 6 squares is a tremendously powerful symbol, containing as it does the old form of the Cubical Cross and the unfolded Calvary Cross. This grade is a synthesising of the candidate's powers in the fires of the Spirit, enabling him to lift the small cross of his personality to receive the exalted symbol of Venus, for only through the door of Love can he pass into the heights. All the great mystery traditions set forth chiefly the mystery of man; and the order in its wisdom chooses the greatest of the four great initiations: the Egyptian, Jewish, Chaldean and Persian, to bring the candidate from darkness to light, to give him a glimpse of his past, and by the power of the Cross to correct those ancient failings – by the power of the Cross to overcome them. By the fire in the heart which purifies the fires of the mind, which enlightens the fire of the will when the Spirit is turned to God, may you be carried up the Holy Mountain.

PORTAL

The candidate's Cross has budded, put on colour, turned inwards for service – he carries the dedicated Cross of the great human orders the Knights of Malta, of St. John of Jerusalem – the Maltese Cross.

He advances alone, he is ready for his personal Gethsemane; he sees three strange officers, and one valiant one, the Hiereus, his own dedicated self.

By the power of his Cross he is permitted to invoke the deity names of the four elements and be sealed by that great ancient form of the Cross, the Kabbalistic Cross – to have the four elements of his body consecrated and strengthened for service. He is ready in the spirit of sacrifice for service, but can he face the World Karma, the world Gethsemane?

Slowly the great monsters of the world's subconscious arise – with such he must be willing to cope. He who would dare beyond his strength, the path of Kaph – Beware! Thunders the valiant one, his own purified lower self. He who would dare beyond his strength the path of Nun – Beware! Again. He who would dare along the middle path, armed with a bright and glowing Cross, the spirit in its centre, receives the confirmation of his aspirations, buries his old self beneath the Cross' shadow.

5=6

And then at the dawn of the cosmic year, when the Cross of wood has become the Cross of Light, we shall discern them – on not only the radiant figure of our Lord, but our own features mingled with His, and the features of our friends; then the divine secret shall have been revealed, and the Cross of transmutation become the weapon of the Warrior of Christ.

This is a stark drama, this drama of the Cross; men flee from it in horror because they cannot bear this tragedy of love. Let us learn the secret of this divine alchemy. We see the sins of the nations before the judgment seat of Pilate, staggering along the Via Dolorosa, becoming absorbed in a multitudinous figure, even you and I my brothers, and countless brothers and sisters, striving to mount Golgotha, striving to lay ourselves upon the Cross.

This meditation upon the drama of the crucifixion is no new philosophical speculation, it is a preparation we are receiving, those added spiritual powers enabling mankind to pass from the state of self-seeking to the stage of enlightenment. By the contemplation of the life and passion of Christ the divine Love is engendered in the crucible of the heart and in that crucible all that is unworthy perishes. In this therefore is the secret of transmutation!

But we, who have been in turn the mystified women, the careless onlookers, the blaspheming thief, if we be content to bear our burdens to carry our Cross, shall see, when that Cross is lifted up on the Golgotha of our woe, our own dear shining Christ appear, and shall pass, with Him, into the paradise of a new day! Gethsemane.

Four timid disciples went to the Mount of Olives – they had an Arab guide, a tall, quiet, dignified man who had a special devotion to our Lord.

They passed by the sleeping disciples, penetrated deeper into the wood, where the young olive trees blustered about a large stone, and there they saw Him lost in an agony of prayer: 'Father, if Thou be willing, remove this cup from me!' Whereon a great multitude arose, the poor, the forlorn, the forsaken, the sinner, the criminals and a great murmuring, a great cry met our ears – and then – the Golden Voice: 'Nevertheless, not my will but Thine be done.' And He was among them – the Healer, the Comforter. There was a flash of light and a drawn sword: 'Come no closer' said a voice. 'Your Lord has conquered.'

We saw no more – not the bewildered disciples, nor the miracle of the High Priest's servant, nor the trial, nor the scourging – but we saw the Cross being lowered, and Jesus received into His Mother's arms – then the slow descent along the stony path to the garden – and we heard the piercing wailing of the Magdalene.

Once more we were in the garden – the moon was rising serene and milk-like, shadowy and gentle like the early church, and the almond trees were in bloom. Presently there arose a little gurgle of water from the brook nearby, the birds stirred, there was a sound of running feet, and the great stone moved away.

This then, Fratres and Sorores, is the ardour and the vision the order gives its children, and those who form His bodyguard in the past, the present and the future have in their hearts the passion and pain of the Cross, the triumph and the majesty of His Resurrection – for all such we give thanks.

To us, Fratres and Sorores, we who are cross-bearers, await the touch of Pentecostal Fire. That Fire which touched the Tree, the Cross, and turned it to a rose – whose shining petals are the adoring saints, whose stem we are, whose thorny stem mayhap – yet carrying the sap of everlasting Love. We have studied the Fatherhood of God, speaking through the Cross – now let us picture the Method of God on the descending Cross-bearers.

ARRANGEMENT OF CANDLES IN SECOND POINT[79]

				One White				
	(I)	(III)	(II)	(IV)	(II)	(VII)	(I)	
One Blue	Two Brown	Four Green	Two Red	One Red	Two Red	Four Green	Two Brown	One Blue
		(VI)	(V)	(VI)				
		Three Yellow	Seven Violet	Three Yellow				

NB: the Roman figures above each set indicate the order of extinguishing.

---

[79] This was sometimes placed in the actual ritual but was not in Percy Wilkinson's copy so was probably dropped by the time he was initiated.

The Following explanation of the symbolism of the Altar and the Candles is not usually read during the Ceremony.

Behold now, the mystery of the thirty-three lights upon the white and gold altar. The altar itself you may perceive is of rhomboidal form, implying thereby that you have consecrated your whole being to the divine inspiration. The five lights in the midst are the five senses and their red colour denotes the passions of which in the past they have been the vehicle, while their exalted position signifies their purification through sacrifice.

The two pairs of brown candles are the four somatic divisions, while the two sets of four are the four Zoa and the Four Archangels of the Revelation, which are their counterparts in the Yetziratic and Briatic worlds, as green is the ethereal counterpart of Earth.

The two threes symbolise the six divisions of Ruach in the Kabbalistic divisions of the soul, the Logos or Microporous.

The seven are the seven chakras, the seven steps to the Throne. And finally the three single lights are the three divisions of the Higher Soul or Spirit – Neshamah, Chiah and Yechidah.

6=5 ADDRESS

By M.C. (Mrs Felkin) / 6.8.1925

I want you to consider the preparation of the Light which the Shekinah carries. Before the Shekinah comes at all into the Rubric she has to prepare the Light. She has to pour forth the oil; she has to mingle the oil with her own blood and kindle the light in the oil. As she pours forth the oil she says: 'The oil is the life of the Tree, let the Tree give its Life.' As she mingles her blood with the oil she says: 'The blood is the life of the Man, let the Man give his Life.' As she kindles the light in the oil she says: 'The Light is the Life of the World, let all the living rejoice.'

Consider the sequence of those three aspects of life. First, the Life of the Tree is the symbol of the whole visible world. Second, the Life of Man represents all living beings on the Earth. Third, the Light which enlightens every man coming into the world. In each case life must be given, must be poured forth in holy sacrifice. For only through giving can we reach joy.

Now consider what Shekinah says as she administers the oil to the postulant. She touches his feet and says: 'The oil is the Life of the Tree, arise and walk.' She touches his solar plexus, which represents the whole life of man, and says: 'The life of the man is thine, receive and give.' She touches his lips and says: 'The Life of the Word is thine, receive the Spirit.' And last, she touches his upraised hands and says: 'The Life of the Stars is thine, be filled with joy.' So you have the giving from the lowest up to the highest blossoms out into joy.

We are all accustomed to the thought that oil is the symbol of joy and peace: and the cup, the alabaster cup, which the Shekinah carries, is the essence of the peace which passes understanding. But if we are truly receiving the ritual, if we are not only passing through it as a curious and interesting experience, we must take the peace of the Shekinah into our hearts and out into the world, it is only for a little time that we can stay withdrawn in the Palace of Mars, in the absorption of the Pastos, we must go forth again, we must arise and shine because the Light has come to us. We must be the alabaster lamps of joy, bearing peace and the light of holy living. It is not the mere passing through of a ritual which can enable any of us to do these things. We do not, in the vault, end the old and begin the new. Each ceremony, each ritual we pass through on the path of initiation, marks the awakening of a new Chakra, a stage in the rising of Kundalini. And as the seed takes weeks, or even months, to germinate, so these rituals must germinate in our hearts and thoughts before they can grow up and blossom. Yet if we pass through with understanding, that seed is planted: it is watered, and it lies with us to cherish its growth. A seed can only grow if it is given peace, quiet and nourishment. If it is too roughly stirred about, if neglected and left dry and unwatered, it will perish. So with us, we must cherish the growth. We must remember that the alabaster lamp is within us, as it is within the hand of the Shekinah.

The path of Mars is war, but the Palace of Mars is peace. It is only when we are ready to fight that we are also ready to dwell in peace. The man who says he is too proud to fight, the pacifist who refuses to fight, while profiting by the battles of others, has no true peace within or without. 'I came not to bring peace, but a sword.'

We must fight with the Sword of the Spirit before we can enter the Peace of the Lord. Only when we are ready to fight, to pour out our own blood if need be, may we dwell in perfect peace. Then the sword of the spirit becomes a shaft of Light, no longer for the wounding of others, but for their enlightenment. The sword must pierce our own hearts if we are to become truly sanctified. Each of us is not only a son of God, but the Mother of God, for within each of us the Christ must be born. Therefore, when the Shekinah withdraws, the Postulant is raised up, his bonds loosened, he is brought out of the Pastos, and he is drawn forth from the Palace of Peace. And that he may have strength and wisdom, he is given the secret food of the Spirit, milk, honey and butter. It is not only by bread and wine that man should live but by the Word of God and the Holy Wisdom. Bearing that Light within him, the Postulant goes out into his daily life prepared to grow into the fullness of the stature of Christ.

6=5 ADDRESS

By M.C. Sunday, 4 November, 1934.

To go more slowly, to think more kindly, to speak more truly, are the prerogatives of old age. I say prerogatives, for when old age has arrived one should be free to choose what is best. To hurry is to miss the tiny things of beauty which strew the way. To think other than kindly is to inflict upon others little pinpricks of pain. Not to think more truly is to deface the wonderful form of Christ, which old age must at least begin to build up in itself.

This is a vignette, of old age – a cameo beaten out of the solid rock of the life now fading behind you. There are some lives beaten out of the rock, some wrought and chiselled in gold and there are some others of each exquisite beauty that it takes a magnifying glass to see their manifold attractions and of this last the mystic is the best exponent. Despise not the contradictions of life – its lights and shades which make character. Seek rather to see in every individual the great personal ideal towards which he is striving and if you do so, your own idea of GOD will become more and more many-sided and with that appreciation will come a variety of power which you did not before possess. For you must apprehend before you can use, you must see before you can transmit, you must feel before you can love.

During this week look upon the tomb as a well of water, into which you can plunge not only your bodies for cleansing but your souls for regeneration. Look upon this 6=5 ceremony as a great cleansing breath of GOD, sweeping away all difficulties in your lives with the impact of that cleansing spring-like freshness which the Shekinah brings in her two hands and be ready to receive each day and every day all along the line the blessing of the moment. The Shekinah moves, spring is here; the Shekinah speaks, the buds burst; the Shekinah shows her lamp and the celestial fires and the terrestrial fires begin to glow in unison. Who are we to be out of focus – out of harmony with the Divine Plan? Gather round our frater, like a close band of brothers, that he may feel the impregnable wall of your friendship and your love in this journey to the grave, and let the Chief remember that, though he is small and weak, yet he is great and strong; though he is tired and old, yet he is young and virile. He has cast about him the cloak of Christ and upon his head is the seal of Knowledge and Understanding. He is no more the lower personality, he is one with the Gods, not in a spirit of vaunting, but in a spirit of loving fellowship. The 2nd adept is as the Chief, though different in that he fixes forever in the candidate's sphere of sensation the clearest truth. The 3rd adept bears the trembling body, sealing it to the triumphant ego.

Now this fresh influx of power which you will receive at dawn will be different in character and you must ray it forth as a child scatters blossoms – a subtlety and fragrance about it which will act as a compelling attraction, drawing those who seek to the feet of the Teacher. Strive therefore to scatter its fragrance and its beauty as a child scatters flowers. The Christ of the new age is the eternally young and the eternally beautiful – the Apollo of the Christian faith. One to whom the young will be able to turn in adoration and joyous service.

6=5 ADDRESS

By M.C. Sunday, 29th November, 1936

With the approach of the 6=5, the thought of transmutation must be present in the minds of the initiates. Year by year, as the soul advances on its quest, it is more and more aware of a change of vibration which occurs within the psychic aura of the initiate.

The first bell sounding at the beginning of the ceremony is an indication that the vibrations of Earth have ceased and the vibrations or the abode between Tiphareth and Geburah are stealing over the consciousness of the disciple. It is with something of a shock that the bell reaches the consciousness of the waiting postulant. He feels it within the heart, because the heart centre is the abode of Tiphareth, and with St. John of the Cross he ventures forth alone, unseen, upon the purgatorial path, which is also the path of balance, towards the unexpected goal. There are great saints who have trodden this path who have made it their special abode, and a study of St. John's writings will reveal to you that he was one of the guardians of this exalted path.

In fear and trembling he leaves his cherished abode. He leaves his known surroundings, he ventures forth unseen, unknown, but within him his heart has become a lantern – a burning light of love which lights his way. It is with anguish that he tries to find familiar landmarks. He is, as it were, disintegrated. There is only a shadowy part of him which treads the path. He is, as yet, unaware that this great drama is the enactment of a secret play between himself and GOD. He sees before him only dimly his other higher bodies, and it is only when he has time to reflect in the silence of the pastos that these other parts of him return and become unified. Yet it is a painful and at the same time a great experience. Slowly the lights are dimmed and the centres of life are muted. There is a little thread only of consciousness which responds to the increasing urgency of the sounding, clanging bells. But with the first sentence, the sound of which is wafted to him from Earth as he speeds on his celestial journey, he realises that there is for him no way of escape into this bliss, but rather that he must ponder upon the urgency of the tasks he should accomplish on his return. It is only when the soul has made that supreme renunciation that the MOTHER appears. So slowly and silently she withdraws, and he returns to life and to the task of living.

The swathing bands go back to the ancient custom of the embalmers, but they have a deeper significance, for they protect the body from too rapid disintegration which would follow if the etheric body were severed too rapidly. They are the shadow of the etheric and serve to effect a more gradual severance than would occur were it omitted. In Egypt the bands were dipped in herbs, spices and gums on which the etheric was fed, for we are more dependent on the purity of the atmosphere than you have any conception of. Therefore is the binding a bar to disintegration, as are also the sentences. The lantern contains a light that can never be extinguished. Hold it high in your hands that its light may fall on all and sundry, that more may follow the gleam.

6=5 ADDRESS

By M.C. Sunday 14th November, 1936

Every secret order expressed some aspect of the Earth's consciousness. As the years advance the aspect may gain deeper and more varied scope, but it is always confined to one aspect, that is the undertone to that great sea of consciousness which is the divine. The work of this order is to illustrate and demonstrate the varied and many wonderful characteristics of the four elements and the countless influences bearing upon them. To do this it is necessary that the member should in his path of initiation be content to learn, not only humbly, but patiently, the elementary knowledge to do with the scientific aspect as well as the more profound Kabbalistic and esoteric. When the esoteric knowledge is superimposed upon an already trained and equipped member we have as a rule a balanced and useful adept, but when this is not so, the result is slow, and only painstaking care can accomplish much in this incarnation.

It may be that the technical knowledge, such as a professional man acquires, is purposely withheld so that more sympathy may be engendered, but whatever the mental equipment, the adept can always, if he strives, attain to a high degree of spiritual light, and that is a treasure which he acquires in this treasure house. From the many coloured planes the Light is focussed upon each candidate at a certain grade and especially after the 6=5, and the spiritual power attained there is so blended and scintillating that thereafter the adept needs to be a centre of life in whatever assembly he chooses to enter. This state of spiritual radiation is always present, but can be increased at will, but there comes with it a great responsibility, for it must always command the attentive attitude of the adept.

You have been told that the sentences are as spirals in the ascending consciousness of the postulant. In reality, they are knots in the rope ladder on which he mounts to spiritual realms, and at each group of sentences the consciousness alters and becomes more illuminated with the divine, less responsive to the human, so that when the least sentence is proclaimed, the postulant is in the proper spiritual condition to contact the Divine Mother.

This ceremony is elaborate and carefully worked out, and you will notice there is nothing left to chance; in other words, the postulant's interior powers are so carefully externalised that the proper results must accrue from such an initiation. The experience of the postulant in the pastos is a foretaste of the experience of the soul at death, when it passes on to that place which has been prepared for it, hence the soul treads no untried path, but when called upon to leave the body, swiftly ascends to its rightful place in peace and gladness.

To some is given the vision of St. Stephen; to others whose eyes are not sufficiently opened on the spiritual plane is given nevertheless a consciousness of life after death in realms beyond this Earth, which sinking deep into the sub-consciousness remains for ever there.

May the peace of GOD, which passes understanding, fill the hearts of all who have passed through this valley of the shadow of death and bring to them illumination and enlightenment.

6=5 ADDRESS

By M.C. 8th November, 1936

Peace profound. In the profound gloom of the tomb the candidate undergoes a complete transformation. Indeed, in that short space of time a recapitulation of all his former deaths is undergone, nay more, for he feels in himself the death of all humanity on this planet. Therefore is the 6=5 grade a much greater and deeper experience than would appear even to the eye of one who views in it the death of the self and resurrection of a new type of life. The 6=5 grade actually accomplishes the flowering of life on this planet – it is the apotheosis of initiations on your Earth. The higher grades can only be given to older initiates because they are, as it were, the habiliments which would only fit on the shoulders of those initiates who have borne them before. The 7=4, the 8=3, the 9=2 do not belong to this Earth as we understand it, but are suggestions great and beautiful, portrayed in ritual as an illustration to which the flower of humanity is pressing.

Therefore, when the candidate enters the pastos, strive if you can to help her, that against the retina of her aura may be etched the profound lessons which not only she has learnt in the past, but which she has been previewing in the dim ages of the Earth's history. It is a great expansion of consciousness, also a tremendous restriction of consciousness in a sense – it is both – and then with the aid of and through the power of Elohim Gibor she is given the strength to return to Earth, which she would not do of her own volition, and to take up the new resurrection life. Elohim Gibor, mighty and terrible, that intangible backbone of personality which defies dissection, is potent to help, but difficult of understanding, and his work in this grade is purposely veiled that it may become an inner secret intercourse between Him and the candidate, that not even a sign or a regretful feeling may cloud the mirror of the candidate's mind and soul.

There are two forces operating in the vault, representative of the Fatherhood and Motherhood of God, without which no birth on any plane can take place. But the MOTHER is the deliverer from darkness and the MOTHER must nourish the child with the divine food and mystery of mysteries, the MOTHER is purposely veiled. Why? That veiling sets the trail for a long process of meditation. Strive, therefore, to lift yourselves from the things of Earth, with its restrictions and its inhibitions, and move freely and graciously in the beautiful plane which the 6=5 symbolises.

6=5 ADDRESS

By M.C.
Dedicated to the Divine Mother

With my mantle I compass the Earth, I am the Star of Night, I am the Pearl of Ocean. I am the Sea. By my compassion I fill the seas and the rivers, the brooks, lakes and rivulets.

I have gathered from the swelling tides, from the ebbing, fainting tides, from the passionate, raging waters, billow heaped upon billow, wave shattered against rock, upon shore, roaring, thundering, flood echoing unto flood. I have gathered all my children to my breast, soothed them to the rhythm of a lullaby, e'en by my down-stealing, soft-distilling tears.

All the griefs and patient suffering, all the hopes and hidden birth-pangs, I have drawn up as a cloud mist, melting into gladness in the sunlight.

Till my joy is consummated my cup runs over with the crimson wine of my heart-blood, for lo! The spirit's sword pierced through and through – a gleam of Light! Whence spring the vital flame, the heaven-born SON.

G.H. S.M.C. MEDITATION, 6=5

5th December, 1939

I will ask you to try to trace the correspondence between the postulant passing through this grade and the world today.

Look back on the immediate past and compare the nations to the postulant preparing for the initiation of death; not knowing what to expect, but feeling that the inevitable experience must be death and the grave.

Look at the Earth itself and see how in every direction are floods, fire, earthquakes, tidal waves. Every catastrophe to which Earth is subject, she has been and is passing through. Trials by fire and water, the two pillars on either side of the entrance.

Compare the attitude of those nations we call democracies – the British Empire, U.S.A., France – with the candidates seated before the two keys; the Hanged Man – enforced self-sacrifice – submerged of all self-will in the great ocean, and the key of Justice – holding the balance and seeking a just way.

Even if you come to individuals, what an extraordinary parallel between the Queen on the throne, holding the seals, with the British premier with the ultimate decision in his hands, who strove, and strove in vain, for peace.

We are apt to put the whole blame on the shoulders of the German nation, and especially on their leader; but remember that we ourselves must bear a share; such a state of things could not be if we, and other nations, had not again and again shown indecision when we should have gone straight forward. Who knows what Karma of the nations are working out if we look back, or how they are interwoven!

If we are to establish right and liberty in the world, we must see that we have our foot on the neck of covetousness and desire. We can hear, if we listen attentively, the sound of the bell marking the passing of time, and that bell is in the hands of the recording angels. We have to look out on one conflict after another and compare them – the destroying of nation after nation, and people after people – compare them with the extinguishing of lights on the altar.

It is said that every nation represents a principle of humanity; and each principle must be first evolved, then established, and then extinguished. It is only by the extinction of the Lower that the Higher can burn with a clear uninterrupted light. No one nation can stand alone, no one nation can dominate the others. We must learn that Humanity is One. There may be head, hands and feet; but the head cannot carry out work if it is not obeyed by the hands and feet, and taken where the work is to be done.

St. Paul said: 'That which is least honourable is given the greatest honour.' Little nations of today – Poland, Finland, Abyssinia, have been given the privilege of suffering for the whole of humanity. Surely we must compare these with the extinction of the dark candles of the flesh, and the scarlet candles of passion and the green candles of psychic vision. We have still candles of the Mind (Lower and Higher), the candles of the Soul, and those of the two great Principles which are symbolised by the Twin Serpents. It may be that we must yet watch the extinction of at least the Candle of the Mind.

Looking today, we cannot fail to be impressed by the lack of any great outstanding intellectual leaders in every country. Yet the three candles of the great forces and the Christ Principle are left unextinguished and inextinguishable. Not even when the Candidate is laid in the Pastos, not even when the salt of the sublimated Body is sprinkled on him, not even then are these three lights put out. The Light of the Spirit goes with him to the grave itself and burns there. We are to remember that Christ descended to Hell, and while there His Spirit illumined Hell itself!

It would seem that we must be very near to the moment when the Candidate is laid in the Pastos and waits the Coming of the Great Mother. Therefore, I ask you all to look forward to the time when the Great Mother will come with the Word of Power on her lips. Arise, shine, for thy light is come. And then it depends on us to see we are ready to obey.

Remember, we are but one small group of an organism far greater than we know. We have been told that even now those great Masters in charge of the destiny of humanity are preparing for coming forth by day. If the work is to be efficient, those privileged to partake of training and preparation, whether in this order or in others, must be ready to obey and co-operate when the sign comes.

The masters are human, though far in advance of us, but they require and demand the help of all able and willing to work for and with them. They ask for no enforced service, but all who are willing may now proclaim their allegiance and willingness.

I will ask you to study the 36 sentences which mark the passing of the hours whilst the postulant remains in the pastos and apply them to our work in this time of preparation. Remember the four statements made as a warning and an injunction. Before the eyes can see they must be incapable of tears. Before the ears can hear they must have been desensitised. Before the voice can speak in the presence of the masters, it must have lost its power to wound. Before the feet can stand in the presence of the master, they must be bathed in the heart's blood.

Die Sol 7-5-16 Michael Sothis Baldur Persis Hyacintha

A.B.S. came in a grey-blue cloak and hood that he has worn once or twice before. Can he give us any teaching about the 6=5?

He speaks of the whole system of the order as it corresponds with the life cycle. Of the 0=0 as being the first awakening; and the four minor grades as corresponding to the four seasons of the year. But those grades are all as it were bringing things to the candidate. All given to the candidate on this material plane. The portal and 5=6 are so to speak the opening of a door or window and showing the candidate something which he looks at. But the 6=5 is the actual raising of the candidate to a different plane himself. Persis got a picture of the candidate looking two ways. In the 6=5 he looks a different way for the first time.

The 33 lights correspond to some cosmic process. As the 33 lights on the altar correspond to the 33 segments of Kundalini and the corresponding divisions of the man, so also they correspond to each 33 centres of life in the cosmic man, Adam Kadmon, Adonai, and those also govern the 33 races and geographical divisions of the globe.

Psychically, as the lights of the lower divisions are extinguished, their light passes on to the higher ones, so that, if we could see the process on the higher plane, we would see that whereas to begin with the White Light burned dimly, smothered underneath the others, and the two blue ones only glimmered faintly, as the others were voluntarily extinguished by the will, which is the third adept, so the higher lights burn more and more brightly and steadily and the second adept, who corresponds to the soul, responds to the demand of the will by helping.

The third adept is the will and gives the command to extinguish, and the second adept is the soul or desire, who passes it on and vivifies it. The chief is the higher genius, the Christ principle, but also the great high priest, who with the swinging incense consecrates the offering of the lower principles. The cosmic correspondence of the three adepti is Sandalphon, Michael and Metatron, the whole being Adonai, just as the three adepti form the one whole candidate. The ceremony could be done in a way to effect the cosmic process.

We five are sitting here moving as one to some point – moving cosmically as it were. This is in the Adam Kadmon form. Stand in Vault in 5 Pent. The person in this grade is beginning for the first time to entering into the pastos, being the conscious muting of humanity which therefore the candidate is then in the position of the Blessed Virgin when she said: 'Behold the Handmaid of the Lord'; therefore the next process is the preparation for the divine birth, which will no longer react upon the candidates themselves but on those who come to them as disciples, not of themselves but of the divine child of whom they are the spiritual guardians. It is the dim and confused perception of this spiritual truth which is manifested in those high grades, which is continually being distorted by those clairvoyants and psychics who have neither the intelligence, intellectual training nor the spiritual development to be able to grasp the true signification, and try to give it a material interpretation, which may become an obsession. For this reason it is necessary to be careful as to those to whom the grades are given.

Personal Preparation of a Candidate for Grades 6=5 and 7=4 of the Order of the R.R. et A.C.

Copied by S.S., September 1951

(Note: what follows may later need some revision. The information dates from about 1625.)

Before the candidate can proceed with the Great Work, or gain from the highest fresh signs of help and further powers to overcome and to attain, it is needful that some very definite bodily and spiritual preparation should be undertaken in order that the candidate may be in a receptive state, with all humility and with a mind free from care and a body purged from gross material surfeit, to receive the next initiation without undue strain or danger either to body or spirit.

A trinity of method is indicated. The method affects the external, internal and spiritual nature. Consider well then, oh candidate, the 14 days' work which it is thy duty – in the fear of God – to endure. (No. of Sephira – 5. 14-5. The 7-4 is 16-7.) For work precedes rest. Effort alone deserves success. Those that ask shall have, but they must knock as well.

The date for the ceremony being known – which date shall be fixed according to ancient rule.

On the first day the candidate shall truly purge his body of all inconvenient dross, by means of a saline water of any convenient natural spring. Also be it noted that if need be from time to time repeat this draught, and definitely upon the 14 day at sunrise.

The candidate shall too upon this first day take five hours during which to meditate in silence, apart from all worldly distractions; he shall duly consider the plan of the preparation and the results to be sought for. The material body shall be clean, therefore at sunrise and at noon and at sunset let ceremonial ablutions take place. During which, pray the Lord of Light to cleanse the heart even as the body is outwardly purified. These ablutions shall take place daily.

The meditation shall be to recall the path hitherto trodden, the knowledge gained shall be recalled. The desires of the candidate shall be fixed upon progress and the life examined, so that the soul's progress may be weighed in the balance of a fair but strict judge.

And now with regard to the candidate's food. It shall be sufficient to keep the body in health, but no kind of surfeit may be present. And the divine food shall be partaken of for the seven days before the ceremony of initiation.

Now the sacred elements are ten in number and are divided thus into a three and a seven.

A Trinity Divine and a Hexagram.

1. The yolk of an egg
2. Milk
3. The best red wine (Laudes wine, pure claret I think.)

4. White grapes
5. Honey
6. Dates
7. Figs
8. Aerated water (a bubbling spring)
9. Pure wheaten bread
10. Pears

(Sacred elements from another source; it was no use writing out a list of forbidden food, e.g. wild boar etc.)

PREPARATION FOR THE 7=4 GRADE

This should extend over a period of four weeks.

1. During this time the postulant should burn incense daily.
2. He should eat beans and peas (the pulse of the bible). Grapes, honey, milk and bread. Very little meat and no pork in any form.
3. Repeat the following daily and learn it perfectly by heart:

    Earthborn and bound our bodies close us in, clogged with red clay and shuttered by our sin – we must arise.
    Flowers bind us round and grasses catch our feet, bird songs allure and blossom scent is sweet – we must arise.
    Mountains may beckon and the seas recall, cloud-forms delude, and rushing streams enthral – we must arise.
    Planets encircle with their spiral light, stars call us upward to our faltering flight – thus we arise.
    Sunrays will lead us higher yet and higher, moonbeams our souls scorch with their purging fire – thus we arise.
    Into the darkness plunge, fearless of pain, coldness and silence cleanse us again – still we arise.
    Open ye gates of light – doors open wide! Gaze we within at the glories ye hide – we have arisen!

4. Get a crystal or moonstone and mark it with sigil of 6=5 name.
5. Write a thesis on Resurrection and Life after Death.
6. Meditate for 40 minutes daily, including prayer.
7. Visit the vault regularly.
8. Study the Tarot keys Fortitude, Hermit and Wheel of Fortune.

Preparation during Four Days immediately preceding Advancement:

This time should be spent in isolation or retreat, if possible on a height.

Bathe ceremonially with hot water and a little soda or ammonia.

Learn correctly so as to use without prompting during the ceremony:

a. Server of Silence is my name.
b. Earth to earth and body to body – in the name of Adonai Ha Aretz, Lord and King of the Earth, I dedicate my body to the service of the highest.
c. Water to water and soul to soul – in the name of the Great Mother, I dedicate my soul to the service of the highest.
d. Fire to fire and life to life – in the name of Jah, eternal, I dedicate my life to the service of the highest.
e. Light to light and spirit to spirit – in the name that may not be spoken, I dedicate my spirit to the service of the highest.

(An indication will be given by an officer at which time of the ceremony these sentences should be spoken.)

Cues for Postulant:

1. When the bell sounds four times he will approach the entrance.
2. When he is asked for his passport he must reply: 'My brow is like unto the kings; my lips are open; my heart is upon its throne.'
3. He will be led into the room and must walk backwards when required.
4. When he is left alone he must repeat the whole of the mantra which he has already learnt, keeping his eyes upon the wheel.
5. Let him remember that the Path of Fortitude can only be trodden by the Hermit.
6. Let him understand that when a door is opened he should prepare to pass through it; he who seeks will find.
7. When he receives a Light, let him say: 'Server of silence is my name.'
8. Only he who hath dedicated his body may obtain communion with his soul; ye are the salt of the Earth; he who renounces Joy, pouring out the wine into the water, shall savour the sweetness

of life, he who shall offer himself as incense cast into the flame shall approach the sanctuary, but before entering therein he must dedicate even his inmost spirit.

PREPARATION FOR RECEIVING THE 8=3 GRADE

We have to lay down one irrevocable law – that he who has resolved, setting all things else aside, to enter the Path of the Quest, must look for his progress in proportion as he pursues holiness for its own sake. He who in the secret orders dreams of the adeptship which they claim, ex hypothesi, to impart to those who can receive and who does not say 'sanctity' in his heart until his lips are cleansed, and then does not say it with his lips, is not so much far from the goal, as without having conceived regarding it.

1. Study the earlier rituals in their order, especially the 5=6, 6=5 and 7=4, and endeavour to trace out the sequence of development through which the initiate passes in receiving them. Do this with special reference to the above quotation. Attend at least one 6=5 and one 7=4 ceremony.
2. Each day for three weeks spend three periods of eight minutes each in contemplation in the following order.
a) Before you rise in the morning review your past life, seeking out and acknowledging the errors you have made. If you can remember any fragments of past lives, collate them with the present one.
b) Between the hours of noon and 3p.m. consider your present mode of life and how you may rectify past errors and bring a more spiritual atmosphere into your existence.
c) Look forward fearlessly into the future.
   Endeavour to comprehend the meaning of repentance and forgiveness of sin – that therein lies the true secret of alchemic transmutation of base metal into pure gold. Consider how you desire to return in another life and how you can create least karma injurious to others so that you may be free to be of the greatest service to God and humanity. Try to understand the meaning of the incarnation and redemption. This should be done after withdrawing to your own chamber at night.
3. Write out notes on the above and, if you wish to, bring them to the chiefs and ask their advice.

7=4 THESIS

By S.S.[80]

The idea of Resurrection appears to become more and more complicated as I progress – the implications appear to become wider and wider. It is as though one were trying to describe one's birth on Earth. At first, it would be comparatively simple. A description of the room or rooms in which early infancy were spent and the one or two people that constituted the people of that world.

Gradually one would be conscious of other beings coming and going, some clearly noticeable and even recognisable, others seen on the fringe of consciousness, as it were. Some would become associated with pleasant experience, others with unpleasant experiences. Gradually the world would enlarge from the simple room or rooms to inside and outside the house, the garden, the world outside the garden and so on. With the enlarging of one's conscious worlds, it would become more and more difficult to describe; more and more complicated.

Therefore, I find the idea of death and resurrection as follows. Once they were merely twee words or sounds, one had no thoughts about them. Then as we one began to think about them, death became associated with terror and evil, and something on which thought was to be avoided if possible and to be pushed very much into the background of life – unpleasant – terrifying. Resurrection was also just another word – it held a promise of hope, one hastily recalled word if one had been so unfortunate as to speak of or think of the word 'death'.

Then gradually one begins to think of a tale of the two phrases together. Instead of death being the end of everything, there was a suggestion that there might be something beyond. Gradually death became a change, not the end. Though one had no idea what form that "change" might take.

Then came the experience of joining the order. The 0=0 was a major and indiscernible experience presenting a vista of BEAUTY in an indescribable way. A vista which seemed to stretch on and on and real yet unreal.

Followed by years of work – working blindly – suffering blindly – but with a feeling that one was following a signposted road – even

---

80 Jack Taylor.

if one could not do more than see the way the signposts pointed or be able to read the writing on them. Sometimes it felt as if one were gradually dying – being crucified. Was this what was meant by death? Was some part of one being crucified? There was no apparent difference in the world about one, so that if this experience was real it was apparently an inner experience. Now and again, there were instantaneous flashes of HOPE. If this process was death, might not there be a process of coming to life somewhere beyond it?

The body grew older. (This was noticeable among other people.) But the mind, although it might grow older in that it became capable of "wider" thinking due to having experienced more consciously, did not seem to age like the body. The brain might grow older and be a part of the physical body, but the mind did not appear to.

Was death only concerned with the physical body? It seemed so. That then was resurrection. The New Testament appeared to suggest very definitely that ultimately the physical body was resurrected also. How could this be if the physical disintegrated into dust? What happened to the mind and the thinking processes? Was the mind analogous to the soul? What was the spirit?

Progress through the order training caused one's thinking to change. One learned of more than one principle. More than one body.

One day in discussion with GH Chief M.P., M.P. remarked, "it sounds rather like a projection of yourself." What did this mean? One had heard of a Higher Self; were there several Higher Selves, so to speak, even as there were several auras?

Come the 5=6 grade, its chief message, apart from a Great Glory, seemed to be humiliation and suffering and sorrow, a weary world that must be pawed through and one in which there was no hope this side of death. The thought of death became the thought of a friend who opened a door into a realm which might be a happier one; it became gradually possible to think of death and suffering as two different things, whereas up to now they had been synonymous.

At odd times, there were psychic experiences – individuals known to be what are termed "dead" appeared, and were able to communicate with one. These experiences became "normal" instead of "awe inspiring" and almost devastating in and by their implication. Gradually it became a part of one's ordinary consciousness to realize that what were normally termed the "dead" and of another and mostly remote world were nothing of the kind, but were frequently in touch with this world.

M.P.'s words "a projection of yourself" recurred and recurred. What did they mean? Why was it that sometimes the "dead" were so close that we could communicate with them and at other times could not? It seemed that this other world might be something in the nature of a dream world, where one moved with the facility of one in a dream and it also seemed that this might be a very much more extensive world than the physical.

The more "adept" amongst the dead appeared to be able to contact us more or less at will, though even they seemed to find that certain times were more favourable than others to make contact with us. Also, there were times when they could be seen and heard and others then one was merely conscious of their presence.

All this suggested that much depended:
(1) On one's mental, emotional and physical state.
(2) On atmosphere or psychic conditions.

Friends from the other side agreed that this was so. Imagination suggested that the physical world might be surrounded by a psychic cloud (of etheric or astral mist) which grew dense or less dense from time to time and that that accounted for the conditions described. If this was so, then it seemed likely that the same fluctuating condition obtained [i.e. existed] in one's own aura.

Furthermore it seemed that the process of order training and suffering might well have had the effect of gradually clarifying the aura, which would mean, quite logically, that if and when that took place we should see "clearly and face to face, whereas now we see through a glass darkly."

What then was this manifestation which appeared from time to time, as one whom I had once known (although the features were not those of anyone known to me on Earth) and which M.P. had referred to as sounding "like a projection of yourself." Could it possibly be a shadow of the Higher Self, so to speak?

If the aura were gradually cleared as above, what about the physical body? Presumably after MANY lives one would acquire a physical body of such ethereal particles that it was under the control of the individual inhabiting it. (It is hard to express this thought.) This body would be under the control of THE SPIRIT or the HIGHER SELF (if the higher self does incarnate). In other words, that individual reaches a Christ-like state so that even if the physical body were destroyed by physical means it could be reassembled or resurrected.

This opened up a vista of ages of incarnations with death as an interval or door between them, or rather the opposite way round, [which] appears to be the better periods of physical existence corresponding to a trancelike or deathlike state, with periods of rest and recuperation (or resurrection?) between them.

What then did the 5=6 grade mean in the light of this? The physical body was fastened on the Cross of Matter and the Higher Self was invoked. Was this then the surrendering of the lower will to that of the higher? If this were so, would this not be a joyous occasion, when the higher rushed down to accept the physical body and imprisoned soul, which was now freely and ceremonially offered and which it could not possess until freely offered?

Was this symbolically the claiming of the soul by Christ? The claiming of the loved one by the beloved? Was it something of THIS KIND that was hinted at in the writings of the mystics and the occultists? If so, WHAT did M.P. mean in his remark about the projection of yourself means? (It was no use asking. One had to wait.)

So to the 6=5. To what did it lead? Would it prove as shattering an experience as the 5=6 had done? The 6=5 proved to be thrilling beyond words. It was REAL; it was TRUE. It meant that the possibilities I had wondered about were actually true and that one day they would be true for me.

Following the ceremony, there was a period of exaltation and after a while came a psychic experience in which I was utterly alone, walking down a pathway between two walls which threatened to close in on me. It was dark and long and terrifying, and there was no help forthcoming. I yelled in the name of Jesus, found comfort, and got through a very long night. While my physical body lay inert, my soul or some part of me went through this dark experience, in which the Holy Name was the only help or support I could find.

Since then there have been times during my waking hours when black depression has surrounded me in a somewhat similar way and furthermore I have wanted to remain silent and dumb. BUT in the midst of this earthly and psychic depression I have known that it would pass, even as I emerged from the experience of the walled passage and from the experience of binding and dumbness in the vault. This knowledge is something indescribable, as also are the psychic experiences I have tried to describe. They are not of the physical world, but they ARE real.

Moreover, since the experience of the 6=5 the experience of seeing "a projection of myself" or experiencing it have become more tangible. In addition, I came to associate them with some pleasant subsequent experience on the physical plane. As though the psychic form, which was that of a woman, was like some sort of guide bringing me good tidings. (Note how this again compared with the experience in vault.) Latterly it has seemed as though this experience has been subjective instead of objective. As though what I had thought of as another personality was newly absorbed into my own personality. If this is true, then it appears to make sense of M.P.'s comment long ago "it sounds like a projection of yourself."

Can it be that it was indeed a faint and shadowy projection, not of the Earthly self, but of the higher self? A hint of experiences to come in some dim and distant future? A shadowing forth of some mystery referred to by the mystics as 'Divine Union'?

If it is, then it changes one's ideas of life and death. They are not two separate states but one combined state which individuals experience more as one or the other (i.e. the individual is more dead or more alive, and the perfect man would be vibrating at a state midway between both, as it were). Resurrection then becomes (in my present state of mind) a process of "becoming alive." What is termed physical life here on Earth is a state more of death than life. In addition, resurrection is not an instantaneous matter but a coming to fuller life by a gradual process which could, of course, become an instantaneous process at any time.

One might hope, then, that the 7=4 might result in the candidate becoming more resurrected than before – becoming more widely conscious than before. It is rather a terrifying thought that, if this be, so the candidate may also have to pass through a deeper experience of death or negativity than before also. But here one is also helped by the knowledge of what has happened before, and by the absolute belief that our Lord has trodden the path before us that we may proceed along it in the shadow of the protection of His Name.

So to summarise, it appears that Life and Death are one and not two. That resurrection is a process of increasing life to balance the state of death or negativity usually experienced by the soul when incarnated on Earth.

S.S.

21. Oct. 1951.

6 Milton Terrace
Napier
20. Oct. 1951

7=4 Grade

GH Soror MC,

Herewith is attached an attempted thesis for the 7=4 grade. If this is found acceptable, would you be good enough to answer the following questions for me?

The postulant should visit the vault regularly. Is it sufficient to visit astrally in view of the difficulties in visiting it physically? What does 'regularly' mean in terms of frequency?

Study the Tarot keys "Fortitude", "Hermit" and "Wheel of Fortune." Is it sufficient that I study these from the "cards" in the Tarot Pack in my possession?

Get a crystal or moonstone and mark it with the sigil of your 6=5 name. Where does one procure a crystal or a moonstone? How does one work out the sigil of a Latin name like Gradyn Summ?

May I be told when or when about the ceremony is likely to take place so that I may try to make preparations accordingly? (My annual leave is now due and I will probably try to put this off if possible so that I can take it at the time of the ceremony.)

Yours fraternally,
S.S.

⟨ IX ⟩ 7=4 RITUAL

**The Mystical Grade
of the
7=4
Being the Grade of the
ROD which BLOSSOMED**

Officers:
The Magus: Grey robe, white head-dress with a gold cord, leopard skin, sandals, spray of almond.
King of Salem: Blue and purple robe, winged sphere, lamen, incense, rose.
Shekinah: Rose coloured tunic, black veil, acacia.
Postulant: (1) White tunic and red shoes.
(2) Brown cloak and cowl, sandals and staff.
(3) Robe of Glory.

Ante-room: Draped in red, Pastos upright and draped in white.
Portal: Sand-coloured with cross of Lights, Ankh and Tat Pillars at the S&N arms of the Cross; Tripod of salt in the West.
Vault: Square, blue with a violet floor, grey veil across East side. White and Gold altar, black and white cross to fold up. Cauldron of bubbling water on the altar. Red Mars symbol on green curtain on the outer side of the vault door.

Four stars: Fomalhaut, 12 rays; Sothis,[81] 24 Rays; Regulus, 36 rays; Aldebaran, 72 rays.
Three Keys: Wheel of Fortune (revolving clockwise), Hermit (Brown Robe), Fortitude (Lion).

---

81   Sothis was crossed out and replaced in hand by Antares.

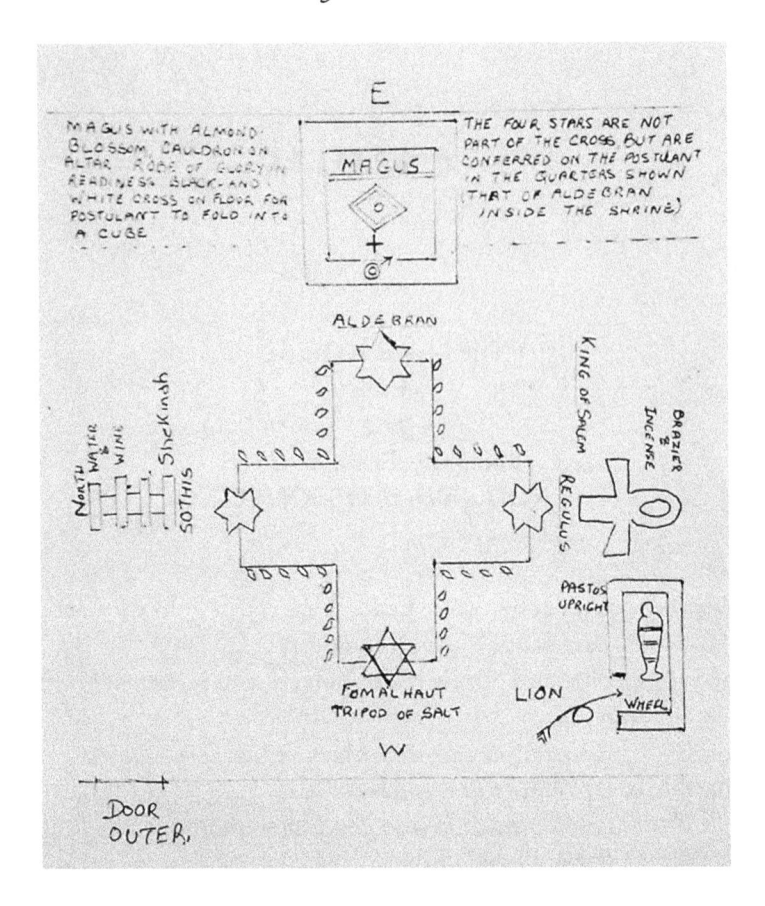

[Diagram of vault layout with annotations including: "MAGUS WITH ALMOND BLOSSOM, CAULDRON ON ALTAR, ROBE OF GLORY IN READINESS, BLACK AND WHITE CROSS ON FLOOR FOR POSTULANT TO FOLD INTO A CUBE"; "THE FOUR STARS ARE NOT PART OF THE CROSS, BUT ARE CONFERRED ON THE POSTULANT IN THE QUARTERS SHOWN (THAT OF ALDEBRAN INSIDE THE SHRINE)"; labels: E, MAGUS, ALDEBRAN, NORTH, WATER, WINE, SHEKINAH, SOTHIS, KING OF SALEM, REGULUS, BRAZIER & INCENSE, PASTOS UPRIGHT, FOMALHAUT TRIPOD OF SALT, LION, WHEEL, W, DOOR OUTER]

OPENING

Vault door is wide open and curtains are drawn back; Magus stands within holding a branch of pink almond blossom in his hand. Shekinah stands by the Tat Pillar with a spray of acacia in her left hand and a lighted lantern in her right. King of Salem stands by Ankh Pillar with a red rose in his left hand and a censer in his right.

Magus: The heavens open and the winds are still and let God's deathless sphere receive the WORD.

King: Oh ADONAI HA ARETZ, MELEK ISRAEL, Thou who appeared unto Moses in the flame of fire in the bush and gave him the law in Sinai – come and redeem us with stretched out arms.

He makes the Sign of Thoth.

Shekinah: Oh Sapentia, Pistis Sophia, Thou who came out of the mouth of the most high, reaching from one and to another, mightily and sweetly ordering all things, come and show us the way of Understanding.

She makes the sign of Hathor.

Magus: Let us give praise to he who is sublime above the heavens and of every nature Lord.

He makes the sign of Horus.

All: Oh Clavis David, Sharbith Israel, thou who open and no man can shut, who shuts and no man can open. Come and bring the prisoner out of the prison house and him that sits in darkness out of the shadow of death.

All repeat the sign of Osiris and face East.

Magus: EL strong and Powerful. El, Lord of Light. Bestow on us thy grade that we in Unity with Thee may impart these Mysteries, which a Father only may bestow on a Son Initiate so that he shall become an Eagle and soar to Heaven and Contemplate your Face.

It is beyond his reach that being beneath the sway of Death he should unaided soar into the Height, together with the golden sparkling of the Brilliancy that knows no Death.

Grant, we beseech thee, most Merciful, that he may be holy even as Thou art Holy, that being made one with Thee he may draw all men unto thee.
Amen

(They prostrate themselves three times.)

POINT 1

Lights are extinguished and the door is set ajar.
BELL IS STRUCK FOUR TIMES.
Postulant approaches the Door and knocks four times.

King: *(Opens door wide)* By what Key would you unlock this door?

Postulant holds out the spray of acacias and replies:

Postulant: My brow is like unto the King's; my lips are opened and my heart is upon its throne.

The King clasps his hand with the 6=5 grip, holds his other arm firmly just above the elbow, draws him into the dark room and guides him backwards in a spiral to the anteroom; he places him upright in the pastos and then binds him:

Around the knees with the amber cord.

King: The feet of Sothis[82] are represented and you are born to their state of rest.

Around the loins with the violet cord.

King: You have inherited Eternity and everlastingness has been bestowed on you.

Around the heart with the black cord.

King: There is nothing hid which shall not be made manifest, nor buried which shall not be raised.

Around the head with the silver cord.

King: You shall be aware that you are the Son of the Father and you know that you are in the City of God and you are that City.

(Start Wheel)

---

82   Sothis was crossed out and replaced in hand by Antares.

7=4 Ritual

He withdraws, leaving the Postulant alone. The door is partly closed showing the Wheel of Fortune Key. One of the Officers reads clearly so that the Postulant may hear through the partially closed door:

Harken now to the Mystery of the Tarot Key before thee and meditate thereon in thy heart.

Is not the tarot itself named from the Rota?

The Wheel of Destiny – of Birth and Rebirth.

Do not the radii spring from the white centre of the divine spirit, passing into the darkness of the womb of the Divine Mother? Even as the Life of man, even as the Life of the Worlds also, which alike pass ever from the Divine Faith into the Divine Mother, that being born of the Virgin they may be crucified upon the Cross of Manifestation and thence commit themselves again upon the Cross of the Father.

Man indeed stands between the Spirit and Matter, between the Angel and the Animal. At the summit of his ascent we behold as in a glass darkly, that the Perfected Being whom our Fathers strove to represent in the Sphinx, compound of the four elements in balanced disposition – the intelligence of Man, the soaring spirit of the Eagle, the fiery heart of the Lion and the firm stability of the Bull. Born of the Spirit he must descend to Malkuth until he is clothed in the coat of skin – the Body which is prepared for him by the humble brothers of the Flesh. And thence shall he arise again bearing with him that creation which groans and travels together with him until now, awaiting redemption.

The Twenty-first Path is the intelligence of Conciliation and it is so called because it receives the Divine Influence which flows into it from its benediction upon all and each existence.

There is a long pause during which the Postulant must repeat to himself the Mantra given to him to learn in his preparation. While he does this he should continue to gaze at the revolving Wheel. In this interval the lights of the cross are arranged in the Portal and the tripod of salt is placed just within the entrance from the ante-room.

The four stars must also be put ready. The green one by the salt, the blue on the tat, the red on the ankh and the silver within the vault.

Mantra
Earth born and bound, our bodies close us in,
Clogged with Red clay, and shuttered by our sin – We must arise.
Flowers bind round and grasses catch our feet,
Bird songs allure and blossom scent is sweet – We must arise.
Mountains may beckon and the seas recall:
Cloud-forms delude and rushing streams enthral – We must arise.
Planets encircle with their spiral light,
Stars call us upward to our faltering flight – Thus we arise.
Sun-rays will lead us higher yet and higher,
Moon-beam our souls scorch with their purging fire – Thus we arise.
Into the Darkness plunge, fearless of pain;
Coldness and silence cleanse us again – Still we arise.
Open ye Gates of Light, Doors open wide;
Gaze we within at the Glories you hide – We have Arisen.

King enters and opens the door but does not withdraw the curtain. He points to the brown cloak, sandals and staff which lie on the floor and says:

King: The Ascent of the Mountain of Initiation must ever be toilsome. Each of us must pass through the Dark Gate of Death before we can attain the summit. Each must treat the fiery path of purgatory, tracing again therein the rescuing symbol of the cross marked therein by lines of flame by the lion of Fortitude.

And to do this the initiate must also be the Hermit, the dweller in the desert, the pilgrim clothed in the brown habit of the earth, yet supported by the firm staff of steadfast will and aspiration seeing the light of inspiration which in due season he will receive from the hand of the Great Mother, a spark of the Indwelling Glory which ever halls the holy places of humanity. Thus may he loose the binding cords of desire and lust, that he may truly dedicate himself body, soul, life and spirit to the living service, and thus may he exchange the robe of Earthly Darkness for the wedding robe of Glory and attain the beatific vision.

The 20th path of the Sepher Yetzirah is called the intelligence of Will and it is so called because it is the means of preparation of all and each created being and by this Intelligence of the secret of all the activities of Spiritual Beings and is so called because of the Influence diffused by it from the most high and exalted supreme Glory.

POINT 2

The Postulant should, without prompting, step forth from the Pastos and take the brown cloak and put it and the sandals on, and take the staff in his right hand. ONE BELL SOUNDS. The door opens revealing a lion[83] in the open doorway. Behind him stands the Shekinah, a lighted lantern in her hand. She holds this out to the Postulant.

Shekinah: He that would be the greatest let him be the Server.

Postulant makes the 6=5 signs and lays his hands on the head of the lion. He takes the lantern and says:

Postulant: Server of Silence is my name.

Shekinah withdraws and the lion disappears thus revealing the tripod of salt. Postulant kneels on both knees, sprinkles salt on himself and says aloud:

Postulant: Earth to Earth and body to body – in the name of ADONAI HA ARETZ Lord and King of Earth, I dedicate my body to the Service of the Highest.

He loosens the amber cord from his knees and lays it across the Salt. King of Salem comes forward and fastens the Green Star on his left knee and says:

King: And behold a Star in the West; even Fomalhaut in his brightness and his rays shall be a guide to your feet.

Tripod is removed. Postulant moves forward, entering the Cross of Light. He passes between the lines of light until his way his barred. He turns to the Tat Pillar with the bowl of water on the top and a cup of white wine on the blue arm. He takes the cup and wets his lips with the wine and then pours the rest into the bowl of water. He falls onto the left knee and cries:

Postulant: Water to Water and Soul to Soul – in the Name of the Great Mother I dedicate my Soul to the Service of the Highest.

---

83 The Whare Ra lion was half the size of the real thing and was quite well made. It disappeared after the Order closed.

He loosens the violet cord from his lions and hangs it across the Tat. Shekinah comes forward and binds the blue star around his waist and raises him saying:

Shekinah: Peace, Peace unto him that is near; let the Light of Sothis[84] bring peace to the Soul.

Postulant turns and goes to the Ankh Pillar. He sprinkles incense on the flame and falls on his right knee and cries:

Postulant: Fire to Fire and Life to Life in the Name of Jah, everlasting, I dedicate my life to the service of the highest.

He loosens the black cord and throws it through the loop of the Ankh. King of Salem comes forward, raises him and binds the red star across his breast saying:

King: Thy Heart is as the Heart of the Lion; and the Star of the King, even Regulus, shall burn on your Breast.

Postulant turns back and is directed to approach the entrance to the Vault where the scarlet Mars on green curtain hangs. He raises the lantern on high, lifts his staff across the threshold before the curtain and cries:

Postulant: Light to Light and Spirit to Spirit in the name of that which not be uttered, I dedicate my Spirit to the service of the most high.

The curtain is withdrawn and Shekinah stands within the Vault. Her veil is now thrown back and she holds in both hands the crystal sphere upon which the sigil of the Postulant is engraved or painted.

Shekinah: I am He and He is I and Lo! The Creator has placed your crystal sphere within the starry heavens.

She gives him the sphere, takes the lantern and places on the right side of the altar. She then turns again and loosens the cord about his brow saying:

Shekinah: Let the Silver cord be loosed.

---

84 Sothis was crossed out and replaced in hand by Antares.

She lays the cord across the left side of the altar and takes the Silver Star and puts it about his brow saying:

Shekinah: I have given unto thee the starry crown of Aldebaran that you may pass on to the Heavenly Path.

POINT 3

King enters Vault and directs Postulant to kneel in the doorway of the vault and draw the cowl of the pilgrim's robe over his eyes. There is a pause. At the end of this time the BELL SOUNDS.

Postulant is raised to his feet and drawn across the threshold with the 7=4 grip. The brown cloak is taken from him and laid aside. At his feet lies a cross of six squares and beyond this is the altar.

King: The Father has given a commandment and the Son has made for me a spiritual body through his own soul.
I am he who has travelled far and who has made the pilgrimage.
Among the stars of heaven and to the Heart of the Great Mother.
She gave birth to me because it was her will to do so.
I am Osiris, the first born of the Gods.
I have become a divine being.
I have renewed by youth as the Eagle.
Behold I was watched and guarded but now I am released.
Behold I was bound with cords but now my Crystal sphere is within the starry heavens.
I have knowledge and I have Truth and movement is restored to my hands and feet.
I have passed through the Gate of Fomalhaut.
I have come forth from the Star Sothis.[85]
I have received the heart of the Lion.
I am crowned with the Crown of 72 rays.
Now let my soul be called into thy presence and my spirit be lain upon the altar.
Oh my Father I have come before thee and thou have caused me to enter the hidden Abode.
Strengthen thou me as thou has strengthened thyself and show thyself to thy Son.

---

85   Sothis was crossed out and replaced with Antares.

Beyond the Sun

```
              White
           Black  Grey
Scarlet   Yellow-Gold   Blue

              Violet

              Citrine
           Olive  Russet
              Black
```

The 7=4 Cross which folds into a black cube with 16 nails

Reverse side is black

Oh thou who returns and withdraws thyself,
Let thy will be done.

Shekinah: Oh Mystery which is without the worlds, because of which all has come into existence,
This is the whole outgoing and the whole up-going which has emanated all emanations and all that is therein, because of which all mysteries exist and all their regions.
Come unto me, oh thou who returns and withdraws himself.
Come unto us for we are your limbs,
Come unto us for we are all One with Thee,
We are all one and the same,
You are the Father and we draw nigh unto thee,
That you may receive this your Son.
Strengthen him as you have strengthened yourself and show yourself to him that your will be done.
We clothe this, your son, in the shining robe of glory!

She puts the Robe on him and points to the cross on the floor.

Shekinah: The last shall be first and the lowest shall be the highest. Malkuth shall be exalted into the Throne of Kether and all shall be consumed and become infinite and holy.

The stone which the builders rejected, the same shall become the corner stone. The cross of suffering is transmuted to the corner stone of the arch and raised above the Earth. The son shall offer that which he has received.

And peradventure then shall he behold the face of his father.

The Postulant must fold up the Cross into a cube and kneel on it supported by the Shekinah and the King. Postulant holds his crystal in both hands and bends his head. There is a pause and then the Magus appears behind the veil.

Magus: Be still my son.
Here the praise giving that keeps the soul in tune – the Hymn of Rebirth – The song of Union
Be still my Son
Thus shalt you know that he is himself

Both things that are and things that are not
The things that are he has made manifest
He keeps things that are not in himself
He is the god beyond all name
He the unmanifest
He the most manifest
He whom the mind alone can contemplate
He is visible to the eyes as well
He is the one of no body
The one of many bodies
No, rather he of Everybody.
Nothing is there which he is not
For all are he and he is all.
Be still my son.

King: All are thee
All are from thee
O thou who gives all and takes nothing
For you have all and nothing is there which you have not
You are whatever I may be
You are whatever I may do
You are whatever I may speak
For you are all and there is nothing else which you are not

Shekinah: You are that which does exist and you are that which does not exist.

You are Mind when you think and Father when you make and GOD when you energise and Good and Maker of All.

Magus: Be still my Son
For I will sing the praise of him who founded all.
Who fixed the Earth and hung up heaven
Who rules the sea, who makes the fire to shine
It is he who is the Eye of the Mind
May be accept the praise of all our powers
Oh life and Light, from us to thee our praises flow
Father I give thanks to you the energy of all our energies.
Take back from me the All into thyself
From you, from your will – to thee the all.

The all that is in us – oh life Preserve!
Oh Light illumine! Oh Creator Inquire!
Father of Lights in who is no shadow of turning receive thy son.

Postulant drops the Crystal into the Cauldron and raises his head. The veil is slightly parted and the Magus touches the Postulant on the heart, lips, eyes and brow with the almond branch and then lays his hand for a moment on the head of the Postulant. There is a pause. Then the Officers help him to rise and then the King shows him the signs of the grade.

Magus: Son, remember you have given your all even to the uttermost. There can be no separateness for thee. Bear this in mind when I give you the watchword of the grade which is ACHAN which signifies Unity and the two numbers 13, which is the number of ACHAD and 31 which is the number of El, the Divine name of this grade. And both these numbers conceal the number 4 which is manifestation. And I greet thee as MENES THEOROS the abider (Dweller) on the mountains.

Remember then Oh Son that in thee shall be manifest the Unity of the Divine One, and in token thereof, let us call upon him in the fourfold, mystic and terrible.

King tells the Postulant to remain kneeling at the altar as long as he desires. The Veil closes and the Magus withdraws and all leave the vault.

COMMENTARY ON THE 7=4 RITUAL

THE STELLA Matutina's 7=4 ritual is a difficult rite to comment upon. It has a role as crowning the entire structure of the Order while at the same time a mystical gateway to what was supposed to go beyond. Although the Order did have a ritual for the 8=3, this was normally administrative and reserved for chiefs. The primary reason for its existence was to enable someone to be initiated into the 7=4 and for the chiefs of the order to feel "above" the great unwashed "below" them. After the 7=4, you were expected to connect to states represented by the three supernal triads.

These were mystical and not magical states and are closer to that of Zen than conventional western ideas. After Whare Ra closed, those who held the 7=4 grade and wished to continue their work would aim to reach these states, and some claimed the 8=3 grade on the basis that they had briefly managed to hold those states and be transformed by them. This seemed to be in line with what Felkin himself meant by touching the states equal to a 10=1, represented by Kether. It was not something that could be held, but even then the mystical impact could be devastating for a psyche which was unprepared. After "touching the feet of Binah," one 7=4 told me that her life turned completely upside down and she entered into the darkest and longest night of the soul she had ever experienced.

The 7=4 ritual had a huge task ahead of itself to prepare and conclude. It did this by forcing the candidate to take a macrocosmic look at the universe using star magic. Star magic is not something touched on within the Golden Dawn system and its appearance here needs some explaining. The ritual initially used the so-called Royal Stars of Fomalhaut, Sirius, Regulus and Aldebaran. The Royal Stars appear to stand aside from the other stars in the sky and were seen by astrologers as important factors for royalty to consider. Since the Magician is becoming, at this point, a form of spiritual royalty these factors are important.

Aldebaran is at 9 degrees of Gemini. It corresponds to the Archangel Michael and rules the vernal equinox as the Watcher of the East. Ptolemy in his *Tetrabiblos* claimed that Aldebaran had the nature of Mars, and the Latin astrological compendium *Liber Hermetis* says that the fixed star has the nature of Venus and Mars combined. It is said to render its natives fortunate and wealthy and provide a talent for administration. It lends courage, eloquence, integrity and popularity but can lead to hot-headedness and licentiousness.

Sirius is at 10 degrees of Cancer and corresponds to the Archangel Gabriel who rules the winter solstice. Astrologers say that the sign is a mixture of Mars and Jupiter. During the day, Sirius can behave more like Jupiter, gifting its natives with leadership ability, wealth and honour, along with the Martian energy. During the night, the Mars force becomes predominant and the star could make someone despotic, insolent, coarse, agitated, and prone to act through passion and resentment.

Later Sirius was replaced by the star Antares. Antares is at 9 degrees of Sagittarius. It corresponds to the Archangel Uriel who rules the autumnal equinox as the Watcher of the West. It forms the centre of Scorpio and is the "heart of the scorpion." A red star, it was regarded by the Greeks as a mixture of Mars and Jupiter and it provides power, esteem, command, rashness, independence, blunt speech, wealth and leadership.

Regulus is at 29 degrees of Leo. It corresponds to the Archangel Raphael. He rules the summer solstice as the Watcher of the North. The star Regulus lies at the centre of the constellation of Leo, and is often known as the "Heart of the Lion." Its name literally means "the star of kings," and it is associated with royalty and power. The Greeks regarded Regulus as a mixture of Mars and Jupiter and believed that those who had this star prominent were esteemed, commanding, independent, outspoken, great-souled and honour-loving, often wealthy and leaders. There is a certain amount of Martian quarrelsomeness involved with this star.

Fomalhaut is at 3 degrees of Pisces. The Archangel Gabriel is associated with Fomalhaut and he rules the as the Watcher of the South. The Greeks saw this star as a mixture of Mercury and Venus, and said it created a learned, philosophical, eloquent, creative, clever, artistic, pleasure-loving, practical, high-minded and successful, but sometimes fickle or promiscuous person. The Greeks said that

Fomalhaut was the mouth of the fish – Piscis Austrinus, into which the water jug of Aquarius is poured.

These are their positions in the sky at night and nothing to do with the directions of the winds or their other elemental associations which we see in the 5=6 or elemental grades, but it is important to note that these are the star representations of the four holy creatures, or the four fixed signs.

In this ritual the Chief Adept has been replaced by the Magus who wears the grey robe, representing Chokmah, a white square on his head, representing Kether, with a gold cord to make the colours of Kether in the Princess scale. He wears a leopard skin which was the Ancient Egyptian robe for a Sem-Priest. The Sem-Priest was a walker between the worlds and a shamanic figure. The leopard skin then indicates that he is supposed to be the guide across the Abyss. He holds a sprig of almond. Almond was connected to the Bible where it was a symbol of watchfulness and promise, due to its early flowering.

The use of hazel has more to do with the legend of Aaron's rod, which was a prototype for magic wands. Aaron's rod, when it was not being turned into a snake, bore sweet almonds on one side and bitter on the other. If the Israelites followed God the sweet almonds would be ripe and edible, but if they disobeyed life would be bitter.

Almond blossom inspired the menorah which stood in the Holy Temple. According to Exodus 25:33 three cups shaped like almond blossoms were on one branch, with a knob and a flower, and three cups shaped like almond blossoms were on the other. On the candlestick were four cups, shaped like almond blossoms, with knobs and flowers.

The other officers include the Shekinah, who now wears a rose tunic and black belt and carries her acacia. Her colours show her to represent the candidate's second order experience.

The King of Salem has his blue and purple robe and winged sphere wand. He is also holding a red rose. In some respects, this later symbol represents the rose which was used in the original 0=0 and is the candidate's outer order experience.

This time the postulant wears a white robe with red shoes. This is an amalgamation of the meaning of the first order and the second order. It symbolically means that he has completed everything.

In the UK the 7=4 vault was set up in the ordinary 5=6 vault by means of a cubical blue tent. At Whare Ra the 7=4 room was permanently set up for the 7=4. But the 6=5 room was hardly used except for the entrance of Shekinah.

The anteroom of the temple was draped in red and has the pastos standing upright in it. The red symbolises the Mars energy of the previous grade. The pastos is upright and draped in white. This indicates that the resurrection process has begun.

The portal hall had sand coloured carpet on the floor. In front of the door there was a cross of made up of lights. To the south and north of the cross were the pillars. There was a tripod of salt in the west, by the door.

The vault had a violet carpet and was draped so that it had four blue walls. On the east side there was a grey veil, and a white and gold altar on which there was a green cup with red Mars symbols on it. An extra veil was hung on the outer side of the vault door.

What is interesting is that the rituals don't mention the use of the side rooms. It would be logical that at least a small part of the ritual would have used that space, if the writer of the ritual knew that it was available. When these rituals were designed, Whare Ra had not been built and so they were written for a ritual space which was not purpose built.

It is my thought that Felkin had thought about adding some material to these rituals that would use these rooms but never did. The other suggestion was that they might have been used by the officers to raise their consciousness to the grade in those rooms before the ritual began. However, Tony Fuller suggested that in New Zealand the 7=4 room was used in the section which was marked as being in the vault.

That is certainly what happened in some post-Whare Ra initiations. In those cases, the 7=4 room was also used for the rite of the link.

The temple opens with Shekinah and the King of Salem standing beside each of the pillars and the Magus standing in the vault. In this case he is representing the Third Order, which the candidate is aspiring to enter.

Unlike the previous grade, where the candidate says nothing, in this grade they are required to remember a long mantra. I found the mantra somewhat stilted, but apparently WB Yeats liked it enough to give it a rewrite, which was never published by him.[86] Yeats' version was:

---

86   Meihuizen, Nicholas. *Yeats and the Drama of Sacred Space*. Amsterdam: Rodopi, 1998. p.125. Print.

> We are weighed down by the blood & the heavy weight of the bones
> We are bound by flowers, & our feet are entangled in the green
> And there is deceit in the singing of birds
> It is time to be done with it all
> The stars call & all the planets
> And the purging fire of the moon
> And yonder in the cold silence of cleansing night
> May the dawn break & gates of day be set wide open.

It is a pity that the Whare Ra or the Stella Matutina did not run with it, although it misses the important lines "we arise" and "we have arisen." It is possible they did not know of its existence as it might have been for his private use.

The function of the mantra is to create a feeling of sadness about the earth and a desire to arise on the spiritual plane. I am not sure that I agree that a desire for spirit is necessarily accompanied with a need to reject the physical. However, this state is something which is common to many mystics and Gnostics.

The postulant is also required to memorise several of the lines and bring an egg shaped crystal, such as a moonstone, upon which they have placed their 6=5 motto and a sigil of the motto drawn from the rose painted on it. The crystal represents your sphere of sensation which goes through its last alchemical purification through the rite.

The paint which contains your name and sigil is literally boiled off the stone in the last stages of the ritual, which means that you have a new motto and a new beginning.[87] Moonstone was commonly used, but some adepts did use other stones that they were more personally attracted to. These stones were then set and worn about the neck during rituals. They have a particular charge and help stabilise the sphere during particularly heavy workings.

The ritual has the three officers give the signs of Thoth, Hathor and Horus. The sign of Thoth involved a drawing down of the word, down the middle pillar from above the crown and out into the hands. This represents a perfected idea coming from the Logos, or the mind of God, crossing the abyss and entering into manifestation. This is performed by the Magus who uses the godform of Thoth.

---

[87] Tony Fuller has Frank Salt's crystal, which he describes as a cube. The motto and the sigil were not boiled off that one, and Fuller says it was not removed from his either. It must have depended on the crystal that people chose, and two people I know had this happen to them.

The sign of Hathor involved placing the left hand on the earth while the right hand reached to heaven. This godform is used by the Shekinah. This moves sums up the second order, by virtue of the fact that it always invokes the higher first and brings it down to earth.

The sign of Horus is given by the King of Salem. It represents the outer order but a turning away from "evil." There is a fourth sign, called the Sign of Osiris, and this is the sign of Harpahkrat but using the left hand instead of the right. It is supposed to indicate Osiris who sees in the great silence the dawning of truth.

Thoth was an important part of the wider Golden Dawn tradition, something which is overlooked by many modern groups. He oversaw all the magic of the Z documents and, by inference, all initiations within the Golden Dawn. He was also supposed to have created Tarot and some people in Whare Ra considered that the Angel HRU, who was set over the secret wisdom and Tarot, was an aspect of this god.

In Hermopolis, Thoth was the most important creator god and Hathor was considered his wife. Thoth was the Logos, the mind of the One Thing. Thoth's previous wife Seshat, the goddess of reading, writing, architecture and arithmetic, was absorbed by Hathor who acquired the role including acting as a witness at the judgement of the dead. Hathor was a sky goddess, known as "Lady of Stars" and "Sovereign of Stars." She ruled Sirius.

The "Horus" mentioned here is not the Horus of Edfu, or Horus the Younger or Elder, but the son of Thoth and Hathor, Re-Horakhty or Ra of the two Horizons – in other words, sunrise and sunset. Re-Horakhty was Ra as a symbolic deity of hope and rebirth. Thoth (Divine Mind) and Hathor (The Universe) combine to give birth (manifest) the solar force on earth.

These agencies are working on the postulant so that he becomes a specialised aspect of the risen Osiris – that of the regenerated Harpahkrat.

The three godforms use the divine name of Chesed, EL, to build a new body for the candidate – he who knows silence and the dawning of truth. This refers to Chokmah, which feeds into Chesed, as the mirror of Kether looking towards the silence of Binah.

The postulant arrives at the door holding the symbol of the previous grade, the acacia. He is asked by the King of Salem how he hopes to enter the grade, and replies that his brow is like the King's, his lips are open and his heart is on its throne. It sounds like the

King James Bible, but it is actually a paraphrase from the Book of the Dead. The chapter of not dying a second time in Khert-neter.

> My heart-case is upon its throne, I know how to utter words. In very truth I am Ra himself. I am not a man of no account. I am not a man to whom violence can be done. Thy father liveth for thee, O son of Nut. I am thy son, O great one, I have seen the hidden things which are thine. I am crowned upon my throne like the king of the gods. I shall not die a second time in Khert-Neter.

This spell was important because it allowed the dead person to become an *akh* or eternal spirit.

The King of Salem takes him, walks him anticlockwise to the anteroom, and places him standing upright in the pastos. The anticlockwise direction is to move him into incarnation and towards the sacrifice and death of Tiphareth. He is then bound with an amber cord around his knees, a violet cord around his groin, a black cord about his heart and a silver cord around his head. The colours here do not fit with the traditional *mintus mundum* and their logic is unclear. They were supposed to represent four mysteries. Amber was supposed to represent the Mysteries of the Souls Unborn. Violet was connected to the Mystery of Incarnation. Black was the Mystery of Death and silver was the Mystery of Eternal Life.

The King of Salem tells the postulant that the Mystery of the Souls Unborn is that the Feet of Sothis[88] are established and you are born into their state of rest. What this suggests is that your Soul comes from Sirius and when you are born this state is passive and needs to be awakened. This is not a literal statement and to understand it you need to comprehend what Sirius represents. The ancient Egyptians believed Sirius was the doorway to the afterlife. In mythology, the dog Sirius is one of the watchmen of the Heavens, fixed in one place at the bridge of the Milky Way, keeping guard over the abyss into incarnation. It was a symbol of the initiate who has succeeded in bridging the lower and higher consciousness. All souls came into being through it and will return out of it. The mystery of the Souls Unborn is that you incarnate into matter and will return the same way you came.

The Mystery of Incarnation, the King of Salem tells the postulant, is that they have inherited eternity, and everlastingness has been

---

88   Sothis or Antares.

bestowed on them. This mystery is that you are a son of a divine being who is eternal. You inherit its characteristics. What you experience on earth is an infinitely small part of you and your divine life.

The Mystery of Death, says the King of Salem, is that nothing hidden shall not be made manifest, and nothing is buried which will not be raised. Death then is an illusion, as is life. If you die you will be raised from death; if you are hidden from the material plane you will be seen. Everything that has died is still around us and has not gone anywhere – it is simply hidden from mortal eyes.

The Mystery of Eternal Life, according to the King of Salem, is that you are a son of god living in an eternal City of God. The City of God was an idea put forward by Augustine of Hippo in the early 5th century AD. His book *The City of God* saw history as being a conflict between the City of Man and the City of God. The City of God is marked by people who forgot earthly pleasure to dedicate themselves to the eternal truths of God. The City of Man consists of people who have immersed themselves in the cares and pleasures of a passing world. Thus to obtain eternal life, it is necessary to focus on divine things which are eternal. The mystery is that you are already a divine being capable of doing this.

The candidate is left alone with an image of a large tarot card, the Wheel of Fortune. At this moment, the god Thoth is placed over him and one of the officers reads to him the description. Unlike the other displays of the Wheel of Fortune, this tarot card had a small engine installed in the back to make the wheel rotate. The effect of this is so that the bound candidate associates the cycles of their lives with the fact that they are bound. Some like to see this as reincarnation and a reminder of the wheel of birth and death of Eastern philosophy, but this is not necessary to an understanding of what is happening. Our lives are made up of countless cycles of repeated mistakes and rises and falls.

There is a long pause here where the candidate repeats the mantra and associates this cycled life with the weariness expressed by the poem.

When the postulant is ready, he is instructed to dress as a hermit, with the brown cloak, sandals and staff. The hermit was a symbol of earthly wisdom, but also someone who had rejected the world. They were attempting, as the bible suggested, to be in the world but not of it. Magically this is interesting. The postulant is not just shown a tarot card, but he is actually becoming it. He is told that his staff represents fire and he is enclosed by the earth seeking divine wisdom.

When he is ready, there is a single bell and he looks up to see Shekinah with a lighted lantern or candle in her hands. This represents the divine wisdom. In front of her is a statue of a lion. This tableau is that of Key 8, Fortitude. The postulant takes the lamp of divine wisdom, places his hand on the lion's head, and gives one of his pre-learnt phrases "the server of silence is my name."

The lion represents the fiery animal self, and the postulant is taming it by silence.

Both the Shekinah and the lion depart and the postulant purifies himself with salt. The salt represents his earthly body which is being dedicated to God. By dedicating our bodies to the One Thing, we align our physical experiences to Divine ones. It means that the mystery of our birth in matter is not a bother, but rather a divine action on earth. The candidate unbinds himself because he no longer sees himself as a victim of matter but taking part in a great experiment.

In return, he is given a green star of 12 rays which he puts on his left (passive) knee which represents Fomalhaut. This placing of a star represents an important transmutation in a candidate's sphere of sensation and its tuning to cosmic forces. The candidate is expected to take on the qualities of this particular star in return for the realisation about his divine life in matter. He should see the purpose of his incarnation to bring the divine Mercury and Venus gifts of being a learned, philosophical, eloquent, creative, clever, artistic, pleasure-loving, practical, high-minded and successful individual. The best material person you can be. This also gives him the power of true movement.

The postulant now enters the Cross of Light. He walks along the avenue of candles[89] until he reaches a crossroads and is barred from walking further towards the east. Disobeying the rules that he was given in the 1=10 grade he turns to the left and comes to the Tat Pillar. The pillar has a bowl of water on it and a cup of white wine. He wets his lips with the wine and pours it into the bowl. While red wine is seen as the blood of sacrifice, white wine is a symbol of clarity. He dedicates his soul to the service of the highest and can take

---

89 Tony Fuller was told by Frank Salt that the coloured lights forming the cross at Whare Ra were Christmas tree lights. But there were different strings of lights forming an Elemental Cross of Lights.

off the binding connected to the Mystery of Incarnation. Realising that he has inherited eternity and everlastingness means that he can truly dedicate himself to his divine destiny. For this dedication, that which bound him is replaced with the gift represented by Antares. He is given the peace of knowing that he is following his divine destiny and whatever assails him shall be part of that destiny. He also manifests the powers of Antares within his sphere of sensation: leadership ability, wealth and honour, along with the Martian drives.

The postulant then walks to the Ankh Pillar, consecrates himself to the service of the One Thing, and is permitted to remove the cord of death around his heart. Once you know that you are divine, you become tuned to your divine self and free from death's rules. It is not that you do not die, as many have suggested about secret chiefs, but that your passing is simply making yourself hidden.

He is now allowed to manifest the powers of Regulus – he will become charismatic, commanding, independent, outspoken, wealthy and honour-loving, with qualities of leadership.

The postulant now returns to the centre and is instructed to walk to the vault where he encounters the scarlet Mars on a green curtain. This is an unusual symbol. Normally you would draw a green Mars on a red background. This would activate the red colour with its flashing complementary. However, in this case you are actually invoking Venus green using a red Mars. This would make for a strongly fiery blend of opposites.

The postulant lays his staff, which is a symbol of his own fiery power, across the door of the vault and raises his light to offer his spirit to the Divine. This indicates that he has learnt the mystery of Eternal Life and has set aside his personal power to manifest that of the One Thing.

Shekinah appears and gives him his crystal sphere, and takes his staff and light and puts them by the altar. The crystal sphere represents the work of the Second Order. He is now purified and ready for further work.

She says "let the silver cord be loosened." This is an interesting use of the term, because the silver cord was supposed to be connected to the body and if it was ever cut then a person would die. This idea was based on Ecclesiastes 12:6 :

> 5 Furthermore, men are afraid of a high place and of terrors on the road; the almond tree blossoms, the grasshopper drags himself along,

and the caperberry is ineffective. For man goes to his eternal home while mourners go about in the street.

6 Remember Him before the silver cord is broken and the golden bowl is crushed, the pitcher by the well is shattered and the wheel at the cistern is crushed; 7 then the dust will return to the earth as it was, and the spirit will return to God who gave it...

It suggests that by knowing the mysteries of eternal life you also go beyond mortal life and concerns. This is also indicated by the fact that the postulant is able to manifest the powers of the Scorpio based Antares which provides power, esteem, command, rashness, independence, blunt speech, wealth and leadership.

All of these stars provide the postulant with the beginnings of a stellar body, one which is particularly suited for his understanding as a royal Son of God.

There is a pause at this point to give the sphere of sensation a little time to recover. The postulant then approaches the vault and kneels. He is raised and then drawn into the vault using the 7=4 grip.

He then sums up his life to Shekinah and is permitted to put on a robe of glory. This is a white robe in which God has interwoven the idea of the 'Robe of Glory' which was originally worn by Adam and Eve before the fall. It was lost when they put on physical bodies.

According to Christian tradition, at the Baptism, Christ laid the Robe of Glory in the river Jordan, making it available once again for humanity. When a person is baptised they put on the 'Robe of Glory'. When the dead rise at the end of days, the just will in all reality re-enter the celestial Paradise, clothed in their Robes of Glory.

He is then instructed to build the cube from the six squares and 16 nails and then kneel upon it. I have written another chapter on the symbolism of this particular act and some of my own discoveries in connection with it.

There are number of prayers while the postulant holds his crystal egg and kneels on the cube. This is giving him the chance to impress his own energy into the crystal and strongly identify himself with it.

The Magus appears in the vault. It is assumed that he had been meditating throughout the ritual in the 7=4 room. He and the other officers pray for the candidate, but at the same time extol him to be still. All the answers and all the evidence required from life are found when you stop living and quieten yourself down.

He is instructed to drop the crystal into the cauldron of boiling and perfumed water. Whare Ra used a small crucible of silver – spherical, with an opening in the top and a small spirit lamp mounted under it. It was filled with boiling water. Just before the candidate entered the Vault, Shekinah put a few drops of rose-water perfume into it. Later Shekinah lifts the cube from the boiling water and gives it to him. She uses tweezers to lift the crystal out.

The Magus then touches the candidate on the heart, lips, eyes and brow with the almond branch. This links the candidate's Neshamah to the Ruach.

The mysteries of the grade are then imparted and the temple is closed by a word of power which is derived from vowels. It is not clear where these come from, or what their use is. However, they are a link to the Greco-Egyptian mysteries in which the vibration of vowels was a key part.

In some instances the sounds may have been designed to mimic elements of Nature, such as the sound of wind or the tune of water. In others, like the various permutations of the seven vowels (AEHIOYΩ) and the commonly repeated divine names of IAΩ and IEOU, the vowel sounds were the magical formula used to invoke the power of the "seven Immortal Gods of the Universe."

According to Aristotle and Hippocrates, the Greek initiates attributed the seven vowels to the seven heavens and planets and a fundamental relationship between the individual heavens or spheres of the seven planets, and the seven sacred vowels.

The first heaven uttered the sound of the sacred vowel A (Alpha); the second heaven, the sacred vowel E (Epsilon); the third, H (Eta); the fourth, I (Iota); the fifth, O (Omicron); the sixth, Y (Upsilon); and the seventh heaven, the sacred vowel Ω (Omega). When these seven heavens sing together, they produce a perfect harmony which ascends as an everlasting praise to the throne of the Creator.

The German occultist and magician Henry Cornelius Agrippa (1486-1535) developed another method in his *De Occulta Philosophia* using the Sepher Yetzirah, where the seven Hebrew Double Letters map in their alphabetic order to the seven planets in their descending order of emanation (Saturn, Jupiter, Mars, Sun, Venus, Mercury and Moon). This Saturn-Bayt order is the predominate system of correspondence between the seven Doubles and the seven planets in traditional Kabbalah; and, through applying the same formula to the Greek vowels and Chaldean planets, Agrippa arrived at the Saturn-Alpha order.

Vowel

A, α	Saturn	Moon
E, ε	Jupiter	Mercury
H, η	Mars	Venus
I, ι	Sun	Sun
O, o	Venus	Mars
Υ, υ	Mercury	Jupiter
Ω, ω	Moon	Saturn

Unfortunately, it is not clear which system Felkin was using. If he used Agrippa, the "terrible name" would be the gods Saturn-Moon, Jupiter-Mercury, Saturn-Moon. Which does not really take us anywhere interesting. Unless someone finds a pattern here which I could not spot, it looks like this particular mystery will remain lost.

⟨ XI ⟩ EXPERIENCE OF THE 7=4

By Fr LiV

OUTSIDE THE temple the sky was dark and clouded. It was night as it was like being in the middle of a very dark storm. Anubis was there between the pillars and was in good humour. He was not standing to attention or particularly rigid. The temple was extremely clear.

I could hear the ritual being spoken, as if far off.

As I said that my brow was like unto the kings etc. there was a feeling of centres opening… brow, lips and heart.

When the King drew me into the temple I was not really aware of his godform or anything. It was dark in the room and it was really like I was being pulled by something invisible quickly and backwards. I almost did not have time to think anything before I was in the Pastos.

The binding was again strange. The King felt human but the cords themselves were brighter, like glowing. When the cord was placed on me I felt a sharp physical pain in my right foot.

The overall effect was one of being alone in this ritual. It was something I got throughout the whole thing. People were there, but ultimately I was working alone with powers that came to me.

The Tarot card and mantra was an interesting experience. I found that as I watched the card the Anubis figure kept ascending towards the sphinx. The mantra itself bought a feeling of sadness. That the world was beautiful but there was a desire to move on, to walk away. The process of calling the planets and then the stars shows the pattern to break free of the wheel of birth and death. I had always felt that the wheel represented cycles, but in fact it represents the up and down of the moon. The goal is to ascend descent and then rise up on a higher arc.

I put on the robes a little early. When the king pointed at them. I also felt that I had a lamp in my hand before I should have. I guess this might have been an association with the Tarot card the Hermit.

The bell sounded and the Lion appeared in the doorway. Shekinah appeared behind it, but similar to the Lady in Black. I was surprised that the lion was lion-coloured and not red. It felt affectionate. I covered myself in the salt. What was odd here was that I felt memories of others who had done the same thing. I saw the same thing happening before in Whare Ra and somewhere else.

The cross of light looked like it should have been made of candles but it felt like stars which hovered about a foot off the ground. I could not see what barred me in the middle. It was like a line (staff sized) surrounded by an ellipse. There was something indefinable when the wine poured into the water. Something happened but I could not see what. When Antares was placed across the loins I felt like I was being rewired. Instead of taking energy from the earth I was taking it from the stars. It did not feel MORE powerful, just cleaner and different. The fire pillar was a similar experience. Again, I had no complete image of the King or Shekinah. They were there, but not. It was as if they were trying to tell me that at this point you are on your own, but assisted. Everything else was so clear and emotional, the fact that I could not see them clearly seemed to be part of the point.

I kept getting images of points of white light, like triangles, or the ends of pentagrams. One in particular was of a single point with two lines coming from it.

The Spirit dedication had power... and when the Mars veil was parted there was a sense of something being opened. Shekinah gave me the crystal and said that it was placed in the starry heavens and I could see that. The sphere of sensation which has been worked on in the Golden Dawn was suddenly thrown upwards and re-oriented by the four stars. When the silver one was removed it was replaced by a silver crown. My brow centre felt like it was being opened (like a rusty muscle).

I could see Sh. and King as they stood on either side of the altar. The King was as Osiris (green faced but with lots of black and gold). Shekinah was as a woman with grey hair. One thing I realised was that Shekinah spoke like Sr _____ .

Intellect was awake in the King's speech and I twigged that he was saying it for me and that I was becoming something cosmic.

The robing was emotional and very bright light. The folding of the cross was also interesting because I could feel that so far everything had been sacrifice. Suddenly I realised that the sacrifice builds to something. As I knelt on it, the walls of the temple faded

Experience of the 7=4

away and I was beneath a night's sky and was at the same time part of it. I was aware of the support of the King and Shekinah, but the Magus appeared as a calming feeling and it was then I think I fully understood the implications of all things being one thing. My 5=6 motto, In Unity I AM, was realised. Hard to explain because it was not a mind fizz or anything… it just was more of an "of course" moment.

The putting of the crystal in the water involved me placing it into a vortex of light where it transmuted. I could feel myself being purified but also the outside of my universe being changed too. The ritual was time and time reinforcing that I was God working within its own sphere of sensation and all things I was seeing were just expressions of myself. It sounds like this was intellectual, but it was not. It was full of paradoxes. I was limited but at the same time limitless. The stone was both my sphere of sensation and that of the universe.

[The stone itself has a 2cm cat's scratch across it because of the boiling and it was still hot half an hour after we took it out of the water. The sigil had been wiped off.]

There was a long pause here, where I seemed to be swamped with lots of white geographical shapes.

⟨XII⟩ THE RITE OF THE LINK

THIS LITTLE ritual provided Felkin with his way to break with Mathers and the Golden Dawn and form his own branch of the Western Mystery Tradition. The Link was acquired from Steiner while Felkin was in Germany and is a magical ritual which connects a person to the Rosicrucian current.

In fact, the ritual is the third and last time that a person encounters the link. It is given to them in their 0=0 and 5=6 at different depths. The link which was passed in the 5=6 ritual gave the person the power to initiate those in the Outer Order. At the 7=4, the link is given to a person so that they can communicate directly with the Rosicrucian current and form their own branch of the tradition.

However, what the Link ceremony did more than anything else was take the Stella Matutina away from the need of masonic authority, lineage or Secret Chiefs or Astral Masters. It plugged in a leader to a spiritual impulse which they could then use to find another expression of the Rosicrucian teaching. Anyone with the link who formed a group would have the ability to have a pure connection to that impulse and could form their own egregore as a method of expression to it.

An egregore is a spirit, similar to the Roman concept of a *lare* in that it forms spontaneously and appears to have a personality. It is formed when a group is started and in psychological terms is called a 'group mind.' In my book *Gathering the Magic* I said that this egregore is made up of the sum total of aspirations and beliefs of all group members, past and present. In psychological terms they refer to it as a 'group mentality'; however, they stop short of describing it as an individual, although some – like British psychoanalyst Wilfred Ruprecht Bion from the Tavistock Clinic who pioneered some work on the 'group mentality' – have found themselves reluctantly labelling it as an entity.

Among his therapy group, Bion found this entity could behave like a primitive human with the entire attendant drives. For example, if the group was attacked they would all behave in a 'flight or fight' reaction against the external foe.

This is all standard stuff. It could be seen in a rowing club or a drama club. Bion noted that an egregore personified the 'basic assumption of the group', and if a person fought against it then a 'group undertow' would drag them in another direction. If they do not go with the flow then the group will enact a fight or flight reaction against them.

Again, this is something that an unscrupulous leader will use. If a second in command can present enough of a case to the group that the leader should be removed, they will work quickly to expel him on the flimsiest of evidence extremely quickly. This can happen intentionally, but sometimes it happens that the second in command is swept along with the group mind if they find that their leader has been misbehaving. In the Golden Dawn revolt of 1901, Florence Farr and William Yeats, who until then had been identified as friends of Samuel Mathers, found themselves with the rest of the mob holding the pitchforks and torches.

Magical groups, because of their dependence on imagination and astral images, develop an unusual form of particularly powerful egregore. It can actually assist them reach higher states and do more than an individual could manage. A group egregore is powered up every time a rite is performed and the longer and more often a group meets the more powerful it becomes, until it has the power to do lots of interesting things – some good, some bad.

Each group has an egoregore and it is part of a larger one for an Order. Often a larger one represents the tradition (in this case the Rosicrucian tradition). When a group is formed its leaders and teachers attempt to form a link first with the tradition and then with a contact which agrees to work with them. This link is then attached to the egregore.

Over the years, egregores will become corrupted. Some of their members, or chiefs, might let the side down. Alternatively, a politically motivated person might try to take over the group. They can also attract astral parasites, which are the astral wildlife which feed off intense generation of energy and emotion. The Golden Dawn had several methods to spring clean every year (the equinox ritual and the use of the HRU and HUA).

While a group is active, it is easy to see how it all works. The difficulty comes when a group breaks up or becomes inactive, as was the case with the Golden Dawn. An egregore stays dormant and reactivates when people identify with it again.

Despite what many might think, working with another group's egregore is easy. It is a matter entirely of identification. If you think that your group is connected to the Golden Dawn, or Gerald Gardner or Aleister Crowley, then it is. It might not be rational, but then again egregores are not intelligent and will associate themselves with whoever asks. If you say that you are a Golden Dawn Order, you are – even if there is a lot of evidence that you are actually four kids with a copy of Regardie. This issue of identification is more important than things like rituals. Rituals might help you focus on an egregore but they are not needed for the egregore. External identification is also important. How outsiders see your group will help define it because an egregore is built by thought, and thought can change it. It is for this reason that the Golden Dawn oath prohibited the disclosure of the name of the temple. It is also the reason why the Golden Dawn changed its name after the Horos Trial. Suddenly its egregore could be modified by the great unwashed.

For Felkin, it meant that he did not have to turn to the egregore of the Golden Dawn, which had been tainted by infighting and public court cases; he could start from scratch, without needing to rewrite the rituals. All that needed to happen was for him to use his link to connect to the second order, and the new link would flow into the first order without needing much change to the rituals. If he wanted to make any changes, he would not get an astral kicking from any conservative early egregore.

Because of his use of the link, Felkin could disconnect his Stella Matutina from the GD egregore, and later disconnected his Smaragdum Thallasses from the SM. The way they did it was by reconnecting their new order to the impulse behind it.

Doing so was a little more problematic than he expected, as the link was a higher level of magic than some people could handle. Christina Stoddard said that Felkin gave it to three Chiefs in London and one immediately went insane and the other became sick. She did not consider that she too had become insane by that point; had she had that level of self-awareness she would probably have thought that the link was completely toxic.

There were different versions of this ritual of the link. The earliest example found (dated 1920) is described as "giving the Etheric Link with C.R.C.", and with the "Ancient Order of the Rose and Cross".

The person has to make an oath of some five clauses, including: "If ever called upon to Rule in this Order I will ever seek to keep it Secret, Pure, and free from all schism". The ceremony then moves to the vault – the Link bestowed here is slightly longer and differs thus:

> "I/we, by the Great Power invested in me/us, do at this solemn hour and in this Sacred Place transmit to our Frater the Etheric Link which we ourselves have duly received. Be thou faithful, be thou brave, be thou true. May the Blessing transmitted from our Father C.R.C. rest upon you now and ever more. Amen. I/we hereby invest you with the power to transmit this Etheric Link to any I/we, give you permission to so honour. Amen."

The Obligation is given upon a sword placed upon the closed pastos placed outside the vault, North and South. "Before admitting the Candidate, Our Father in God should be called within the Vault by his full name three times, after bringing down the D.W.B. after full L.V.X. signs."

It is not clear how long this version of the Link was used, as the one given below is shorter and simpler. Initially the link was given at 5=6 to those who were expected to initiate people as Hierophants. This meant that those who were initiating were actually connecting to this general Rosicrucian current during the 0=0. However, the ritual was later only given to those who were 7=4 and only those who were likely to end up as chiefs in the Order. Pat Zalewski thinks that this is because later in Whare Ra's history all the Hierophants were 7=4 anyway, but I think there might be another reason.

The introduction of the Etheric Link within the Stella Matutina was probably the reason why Felkin lost control of the English temples. More than just making unprepared people insane, it would have been pumping new ideas and methods into people who were ill-equipped to handle them and lacking real dedication to do so. I was warned by Barbara Nairn that some of the people who received the link within the Order had become unbalanced afterwards because they could not handle the load. This included some of the people who were given it after Whare Ra closed.

"At the point you are given the link, you are expected to have done the work on yourself and not allow your ego to get in the way of your work. If you could not then the link would overpower you," she told me.

I know of several people outside Whare Ra who attempted to get the link either before they were ready, or simply by performing the ritual in Pat Zalewski's book. Most of the time nothing happened, but several people had the impression of an old man being in the room looking at them critically and they did not like the experience. Equally, I have spoken to those who received the link in other situations who found it a fascinating experience that did them no harm at all. This would suggest to me that the link is protected or that it is intelligent and when you are ready to receive it, you get it. Those who received the link legitimately described themselves as looking at a vortex which was a gateway somewhere else.

In a paper Pat Zalewski gave to his Thoth-Hermes Temple, he said that the Link was an "astral tunnel" which allowed access to certain regions of the astral plane where a contingency of astral entities govern their respective areas.

"If there are enough links to humankind, the more energy is released to accomplish things of the Great Work," Zalewski wrote.

The idea of bestowing an Etheric Link killed off those who believed that it was possible to form a magical group based on the idea of paper lineage. Paper lineage is a masonic, anti-magic atrocity. It says that someone is able to form a group without doing any work because another person thinks that they are worthy of a certificate to start a group. In fact, the Order of the Golden Dawn was formed based on such a concept. Westcott and Mathers were never initiated into the Golden Dawn but claimed they had the right to form such a group because they had authority in the form of letters from Fr Sprengel. Westcott and Mathers were brilliant magicians, and Mathers went on to form a link of his own to the Rosicrucian tradition, but the idea that you can be named a $7=4$ and then start a magic group is absurd. Nevertheless, there are those who have formed their groups based on such paper lineages, sometimes actually buying them and passing them over kitchen tables with a cobbled-together ritual.

The Link idea did away with this concept. It could only be passed on to someone who was a $7=4$ in that tradition by someone who was "slightly above" a $7=4$ themselves. This means that no one can claim to have reactivated the Whare Ra current or Order unless they have been given a link by a human who also had it. In the case of Whare Ra, I know of a few who are authorised to do so. Jack Taylor conferred it upon his students Pat and Christine Zalewski; Frank Salt did likewise to Tony Fuller. I know that Pat has passed the link on to one of his students, who had attained the correct grade; I am uncertain if Tony Fuller has. Others hold the link and have passed it on but I am not at liberty to say who they are.

The link was given to those who the Whare Ra chiefs considered leaders. In theory, it was supposed to be given to those who would be chiefs, or potential chiefs, but this was not always the case. Although Mrs Felkin admired Jack Taylor, she was unlikely to appoint him as a chief of Whare Ra (whatever he might have thought). This was because the very skills which made him a great magician also made him unwilling to play the necessary political games to hold the order together. Yet he was given the link by her after his 7=4.

Unless they wish it, the link does not even require them to open a group connected to the Whare Ra egregore. It only requires them to be connected to the source which inspired Whare Ra.

There are those, including Pat Zalewski, who believe that the link is only a connection with Steiner and therefore not particularly important. Pat and I agree on many things but this is not one of them. This is because in my view the link was written to connect Steiner's group to the Rosicrucian current and so passes well beyond him and into the roots of the original Order. In fact, exploring the roots of the link will take you even further back into the roots of Rosicrucianism and into prehistory.

One thing about the link that Zalewski and I do agree on is that you can form your own link to this particular spiritual impulse and form a group based upon it. You will not, however, be able to claim lineage from Whare Ra or Smaragdum Thallasses.

I was told that in Whare Ra the Link Ritual was performed in the hidden 7=4 room after the 7=4 initiation. There is no proof of this, but it would be logical. The rite was carried out by the 5=6 officers: Chief Adept, Second Adept and Third Adept.

Tony Fuller has also found evidence that under the early days of the Stella Matutina the link rite was awarded either at 5=6 or for anyone in the second order who the chiefs considered worthy. The logic was that to be an effective outer order hierophant you would need to be linked to the current of the order. That idea was abandoned sometime after his death.

THE TRANSMISSION OF THE ETHERIC LINK

Chief Adept – 2nd Adept – 3rd Adept

Note: The pastos was placed in the portal for this ceremony and the altar moved to the extreme East; and three candles placed upon it. The incense was burning. The candidate waited in the Portal of the Vault.

Chief Adept: V.H. Third Adept, who is he that waiteth without the Portal?

3rd Adept: Our Frater et Soror _____, who hath attained unto the High Grade of 7=4.

Chief Adept: Go then, V.H. Associate Adept, and see that it is in truth our Frater. Test him if he be well prepared to proceed with this ceremony, being in a calm and recollected frame of mind, that we may bestow upon him in full power the Link which we have commissioned to transmit to him.

Instruct him to enter this hall of the Adepti, his hands meekly folded upon his breast; let him say clearly and humbly, "I hereby request you to bestow upon me the true Etheric Link which unites us in unbroken succession with our Founder and Father Christian Rosencreutz and His Companions. May he transmit therewith the Spiritual Knowledge and Power of Healing and Comfort to the sick and sorry, and may I be enabled to use those gifts for the good of the Rosicrucian Order to which I have the honour to belong. I pledge myself to use this Link according to the Ancient Traditions of the Order, and I proclaim my sincere belief in the person known to us as Christian Rosencreutz, who founded the Order to which I have the honour to belong."

V.H. 2nd Adept, assist the Third Adept in the Reception of our Frater.

3rd Adept goes out, prepares Postulant, and sees that he is robed in White, and he gives him the petition, and guards the Portal.

Postulant gives !!! !!!

2nd Adept admits them. Postulant reads petition.

The Rite of the Link

Chief Adept: V.H. Frater et Soror, since the days when our Founder and Father C.R.C. dwelt upon this Earth, He has been able, by His great advance, to exercise supreme rule over the Order called by His name. He and certain of His followers who have passed through the Veil form a circle which continuously directs the growth and development of this Order, aiding its Rulers and inspiring them. At intervals of 120 years, this supervision becomes for a time more definite, and has been used to modify and reconstitute that it may be constantly adapted to the needs of each new age.

In the year of Our Lord 1890, this revival and reconstitution of the Order took place. Under the new conditions, no written mandate was issued to the Rulers of the Temples or Groups, and it is therefore more necessary that the purely Etheric Link should, at the discretion of those who already hold it, be transmitted to such Rulers and Adepti as may be considered suitable. For this reason, it is now offered to you. We have been given the Power to transmit it and the privilege of conveying it to you, and through you to others who may be judged worthy. We do this therefore on the understanding that you will exercise due care and conscientious discrimination in the transmission of this Link to others; that in doing this, you will call to your aid Two Fraters who have also received it from us, so that you form a Triangle of Power. Should one of the three be removed from this plane, let the remaining two select a discreet and loyal person as successor. You are only empowered to transmit this Link to members of the R.R. et A.C.

In receiving this Link and those Higher Grades which we are in a position to bestow upon you, you will in truth become connected with the modern successors of the Original and True Rosicrucian Order. That Order which was founded in Europe in 1250, and was duly manifest in 1405 as is transcribed in our Ritual of the 5=6 Grade.

I now charge you to answer truly under those conditions. Are you willing to receive this LINK, and never to reveal when, where, or from whom you have received it?

Postulant: I willingly accept the conditions and pledge my honour that I will faithfully observe them."

Chief Adept: Approach then the Vault, my Frater, and kneel within its Threshold while we invoke our Father Christian Rosencreutz.

Chiefs enter the Vault and Postulant follows and kneels on the Threshold facing East. Chief Adept stands east of him, facing East. 2nd Adept in S. East. 3rd Adept in N. East. They stretch out their right hands towards the Centre East holding their Wands.

Chief Adept: Christian Rosencreutz.

2nd Adept: Christian Rosencreutz.

3rd Adept: Christian Rosencreutz.

All: Christian Rosencreutz, we invoke Thee to manifest Thyself and to transmit through us the ETHERIC LINK with thyself to this our Frater _____ that he may indeed become Thy son and spiritual heir.

There is a Pause; the three Officers turn slowly, form a Triangle about the Postulant. They lay aside their Wands and Ankhs. Postulant is directed to place his left hand on Chief's breast, his right hand in the Chief's right hand. 2nd and 3rd place their hands: one on the head of Postulant over Chief's left hand, and the other on Chief's back.

All: I (we) by the Power transmitted to me (us) do hereby transmit to you Frater   the ETHERIC LINK with our Father CHRISTIAN ROSENCREUTZ, and the Rosicrucian Order founded by Him.

(*Pause*)

Adepti withdraw their hands and leave the Vault. Postulant remains kneeling. The Door is closed upon him, and he is left alone for 10 minutes. The Chief then goes into the Vault, raises Postulant by placing his hand on his head, saying:

Chief Adept: May you be brave. May you be faithful. May you be true.

All present exchange the Full Grip across the Pastos, then form a circle and do full 7=4 Signs.

COMMENTARY

The ritual uses the second order officers rather than those who were taking part in the 7=4 rite. While the officers needed to be high grade, the effect of the link is through the vault of CRC and the Second Order. The vault was a key feature of all Second Order workings and was used even if it was draped with different colours. The vault was also placed at Tiphareth, both within the physical order and the candidate's sphere of sensation. When correctly placed it can be seen in the postulant's heart centre and in the East of the Pastos in any second order workings. The link therefore must be connected through the middle pillar to the candidate.

The petition is read out and then the Chief Adept informs the postulant that every 120 years the link becomes stronger and initiates a modification to the order so that it can modify and reconstitute, that it may be constantly adapted to the needs of each new age.

It says that the last time this happened was 1890, which was when Mathers created the Second Order of the Golden Dawn. But it says it will reform again in 120 years, which was 2010. This pattern does seem to make a lot of sense to us, if only because that is when the Magical Order of the Aurora Aurea's vault was built. Please be aware I am not making any claims here, it was just a personal coincidence and we had not received the link. I think you can find yourself part of any big cycle if you point your mind to it and play around with dates.

The link is formed by vibrating the name Christian Rosencreutz and placing it within the postulant's sphere of sensation. They then place hands upon him in a manner similar to the Christian priesthood.

The ritual says that the postulant is in the vault at this point and is left alone for ten minutes. This is because they are supposed to be exploring where the link takes them. Again, this is confusing, because more than one person told me that the ritual was conducted in the 7=4 room and they were led back to the vault afterwards for a few minutes.

EXPERIENCE OF THE LINK

By Fr LiV

The chamber was in darkness and I did not see much other than the white candle light for the first part.

I found myself intellectually processing what the Magus said. But when I started thinking about my next step, I could not find any answers. Most of them seemed too small or ego based. I thought of the Order, I thought about what I wanted, but after what I had experienced, it all seemed pointless in comparison to what I felt from the 7=4.

I thought about what I needed, but my future direction seemed to be literally into the darkness. Some of that, I felt, was not up to me.

Anyway suddenly the room was filled with seven flames (they were human sized). Rather than being pure colours they were like a cross section of several colours, but flame shaped.

They stayed in one position and appeared to be waiting. Then there came another being which was more angelic.[90] It was more made out of bits of symbols and reminded me a bit of the Hermetic Arcanum diagram (it was round and spiky with rays of teaching and symbols coming from it). It started to spin and it opened like a multi-coloured tunnel. I was aware that hands had been placed upon me but I did not really feel like I was there. I was travelling down the tunnel. I saw images of members that I knew and then others, older, who I did not recognise. I continued along the tunnel and I saw various different RC orders through history. Still I went backwards until I emerged in a hot steaming climate by a huge river. In the middle of the river was an Island.

Landing on the water was a huge bird. However, I felt it more than anything did. It was pure spirit. I felt a hand on my shoulder and it was _____ in a human form. He was dressed in a kilt. I tested him with the 7=4 signs and he replied.

"The Link connects you to the beginning, when the bird first landed on this rock. From this point begins the long unbroken chain of adepts of which you are the latest link. The order might change as my teachings adapt to different epochs, but while humans and their orders will die, the golden chain will never be broken.

---

90 Footnote – the link as an angelic being, which also must evolve and develop.

"I will teach you."

He held up a symbol [not listed] and said:

"By this word _____ you will open the vortex and connect to the source of the chain."

I came aware that the hands had come off me and I had been left to pray. The vision was extremely clear and very emotive.

LIGHT IN EXTENSION

PAPERS INSPIRED BY THE 6=5 AND 7=4

BY
NICK FARRELL

⟨XIII⟩ ATTUNING TO CHESED

1. Cabbalistic cross.

2. Move awareness to a golden heart centre and vibrate YHVH Aloah Ve Daath.

3. Visualise a scarlet sphere on your right shoulder and a royal blue sphere on your left.

4. Move your awareness to your left shoulder and allow your sphere of sensation to turn blue.

5. While visualising the blue sphere vibrate the name *El* four times. Try to feel, if possible, the compassion and love of Chesed.

6. See a door before you with a blue crucifix upon it. Do the sign of the Portal at it and see it fold up into a blue cube. As this happens feel that you are unbalancing slightly so that the more Geburah side of your nature is shifting to its opposite.

7. Step through the door and you will find yourself on the top of TeMata Peak looking out over the land and towards the sea. On your right hand you see the figure of the Hermit. Go to him and ask that he allows you to become an expression of Chesed.

8. He raises his staff and holds up his lantern. In the centre is a bright blue cube which spins slowly, radiating light. The cube moves from the lantern and into your sphere of sensation. Allow yourself to melt into it, until you become a radiating blue cube.

9. The Hermit appears to get bigger, and you move into his lamp where you radiate compassion upon the land. Hold this for as long as possible.

10. Allow the scene to fade into blue and become aware that you, still as a blue cube, are now within your heart centre.

11. Say to yourself: "From the exhaustless riches of its Limitless Substance, I draw all things needful, both spiritual and material."

12. Do a cabbalistic cross and become aware of this time and space.

⟨XIV⟩ BECOMING THE STAR CHILD

In the film *2001: A Space Odyssey*, a human is transformed from a mortal into a Star Child. In the Golden Dawn this 'Star Child' was called the 'Babe of the Abyss' and they made it a grade equal to Da'ath on the Tree of Life. Many Golden Dawn groups say that it is impossible to attain this grade while you are still alive and it can only be managed by an advanced magician after they've died.

In some ways they were right.

If you literally became the Star Child, or the Babe of the Abyss, you would be a god. But then if you take the Roman Catholic Communion literally, you are eating the blood and body of Jesus in a cannibalistic rite which does not allow a vegetarian option. Literalism is the biggest curse in mysticism and magic.

The most detailed account of someone trying to cross the Abyss was written by Aleister Crowley, who seems to have either taken the idea too literally, or written down it down in such a way that many of his students think it should be approached that way. To be fair to him, Crowley admitted the concept was difficult to explain:

"It corresponds more or less to the gap in thought between the Real, which is ideal, and the Unreal, which is actual," he wrote. This sounds closer to what is being said in this essay, but then he went and spoilt his definition by saying that "in the Abyss all things exist, indeed, at least in posse, but are without any possible meaning; for they lack the substratum of spiritual Reality. They are appearances without Law. They are thus Insane Delusions. Now the Abyss being thus the great storehouse of Phenomena, it is the source of all impressions."

This implies that the Abyss is a spiritual location and has things inside it which, according to Crowley, are not that pleasant. Crowley claimed that he crossed the Abyss by taking a packed lunch into the Sahara, allowing the worst demon in his Enochian filofax to possess him and rape the poet Victor Benjamin Neuburg. Somewhere along the line something went wrong, but Crowley did not admit it.

Crossing the Abyss is part of many mystical spiritual religions. It represents that state where the personality is jettisoned and the microcosmic mind merges briefly with that of the infinite macrocosmic one. This is sometimes called Cosmic Consciousness. It is not only possible to catch glimmers of this state, but it is important for any magician to do so.

It is by doing this that we see how the magician ends up becoming a mystic.

It is a serious and difficult path and one which should not be lightly attempted. It does often create a psychological backlash from the personality and a feeling of sadness when dealing with the material world. At its deeper levels of experience, a more mystical soul might feel that they have achieved all that is important to them and they might reach the state and die.

But a magician, who is probably more optimistic than your average mystic when it comes to the created world, looks back upon it and returns. They stand between these two states and manage to become both at once. This dual state of consciousness looks towards the higher, more abstract worlds of Binah, Chokmah and Kether and becomes a conduit for them.

Being a 'Babe of the Abyss' or a 'Star Child' is not a mystical state that can be held.

Once the experience is over, the shadow play on the back of the cave wall takes over. To get back into that state the magician must force themselves back. But the more it is practised the easier it becomes. The Star Child grows within the magician over time and through repeated contact with the Absolute. It is able to exist in both the abstract world and the mundane.

Arthurian legend is full of symbols of Sword Bridges which need to be crossed to get to the Holy Grail. Obviously crossing anything that thin and sharp requires balance. You cannot be too attached to the material world or that will hold you back, and you cannot hang on to the world of spirit because that will take you over completely (you will be like Galahad who sees the Grail and then dies. To a mystic this is the perfect death, but the magician has real work to do and cannot afford the luxury).

The issue of non-attachment to matter is a tricky one. Many mystics hate matter. Some Gnostics were convinced that the Devil must have created it to trap our souls and prevent us from seeing divine perfection. But there is a certain spiritual feeling which does lead both mystic and magician across the Abyss.

This was expressed in the mantra which was given to those reaching the 7=4 grade in the Golden Dawn offshoot the Stella Matutina, which was an inspiration for the poet WB Yeats.

> Earth born and bound, our bodies close us in,
> Clogged with Red clay, and shuttered by our sin – We must arise.
>
> Flowers bind round and grasses catch our feet,
> Bird songs allure and blossom scent is sweet – We must arise.
> Mountains may beckon and the seas recall:
>
> Cloud-forms delude and rushing streams enthral – We must arise.
>
> Planets encircle with their spiral light,
> Stars call us upward to our faltering flight – Thus we arise.
> Sun-rays will lead us higher yet and higher,
> Moon-beam our souls scorch with their purging fire – Thus we arise.
>
> Into the Darkness plunge, fearless of pain;
> Coldness and silence cleanse us again – Still we arise.
> Open ye Gates of Light, Doors open wide;
> Gaze we within at the Glories you hide – We have Arisen.

This is a state where you feel you have done everything and realise that the material world is dissatisfying. This is not a rejection of the material world, which would be just as wrong as a rejection of the world of spirit. Both are fragments of the One Thing, and if you want to be Star Child you have get beyond fragments and ditch a lot of dualistic thinking.

What is needed is a realisation that what you are watching is a shadow play and you can take your chains off whenever you like. It happens to everyone at a certain point, but not everyone gets their chance to do something about it.

The spiritual process of "crossing the Abyss" initially means starting to observe the world totally without involvement, emotion or preconceptions. This is done whenever it is possible until it becomes second nature.

Observation without attachment takes you to a state which you will not have been in since you were a child. A child sees the world as being entirely focused on them. If a person disappears from sight, there is no proof that they actually exist any longer, they 'disappear'. Perspective changes too. You will notice that all points in your vision stretch away to a vanishing point which stems entirely from you.

This might seem like a case of being egotistical, but with further meditation you see that the ego is what you say you are, rather than what you really are. There is little proof that others actually exist and they might simply be shadows on the wall of the cave.

This sometimes leads to a feeling of isolation from humanity and an understanding that all around you is like the plot of a bad film, which the real you is watching. In fact the biggest danger is that as you practice watching, you become more cynical and stop caring about the rest of the world. But before that leads to a rejection of the material world, you use it to provide momentum to search for the Divine One.

But the problem for the magician is that he has gone so far by using symbols.

True, they might have come from the Divine, but they cannot take you into the macrocosmic divine states which formed them. Once the macrocosmic consciousness is seen, then all symbols become null and it takes a new consciousness to understand what is happening.

This half-world has all sorts of different symbolic metaphors. In traditional Kabbalah you cross over a desert, where you are tempted by the devil, and find an abyss which you must get across, usually by casting yourself into it and having faith that God will hold you up.

A literal understanding of this is probably the reason why Crowley went into the desert (although he did not throw himself off any cliffs) but in fact what happens is that each person is given an image that is unique to them. Explaining this is tricky because the temptation is to say that the experience is psychological, which it is not. It is a vision which might be interpreted as psychological after the dust has settled, and the records are looked at. But to the person who experiences it, the vision is real and impersonal. It overwhelms.

I encountered my own Abyss in a minor way when I was happily married to a nice non-magical person. I had reached a certain point in my magical life where I was simply writing and initiating people into the magical group to which I belonged, but living a normal 'muggle' life.

One winter's day I was walking with my wife down a city street when I just 'stopped'. I didn't faint, I did not fall unconscious. As far as I was concerned, my awareness stayed the same but time moved. I opened my eyes and I was lying on the ground. My shoe had come off. From my perspective the scene changed and I was in an ambulance. There was no pain, or fear. I was warm and happy. Then time moved again. Next I appeared in the hospital. As far as the doctors were concerned I had had a grand mal epileptic fit, but no one could actually say why or how, and I have not had one since.

My biggest fear has always been that I would lose my mind and reasoning, and that death might end up as some oblivion. But when I experienced it there was no fear. Mind created reality and placed it in a neat order. If this was switched off then time slipped. I had briefly been shown how the universe worked on a macrocosmic level.

Many people think that when they have visions there should be a cast of a thousand angels and a bearded bloke on a throne. I had not *seen* anything but what I *experienced* was macrocosmic and it bought me out of myself.

I decided it was pointless playing at magic, I had to become the magic, and that would mean some drastic changes. It took some time for these changes to happen, and the universe I had created had to be slowly destroyed and a new one created. I failed a couple of times before I got it right, but it is safe to say that after the vision, nothing was the same. That was my first experience of the Abyss and it was also a direct demonstration and 'unvarnished' by symbol.

What follows is a pathworking which will give you an idea of a sequence which can be followed.

It is a training pathworking, so that you may understand the symbolism involved. It is only a starting point and not meant to be taken literally. As I have said, to truly approach the Abyss you have to use that symbolism in your own way.

Once you get to that state you will have to abandon symbolism to really comprehend it. The training pathworking will have an effect; it will open the way for you to experience the Abyss and start to understand the divine consciousness. I suggest that this one is read to you, or you record it on tape.

The pathworking should be performed in sacred space and you should have repeated the above mantra at least ten times before you start.

STAR CHILD

Before you is a door. Upon the door is the image of a baby with stars in its eyes.

Focus on that image and let the door fade until it opens into a scene of astral mist.

You step through the door and the mist clears. Look at your feet. You are standing in the desert. It is not the sort of sandy desert of the Sahara. It is a hard, hot stone desert, devoid of life.

You are dressed in a plain brown robe which is the colour of the earth, and in your hand you hold a staff. The staff represents your steadfast will and aspiration.

You look behind you. There is the city of manifestation. It is bright, with flashing lights. In this city, from which you have come, you know people will be busy with their lives, chasing amusement, filling their lives with whatever they define as meaning. Shadows. You have played with the shadows and now even your body feels like a tomb. Now you must escape. In your hand is the lamp in which is the spark of the Indwelling Glory leading you towards something new.

You walk into the desert. Never to return the same again.

Walking in the heat. You have no water, no food; you don't feel you need these things. Dust in your mouth. Dryness. The lamp you carry feels heavy. Truth be known you have been walking for so long that you have even forgotten what the lamp you hold looks like. Your eyes are fixed on the horizon. One foot trudges wearily after the other. What is it that you are heading toward? You have no idea.

On the horizon you see a building and you head towards it. If it gives you anything, it will give you shelter from the sun. But as you come closer you see that it is a mausoleum and there is something living there.

As you get closer you see the Jackal headed Guardian of the Necropolis, Anubis.

He carries a sword and has the job of protecting the mysteries from the profane, or unbalanced forces that would seek to destroy them. He wears a white kilt with a lion's tail at the back. He carries a sword with a red hilt and wears a black and white nemyss. He has a necklace of black and white beads. His head is black with golden eye make-up.

You take a deep breath said say:

"As I approach the Gate of the Mysteries,
I meet its Guardian and pass without
Fear, for we are the one and the same.
I invoke thee oh Guardian of the Sacred Mysteries
Come forth and judge my soul, oh Anubis
Protect me as I enter the holiest of holies
Speak for me before the Throne of Truth
For I am like unto thee
A manifestation of the Most High.
Take me in your arms
As the tempest rages
Uphold me as I reach toward the stars
For thou art the defender of the sacred circle
My strength and refuge."

He bows to you and takes you by the hand into the tomb. All around you on the walls are images of your life. Then you realise. This tomb is yours and Anubis is death.

You do not have much time to worry about this before you come to the sarcophagus itself. On it is a realistic depiction of your own face, dressed in the form of Osiris.

Anubis looks at you.

"It is time," he says. "Your life is over and this personality has done all it can. If you would become a Babe of the Abyss, its time is over and must pass."

You nod and open the sarcophagus. It has been a full life, but hard, and you must now pass on. You hand your lamp and staff to Anubis and lie down in the sarcophagus.

It does not feel uncomfortable. It is like getting into bed after a hard day of work.

You shut your eyes and the next moment time moves.

You are standing outside the coffin looking down at the image. Anubis is there and he hands you the lamp.

What happened?

"You died," says Anubis. "The old self is no longer, the personality which held it is being absorbed into the Universal Mind as a memory. It has done its work."

You do not feel sad. In fact you do not feel anything, nor do you think. You just are there. It is an odd sensation. You do not think or feel any more. That was part of the personality. You can feel expansive. Like you have just escaped from a confined space. Anubis has changed too. He still hold your lamp but your staff has become a caduceus.

The phrase "He who is Upon the Mountain" comes into your head and you feel moved to say the following:

"O Thou Lord of the Hallowed Land,
Sky hunter of dawn
Master of the feather of truth;
I call upon thee as a son (or daughter) calls to a father.
Hear my call and indwell my Soul-Temple.
Extend thy hand through the veils of time.
O Anpu who stands upon the Mountain,
Thou who are upon the pillar of the north,
Hear my call and indwell my Soul-Temple.
O Sah who guards the heavens at night-time,
Shine thy beams of Divine Light upon this supplicate.
Here my call and indwell my Soul-Temple.
I have cleansed myself in thy sacred lake,
I have offered unto thee incense,
Now indwell my Soul-Temple with Holy Fire.
The Paths to the Gate are cleared,
Anpu is within his House, he puts
His hands on the Lord of the Gods,
Magic and protection are knit about him.
O Great One who became Sky,
You are strong, you are mighty,
You fill every place with your beauty,
The whole earth is beneath you, you possess it!
As you enfold earth and all things in your arms,
An indestructible star within you!
The Sky is cleared, the Horizon dwellers
Rejoice, for Ra arises from the Double gates.
For I am the Companion of Anpu
Within the secret places of the Great Hall."

Becoming the Star Child

Time moves but you stay still. You are no longer in the tomb but in the desert.

Before you are seven flames, each a different colour of the rainbow. Violet, Indigo, Blue, Green, Yellow, Orange and Red. These are the gods of the earth, each holy and pure in their own way. Each stands over you and you feel a little of its power given to you. It strengthens you. You start to remember.

You crossed this way before as you walked to the city to live your life. But you forgot. Now you start to remember who you really are.

Time moves again.

You are standing on the edge of a cliff. It descends into darkness. In front of you the air shimmers like heat on a hot road. You look up and the shimmering extends into infinity. One step forward and you could be swept upwards or fall downwards.

You look across the abyss and you see that on the other side it is darkness. Not an empty darkness, but a darkness which contains all. You know that darkness is your real home and you want to return to it. That longing seems to seize you and you realise that all you have to do is surrender to it and you will come home. You feel a hand on your shoulder. It is Anubis.

"Your task is not to return, unless you want to, but to become something new. That is much harder."

You nod. Without thinking you take the lamp from Anubis and cast it into the void.

Instead of falling it floats between the two cliff faces.

You focus your mind on that point of light, which stands out against the darkness. Suddenly you are floating above the abyss. You look across and you see the shadowy form of yourself standing next to Anubis. But you are also aware of the darkness at your back. You shut your eyes and try to surrender to it. It feels like a stream of blackness, of potential. You melt into it and expand into it.

You are not.
You are aware of symbols forming within you.
Ideas, new teachings, new beginnings.
They flow through you like a river.
Your eyes have become stars.
You become the universe.
Ever forming, ever changing.

Your brown robe has become a white robe of glory
And you have the stars in your hands.
Before you is the globe of the earth.
You know that on that globe is the city of manifestation.
From behind you, from the divine potential, you have a new idea.
A new way that this universe will go.
You are the magician shifting the elements.

You feel yourself begin to re-assemble and then you are reborn in this time and this place and in this reality.

‹XV› THE CROSS AND 16 NAILS

In the 7=4 ritual which was used by Whare Ra and the Stella Matutina there was an unusual piece of DIY where the candidate had to build a box from six squares.

In the ritual the candidate sees six black squares on the ground and is given 16 nails. The outside of the 7=4 cube is black, denoting matter. The 16 nails are four inch, or equivalent metric, with holes drilled in the edges of the cube so that when they are fitted it is stable. The 16 nails correspond to the 16 outgoing Rays from the Earth as used in Geomancy. By folding the cross up, the candidate discovers that the outside of the box is white. After the cube is built he is expected to stand on it.

Later on the candidate is given a list of things that the nails are supposed to represent. The nails themselves were supposed to be made of forged iron to represent transmutation of the personality. Each one was supposed to represent one of 16 sins which were transmuted to something better.

The sins listed were:

>   Passion which was transmuted to patience
>   Lust to love
>   Drunkenness to gluttony after righteousness
>   Fearfulness to faith
>   Wavering to steadfastness
>   Self-righteousness to divine righteousness
>   Pride to humility
>   "The vain glorious" to a chill
>   Hardness of heart to mercy
>   Violence to meekness
>   Malice to charity
>   Wrath to peace-making
>   Dishonesty to supreme truth
>   Darkness to light

This leaves two nails missing (probably a transcription error). There is a lot of repetition in the list. Some of the sins are the classic seven deadly ones and some of the antidotes were not connected either. For example, drunkenness is not a repressed desire for God.

There are some other problems too. The number 16 does not fit into any list of angels, demons or gods. It would fit into the Enochian tablet sub-quadrants, but the entities there are not connected to those particular "sins."

It is important to realise when looking at this particular sub-ritual, that the 7=4 was channelled and rarely performed. As a result it did not get the full impact of magical thought. Felkin's contact might have given the outline, but he never fleshed it out.

One of the side effects of the 6=5 is a dark night of the soul where the parts of yourself are stripped away. This places a huge amount of stress on the psyche. One Whare Ra adept told me that unlike the other grades this one often resulted in insanity, as a person's demons came bubbling to the surface to demand attention. By the time a person comes to the 7=4 grade they are exhausted.

This is not a state of joy, but one of rejection of matter. This would seem like an obvious spiritual state to be in after a dark night of the soul. But the box ritual says something different.

You are looking at the blackness of the cross and are expected to transform it into a white cube. As the ritual says:

> "The last shall be first and the lowest shall be the highest. Malkuth shall be exalted into the Throne of Kether and all shall be consumed and become infinite and holy.
> The stone which the builders rejected, the same shall become the corner stone. The cross of suffering is transmuted to the corner stone of the arch and raised above the Earth. The son shall offer that which he has received."

In this sub-ritual, then, is a cure for the dark night of the soul and the formula for crossing the Abyss. Curiously, it is not a high spiritual formula but one of deep magical personality work, admittedly on a higher level.

Now we come to my approach to this process.

The clue here is the numbers 6 and 16 and the fact that you are making a cube, which was the perfected personality.

According to Agrippa, 6 was the number of the planets which were on the ecliptic. These are Saturn, Jupiter, Venus, Mars, Mercury and the Moon. The Solar force is absent, but is created by the generation of all six planets. This would be the same formula used to the frustration of those who have to perform the lesser banishing ritual of the hexagram.

The process of folding up the cube does two things:

1. It connects the lower square to the upper square and uses the other squares to support it.
2. It generates an unseen solar force in the box's centre.

Standing upon it is a way of saying: "I have done the transmutation, spirit is in the heart of the personality and now I use this as my foundation."

The 16 nails are supposed to represent transmuted sins which hold the box together. But they are more than that – they are elemental forces which have been placed under the control of the magician in their 6=5 work.

To make matters more interesting, there are 16 of them – and since the sub-quadrants of the Enochian tablets do not normally translate into "sins" we have to look to something that has positive and negative traits, and to this there is only one candidate: Geomancy.

While the Geomantic symbols are traditionally used for divination, they have a powerful effect on the personality. Since the symbols have their positive and negative aspects, it makes more sense for them to be an important key to nailing up the box.

Geomancy uses seven double sets of planetary attributions, and then two which represent the nodes of the planets.

The double sets of planetary attributions give us the planetary force and their underworld equivalents. The underworld is a very important part of magic which sadly has been under-developed by modern magicians. There are those who claim that the underworld forces are demonic, or, at best, unconscious complexes. This is only partly true, as they are vital to development of advanced magicians. Whare Ra was aware of this and defaulted to the use of Goetia in the 6=5 under very controlled circumstances. Others felt that it was enough to do the Abramelin system to make a contact with the underworld forces.

In my experience it is better to approach this using godforms, as they tend to be a little friendlier. But they still bring in a tremendous burst of power which is not for beginners. For the purposes of this I arranged this so:

Square Connected	Geomantic Figure	Celestial God	Underworld God
Top to bottom	Caput Draconis	Janus	
	Cauda Draconis		Vesta
Saturn to Jupiter	Tristia	Saturn	
Saturn to Mars	Carcer		Hekate-Brimo
Jupiter to Venus	Aquisto		Zeus-Typhon/ Hades
	Laetitia	Jupiter	
Jupiter to Moon	Fortuna Major	Helios	
Mars to Moon	Fortuna Minor		Apollo Soranus
Venus to Saturn	Puella	Venus	
	Amisso		Venus Cthonios
Mars to Venus	Puer	Mars	
	Rubeus		Dionysos
Mercury to Venus	Albus	Hermes	
	Conjucto		Hermes Cthonios
Moon to Mercury	Via	Selene	
	Populus		Proserpina

This gives the adept a sequence of symbols and gods for invocation that will, over the course of 16 workings, enable him to roll the cross of suffering into a cube upon which he can kneel.

⟨XVI⟩ INNER TEMPLES

BELOW IS an unpublished Whare Ra document. It is has close similarities to a paper written by Dion Fortune and is related to what I call the Inner Temple method. Fortune said that she acquired the Inner Temple method from the AO Chief Maiya Tranchell-Hayes where it was a Second Order AO procedure. Since this paper was written after the split and is an ST document, it indicates that the idea had a common source and that both sides of the divide used Astral Temples for ritual and teaching. You can see hints of it in the Flying Rolls and the Z-documents.

The idea of using the astral counterparts of important landmarks was very important to Dion Fortune's work. She used the astral aspects of Glastonbury Tor, but she had the additional advantage of living there.

As this paper points out, these are powerful sites to work for humanity, rather than for individuals. Rituals which take place at these levels can help humanity.

To seek out these places, even using this paper as a guide, is a lot of work. Even then they are 'protected' by their own guardians. If you do find your way into one, it pays to be very, very polite. If you find entrance is easy then you are in the wrong place.

This Inner Temple was used widely in Whare Ra, and in both the First and Second Orders. When Tony Fuller was talking to the elderly Whare Ra members they would speak in hushed tones about the visiting the 'White Temple.'

Even Frank Salt, who was sometimes rather dismissive of 'astral travelling' and 'visions' also regarded it highly.[91]

---

91 In a letter to Tony Fuller, Frank Salt replied to a question about visiting an astral 'White Temple'. He said: "The White Temple you refer to does exist, not over Egypt but is the 'Aur' of Chaldea referred to in Genesis 15:7. I was taken there, not so much for my edification, but as a means by which the Chiefs tested my aptitude for progress. This is an occult matter and is best kept so."

"When I first knew him he would not speak of it, but after a couple of years, and oblique references, opened up more," Fuller said.

This is because such temples were places to meet contacts and teachers behind the Order. They also act as training grounds, where these beings show practical methods. Such places often are where people's unconscious minds first meet consciousness outside themselves. It is this consciousness which will take them further in magic, well beyond what has been written down, and form the basis of their own oral teaching.

There was more than one Astral Temple visited by Whare Ra adepts. One transcript in Whare Ra records recounted an attempted journey to a temple on "Borders of China and Tibet." The description runs for five pages and it was submitted to Mrs Felkin for her appraisal. She has written masses of comments on nearly every page, with suggestions made of what she thought was a more correct interpretation. This was because the person was describing something subjectively, in her own unconscious symbolic language. Mrs Felkin was doing what many teachers do when students present them with such material – interpret what they actually saw, rather than what they thought they saw.

THE TEMPLES OF THE EARTH (M.C.)

There are certain areas on the earth's surface which are surcharged with ritual force. These we call 'Temples', for on them, or most of them, men have erected buildings set aside for Spiritual Teaching.

It seems probable that in the first place such areas were marked by some natural phenomenon, such as flames or hot springs in some cases. At all events they have formed sanctuaries for the wild creatures in time of stress.

Having once been recognised and dedicated by man, they continue to be used by whatever form of religion prevails at any given time. As for instance the site of St. Paul's and Westminster Abbey, which are known to have been Temples of the Sun and Moon, in pre-Christian days. There are at least 12 such sites and there may be many more. It seems likely that our own Temple at Whare Ra is such a spot.

These areas have, from time immemorial, been associated with the Astrological Signs and Planets. We know of one on the bank of the Euphrates, which is dedicated to the Sun.

One on the Ruenzori Mountains (between Lakes Albert and Victoria), which is associated with the Moon. One in Central Europe, which is linked with Venus. And another in North Italy linked with Mercury.

There are some others in China and elsewhere.

Mesopotamia (Sun) Northern Persia (Mars) North Asia (Saturn) Mountains between China and Tibet (Jupiter).

To contact any of these, it is necessary to be quite clear which you desire to visit, and how you would reach it if you were travelling there by ordinary methods.

In these days we can go almost anywhere by air, therefore you can imagine yourself entering an aeroplane.

First protect yourself by the Banishing Ritual of the Pentagram.

Then enter your plane and behave exactly as though you were going an actual physical journey. Follow mentally the route you have already plotted out. Descend at a convenient distance from the selected site and then endeavour to see, with the interior eyes, what is before you.

It may be added that all these sites are distinguished by the presence of mountains, water (either river, lake or springs). Pure invigorating air and abundant light.

So far Whare Ra has lacked the near presence of water. The Order should aim at boring for this, is as there is at least one underground stream and there may be two.

One of the easiest Temples to reach is the Sun Temple on the Euphrates. It is simple to follow the course of the river until you are on top of a hill in a loop of the river. After a short distance a canal cuts it off from the surrounding ground and it is therefore approached by crossing a bridge either North or South of the building and climbing steps. On the South side, steps begin on the far side of the stream and thus form a bridge in themselves.

On the Northern side the bridge crosses the stream first and the steps are broken into three sets of twelve, seven and three, each marked by a square landing and supports. The lowest of these is a pair of obelisks, the second two palms, the third two lion-headed sphinxes.

The southern approach is unbroken and has a hundred steps with a balustrade on each side. At the top either side there are great doors opening down the middle and giving entrance to a large square portico: on the inner side of which hang heavy embroidered curtains.

The aspirant must be ready with all his Order Signs, Grips and Passwords. If he is a Mason he had better be ready with these also.

Remember that you must always enter such a place with the saluting sign and the sign of Silence. Stand still and await further guidance and instruction; use your eyes and intelligence, make a careful note of whatever you see or hear, so that you can write out a short, clear account when you return.

Remember that these Temples are not simply astral, you should receive spiritual vibrations from them: and the Teaching should not be merely personal.

These places are cosmic and are concerned with world affairs, not petty personal contacts. Most of them seem to use some form of ceremonial: and you may be called upon to take part in this, but if so it is for definite reason and purpose.

⟨XVII⟩ ADDITIONAL WHARE RA MATERIAL

THIS CHAPTER is a collection of papers from Whare Ra which I have obtained over the years – mostly from Percy Wilkinson's collection, although some of it comes from other sources. It is the tip of the iceberg of Whare Ra material, but should give some idea as to the sort of approach the group was taking. It will also serve to preserve this material for those who need it.

The following was one of about 10 basic 'practical studies' for 0=0 and 1=10, issued at Whare Ra in the 1950s, and which may be of interest.

H.O. 49

PRACTICAL STUDIES

Most of our Order material can be freely read by anyone these days as so much has been published. The question arises whether initiation can take place entirely without Temple ceremonial. Regular and sequential meditations on the Paths of the Tree can result in self-initiation, but it is a much slower process than that of ritual initiation. In the latter, a link is made for the candidate between the microcosmic Sephiroth and the macrocosmic Sephiroth, and symbols of forces are impressed upon his/her aura. The candidate then finds it much easier to bring these forces into fuller activity through study of ritual, meditation, and work on the practical exercises. The object of all this is an increase in consciousness and a greater understanding of himself (herself), his environment, and the whole universe. This has remained valid throughout the ages. Each part of the Soul, and each Elemental aspect of the entire being must be strengthened and transmuted, and brought into harmony with the others. Integration must be the rule, not pathology. In such a vehicle, consecrated and made truly holy by this equilibration, the Higher Genius may find a worthy and fit dwelling. This is true initiation.

As the Tree of Life is a pattern of the forces that are active (or potential) both in ourselves and in life as a whole, it is never outdated. It keeps pace with modern living and the problems of our time.

The vandalism and useless destructiveness that we see so much of to-day can be understood as an excess of the dynamic energy which originates in Chokmah. In a free state it can be dangerous. From Chokmah it must flow into Binah to receive the discipline of form and purpose. "Liberty is the luxury of self-discipline". The force of a Sephirah on one side of the Tree needs to be balanced by a force on the opposite side… Then there is a state of equilibrium. But then there is an interesting point – equilibrium is virtually a state of rest, and rest is not progress. Standing with the feet together is a position of balance, but it does not take you anywhere. When you take one foot off the ground to step forward you are really in a state of imbalance until that foot gets on the ground again. So a certain amount of unbalance has to be risked in order to progress. By examining the rise and fall of different civilisations of the past we can see how this happens. And the situation of our present times can be better understood. The Path of Daleth connects Chokmah and Binah. The Sepher Yetzirah calls it 'Luminous Intelligence'. It is the subconsciousness which enlightens by its method of deduction from our observations.

A PIECE OF WHARE RA 'ORAL TEACHING'[92]
OF THE FOUR CUPS IN THE TEMPLE (& OTHER MATTERS)

The Cup of the Stolistes is described in the Rituals as a hemisphere mounted on a spherical stem with a triangular pyramid base whose four sides form a tetrahedron. At Whare Ra it is of silver, made to exact specification. The Cup or chalice used on the altar is like a champagne glass, a mammary in symbolism. The Cup in the West Watch-tower is of beaten silver in the form of a half-open lotus, having a triple stem terminating in three leaves as its base. It is always left containing Water and specifically used by the Hiereus to make the Sign of the Eagle in the aura of the candidate. The Fourth Cup is placed on the Sign of Scorpio on the Inner Altar. Its shape is different – it is of alabaster, deep and narrow with a serrated lip. It

---

92 Thanks to Tony Fuller for this nugget.

stands about nine inches high, tapered inwards at the top and with a circular base.

The reasons for these specific forms will become clear to the contemplative aspirant if he pursues his speculations. The dagger used in conjunction with the Inner Cup has the usual Cross form of handle; the blade straight but tapered. It lies on the Sign of Aquarius on the Inner Altar. The coloured Crook and Scourge lie crossed at the yellow bands on the Inner Altar (Leo and Sol). Cups of any material other than alabaster and silver may be used, but it is well that the candidate be informed of the optimum substance and of their lunar significance.

The Crucifix on the letter Shin on the Inner altar is of ebony with a symbolic Rose (usually of Five Petals) behind the Figure. Consistent with Order principles, it is left to the Aspirant to ask only himself what each Symbol represents – and although in some cases suggestions do appear in some Rituals it is still over to the Aspirant to wonder and to suggest the full significance of all Symbolism for himself but not to "teach" anyone else, thus limiting the full impact of that symbolism.

The Chain used in Inner ceremonies is a light one of even oval links to hang from the neck to the loins, and kept on the Sign of Taurus on the Inner altar. The Censer used in the Outer may be stood on the Sign of Leo on the Inner altar, or a cup-shaped brazier with burning incense may be used, but it is a brazier rather than a cup.

The designated wording on the Inner Altar should be well considered by the Aspirant. The Inner Altar is a circular table on four legs straddling the Pastos with a black drape to floor length over the Pastos. The *Minutum Mundum* diagram should be carefully drawn, but not used by the spirant as a firm guide to colours. He must find and mix his own colours. All diagrams are similarly not to be taken as "correct" colouring.

G.H. Frater O.S.U.

WHARE RA – SHORT NOTES ON THE 1=10 CEREMONY

In the 1=10 ceremony we enter the Tree; here the will has to decide by which path to travel, and finally enters the Path of Equilibrium, between Good and Evil. The Baptist Church is the only one which places this choice in a dramatic form. In the Mystery Plays of medieval times the people were taught Spiritual Truth in material forms. The Devil, the Angels, Archangels, the choice of good and evil, and the Elemental forces, were all represented. Wind and Fire were brought into manifestation by Magical Formulae, The Feasts of Asses and the Feasts of Fools were Bacchanalian, to show by contrast the difference between sacred and profane. Then the description of the Garden of Eden is read with the Tree of Knowledge of Good and Evil, the account of man's fall; showing the same truth of choice as given in the Paths.

The Garden of Eden was not on Earth but on the Astral Plane or in Heaven. The Fall of the Angels ante-dated the Fall of man. The coats of skins were the material bodies prepared for them to incarnate in.

Either the bodies by evolution were prepared and ready for them, or they had to wait until these bodies were evolved to incarnate upon the earth. The Ceremonies take place on the Astral Plane as well as on the material, the vibrations caused by the knocks attract the Spiritual Forces into the material Temple. The diagram of the 7 Branched Candlestick, and the Shewbread, are shown; symbols of the 7 Creative Spirits, the Planets, the Zodiac, the powers ruling man. Their powers were known to the Hebrews and all the ancient religions, they are mighty beings working on and in, man. Astrology was studied from the most ancient times, the experts could, after setting up the Horoscope, pass through it, see the truth without calculating the time) trine, square and sextile. All 5=6 members should be able to do a divination in the Tarot, Astrology and Geomancy, and get the same answer in each. All these methods keep the mind occupied in order to leave the subconscious mind free to find the answer. Mystic Titles of Malkuth are given – taken from ancient religions and literature up to the Christian period. By meditation, their meaning should be discovered. We learn that the Earth has a soul, and all the animal and vegetable world; and are introduced to Auriel the Angel of the Earth, the Elementals and the Gnomes. The Gnomes and the Elemental Spirits did not partake in the Fall. They know far more than we do about the Earth.

They are intelligent beings and long for higher development; they rise by their blind obedience and labour. The Rituals are the condensed wisdom drawn from all the ancient religions, and need study and meditation to get at the truth therein.

Most likely the round earth (out of which our earth arose) was the result of the Fall of the Angels.

The race of Adam fell, the one man representative can – Jesus Christ restored all by His Incarnation and redemption, before Christ, the two higher principles, the Spiritual Man and the Higher Genius could not be reached during earth life, except for one or two exceptions (Enoch & Elijah). The Holy of Holies represented Divine Nature, the two higher principles were shown by the two Cherubim, the Divine Spirit the Shekinah dwelt with them.

The Holy Place may be said to represent the human, the powers that work on, and in, man – the Zodiac, the Planets, the Altar of Incense, worship, the highest exercise of the being of man

WHARE RA – SHORT NOTES ON THE 2=9 CEREMONY

When the Chief entered the Order no perfect copy of Ritual or Lecture was given out, no typed copies were allowed. Each Member had to attend all the Ceremonies, and correct his Ritual until it was perfect; he could not take another Grade until this was done.

The words first spoken to the Candidate: "quit the material and seek the Spiritual", give the key to the whole Ceremony. Learning no longer must be sought for material gain or advancement, no self-seeking must influence the Candidate in his search for the true wisdom. Anubis the Guardian leads the Aspirant from the material to the spiritual.

The Sphinx of Egypt. There were other Sphinxes besides the Great Sphinx, one the syntheses of the Elements, Man, Bull, Lion, Eagle, the goddess of Air, who drew back the veil which hid the rising Sun.

The Soul asks for help, "Give me your hands, ye Lords of Truth, for I am made as ye." The soul claims kinship with the Spiritual helpers, as she came from the Spiritual Realm to incarnate in a material world, to transmute the material into the spiritual. The diagrams and speeches are full of names from many sources; it needs knowledge of ancient mythology and history to understand them. The Candidate should look them up, study and meditate upon them, to gain real knowledge of their meaning. The Jews had to go to Egypt to learn the ancient wisdom, and from the Hieroglyphics Moses was told to construct the Hebrew Alphabet.

The higher mathematics in ancient times were part of the secret knowledge; they are being studied and applied by scientists at the present time. This has led to the wonderful discoveries of late years.

Reinforced concrete is an example; by the union of two opposites, with concrete and steel, the concrete can be made strong enough to stand any strain without crumbling.

ADDRESS BY MRS FELKIN

14th July, 1952.

GROUP WORK

Most of you have already heard me speak quite often of the importance of working in groups. You will see in the letter you have just been given that the idea of group working has grown up very much since Mr Felkin and I joined the Order nearly 50 years ago. In those days at home in England, the members of the Order were scattered about and they had been left very much to the idea of individual work. Those of you who are familiar with the working of the churches of almost any denomination will realise that even today the church teaches that the important thing is the salvation of the individual soul. They couple with that the importance of service. The great missionary churches develop that to a much further extent, and especially – I don't want to be invidious but I should say especially the Roman church and the Presbyterians, who have coupled medical work with religious teaching almost from the beginning of their service as missionaries.

But as a whole you find that religious teaching is "Save your soul." I do not think that that is the teaching of our Lord. I do not remember that He ever says that it is important. On the contrary He says "He that loses his soul for my sake" (the ordinary translation is "He that loses his life or giveth his life," but the Greek word is "soul") He that loseth his soul for my sake. And following on from that you come to the thought that much more important than the individual soul is humanity as a whole.

Bound together in the bonds of brotherhood. We may fight and struggle one nation against the other but we cannot get away from the fact that all men are brothers, and if we are brothers then we must learn to work as a family works – in a group. The family is the unit, and from that you go on to the greater family, which is the formation of groups by mutual interests. Now in forming a group you have to try to reflect the great natural laws. The whole of the Order is based on this realisation of the cosmic laws and the example with which we are most familiar is the working of the constellations and the planets. We know that both constellations and planets circle round a common centre. The ancients, by which I mean the Egyptians and further back, knew that the Sun was a centre of the planetary system, but in later days, in what we call the Middle Ages, this was forgotten and man was taught that the earth itself was the centre; and for ordinary practical purposes, in astrology for instance, we still regard the earth as a centre just as each one of us regards ourselves as the centre of our own circle. There must always be a centre of the circle revolving round it. So we see the earth as a centre with the signs of the Zodiac circling round in the great wheel. But because we are not really in the centre, and because the earth is tilted on her axis, therefore the signs appear to open and shut as a fan does. There are signs of long ascension and signs of short ascension, depending upon what part of the earth we happen to occupy.

Therefore as a model of the group you have the earth and the signs of the Zodiac, the planets and the luminaries, and when you begin to study these with the idea of forming groups you realise that you have groups within the Zodiacal signs. There are the groups of the four elements, earth, air, fire, water. There are also groups of the triplicities, say, three signs belonging to one element; and there is another triad formed by the decanates, that is to say, each sign is divided into groups of 10 degrees. Each decanate has its own characteristics and its own ruling planet. And we have the luminaries; so that gives us the smallest possible group of two. But the signs of the Zodiac also fall into groups of two, which we call the day and the night signs, positive and negative, donative and receptive, masculine and feminine. Studying all these things you find your foundation for forming a working group.

Any kind of occult work must be based on the cosmic laws, so, taking two to begin with you have man and woman – perhaps husband and wife, perhaps friends, but in either case they should balance each other, complement each other. A good group should always be made up of differing elements, so that the triplicity is not such a good group practically as the three decanates, which gives the three aspects of one sign. When you form a triangle, a group, it should be modelled on the idea of one particular sign with its decanates, with the three planets which dominate those decanates. Or, if you have a group of four, then you take the four elements, all of them differing from the others and two definitely complementary. Taken from this point of view, you do not regard fire and water as antagonistic but each as supplementing the work of the other. Those of you who are gardeners know very well that your plants will not flourish if they are given all sun and no water, neither will they thrive if they are given all water and no sun. The two must balance.

And to make the perfect group you must also have the earth and the air. For that reason it is a good plan to learn as much as you can about your own astrological formula.

A great many people do not know what time they were born and therefore they cannot cast an accurate horoscope. But practically everybody does know on what day and what month they were born in and knowing that they know also what sign the sun was in at that time. From studying the position of the sign of the sun and the time of year, you can work out a fairly good idea of what sign the moon is in. You know, for instance, that the new moon is in conjunction with the sun, that the full moon is in opposition, and from that you can calculate fairly well the relative positions of sun and moon. So if you take the larger group of twelve, it should, as far as is possible, be formed from those whose sun is in the twelve different signs. And if you take the trouble to work it out you can also reckon the aspect (roughly) of the moon; and if you study the ephemeris carefully you will find out what signs the different planets are occupying; and when you know all that you can begin to fit your various horoscopes in with each other. If you do know exactly the time you were born, and therefore can set up your horoscope correctly, and if you have a kind friend who will give the time and energy to do you a progressed horoscope, you can learn a good deal more. But even with the rougher map you can find an extremely interesting result in comparing the maps of the other members of your group with your own. I speak from experience because I did that quite a lot at one time with very notable results. Still, you do not all want to go to all that time and trouble, but you can all find the sign occupied by your sun and begin to consider the relative values of other members with whom you work as a group.

The Order itself forms a greater group which you might compare, as far as we are concerned, with the 36 decanates; and one very valuable conclusion is that each member contributes something which no other member can give. It is not a question of personal likes or dislikes but of realising the value, the mutual value, of working with people of different temperaments who therefore see things from a different angle from your own. If you have mixed much with members of what we call the Arts – music, painting, sculpture, architecture, literature – you will know that anyone who has devoted the greater part of their lives to one central subject develops a quite different way of looking at the world from other people. It is a very ordinary example to say that if three or four people of different professions go for a walk together, each will come back with a different impression of the country they have gone through. The painter will bring back the memory of all the wonderful colours he has seen – the lights and shadows. The sculptor may hardly notice the colour but he will have been impressed by the shapes of things; and the musician may have been so absorbed in listening to the sounds of the birds, the wind in the trees, the ripple of water, and all the thousands of sounds which you lucky people with ears must hear whenever you go out. But if they all compare notes and put them together, then they get a real picture of what they have seen and experienced; it is in the round instead of in the flat. And it is the same, much more it is the same when you pass beyond material experience and begin to work on what we call the higher planes.

Those who are clairvoyant should be particularly anxious to work in groups and to compare notes of what the different members of the group get. Even with our physical eyes it is extremely difficult to get a really accurate memory picture. If you recall something you have seen or perhaps a book you have read, you think you remember it perfectly clearly. But if you re-read the book, or if you go back a few years later and see the same place again, you find how very much you have forgotten and how very often you have seen quite wrongly. You have missed out bits and perhaps you have put in bits that were not really there. And if that is the case on the material plane it is much, much more so when we go on to the Astral. Remember that you are warned quite early in your Order studies that the Astral is the plane of illusion.

You see things because you have preconceived ideas. You hear things because you want to hear them. And it is only by checking up again and again, over and over again, that you can arrive at anything approaching accuracy. But if several people are working together, the very fact that each one is almost certain to make different mistakes from the others gives them a value as checks – controls, as the scientists call it. But there is more than that. It is not only that the group has value in building up within itself: but also, if you form a group like the Triangles of the Great Invocation, then you Increase the creative power not threefold but multi-fold. Three working together can form a tremendous centre of force and, agreeing upon their objective, they can send that force out to accomplish a definite purpose. If that is the case with a Triangle, we must believe that it is far more when the larger group such as the Order works together in harmony. Remember the difference between harmony and unison. It is not unison we seek but the harmony of different colours which make a picture, the different notes which make music. You know the difference in power between one person singing to themselves or one person picking out a tune on the piano, and a great orchestra playing, each one contributing his own particular part in the music of the whole. That is harmony. And what the orchestra does in music the Order ought to be doing in the spiritual plane. But we can only accomplish that if we learn to recognise the value of the others, if we learn to work harmoniously with loving kindness and brotherhood. You know there are some of the great symphonies and concertos which use not only strings, wind instruments, piano – they also use the drums and xylophone. And because those instruments have their own peculiar character, therefore they give something to the whole symphony which even the finest violin or the purest note of flute or oboe cannot contribute.

I remember a story of one of the great conductors when I was young who had to take his orchestra from one great city to another – London, Edinburgh, Glasgow, Manchester, and, I think, Birmingham. One night when they had arrived at the end of the journey and they were just about to go into the concert hall a man came up to the conductor in great distress and said, "Sir, I have lost my xylophone – I have not got one!" "Oh well," said Henschell, "take the leg of the chair, and strike that. Xylophone only means wood." The man took the leg of a chair and struck it and it had a perfectly good effect. The moral is that even the leg of a chair may be made to contribute to the music of the whole orchestra, and even those who seem to be giving very little to the whole are contributing their quota – that which nobody else can give. We are not all clairvoyant; we are not all clairaudient, but each of us has some special capacity, some quality, that nobody else has, and in forming the group you have to realise and accept the value of those who seem to be giving least.

That does not mean that any of us is to be content with giving less than the greatest of which we are capable. Nobody should rest content and say "Oh I cannot do any more." We can always do a little bit more; and it is often the little bit more which is given at great cost to ourselves which is most valuable in the whole result.

MEDITATION

Address by M.C.

One hundred years ago was written an occult work by Fabre d'Olivet called *Hermeneutic Interpretation of the Social State of Man* and it is an extraordinarily good definition of meditation. Twelve qualities are mentioned as being necessary: attention and perception, reflection and repetition, compassion and judgement, retention and memory, discernment and comprehension, creation and imagination.

The majority of people when first told to meditate imagine that it means sitting quiet and allowing ideas to drift in the mind. This of course is not meditation. Meditation is in fact one of the most difficult forms of occult study; as you have been told before, deep and regular breathing will assist in inducing tranquillity, and for meditation to be effective it is necessary to put aside the affairs of ordinary life to dismiss life worries.

It is not the great worries which we all have now and then to face that really causes distraction, it is in the innumerable and perpetual small affairs and the more we desire to concentrate upon really vital things, upon the spiritual life, the more does Satan find occasion to hinder us. Those of you who have passed through several grades will remember that one of the special forms of evil and adverse Sephiroth is designated "the hinders" and they are continually trying to get the better of us: "too busy" – "no quiet"– there are lots of excuses but if you make your mind up firmly once and for all that you are going to set apart a special time every day for meditation, the hinders will take a back seat and the way will open. But so long as you are of two minds and try to serve two masters neither will get full service.

The first qualification mentioned is attention. Attention must be directed to *do* work it is intended to do. But there is more, in that attention is coupled with perception. The mind being directed to outward things as affecting the inner, attention must be paid to ordinary duties, but as we are set apart for spiritual work these central things must be drawn into the services of the interior life.

Therefore cultivate perception which implies a certain abstract way of looking at things as opposed to concrete attention when doing them. Most of the ordinary work of daily life such as washing up etc. may be brought into service of the spiritual life if we can find a point of contact. What may appeal to one in this respect may not appeal to another. But you will recollect that for thirty years our Lord's Mother did all these things and was busy about the house and she is the type of spiritual Womanhood of humanity related to the divine.

Then there is refection and repetition; the considering of the matter turning over in the mind, and as a cow chews the cud so must we get the full meaning.

It is not enough to look; the different points of view must be reflected upon until the whole becomes a part of ourselves. What is reflected upon our auras or spheres of sensation remains as trace or symbol; it is not merely a literal picture but contains also latent ideas of the practice, because the aura reflects not only the physical but also the mental and the spiritual. The akashic records are the sphere of sensation of the world, and whatever is done, said or thought is reflected and preserved therein.

It is no empty phrase that every idle word must be accounted for. Reflection therefore does not mean a mere passing picture as mirrored in still water; it indicates something permanent.

Compassion and judgement; it is not sufficient to accept an idea presented to you, it must be compassed with others' ideas. Children are not sent to school with the idea so much of learning out of books, that could be done at home, as of rubbing up against other children; and herein lies the true value of reading. Because it is in a book does not mean that it is necessarily true. Diametrically opposite statements are found in books but each may contain valuable lights on the truth. Statements need not be accepted at face value; use judgement and discrimination and you will eventually find out what is true for you.

We are limited in our capacities and can only assimilate a limited amount of truth. That is to say, when working clairvoyantly we work in groups; each sees from a different angle, and when all points are compassed something like the truth is arrived at. In clairvoyant work we are on a little known plane and therefore are more liable to illusion than on the material plane, and it is necessary to learn to see before we can hope to see accurately.

On the material plane, an artist – that is, one who is trained to see – sees much more in a landscape, for instance, than the ordinary observer. A baby is more is less blind when born, it can practically only distinguish light. We are more or less babies at the stage of seeing light, something or some power that is beyond our reach. It is only when that light becomes clear and a guiding light that we are entitled to call ourselves an initiate. It is not one who has absorbed a vast quantity of wisdom but one who had begun to see and follow the light. Therefore meditation is concentration upon the light. If we should find spiritual light within we must recognise the light without.

All infants have two sensations when born, the need for the air they must breathe and the need for food. Both are supplied to him from outside. So if we are to grow we must fill our spiritual lungs with air of divine flame and satisfy our spiritual desires with nourishment. When we have existence, air and nourishment, we can proceed absorbing and digesting retention and memory we must consciously retain and remember. Most occultists hold that our actual thoughts and ideas and experiences are not of the brain but of the sphere of sensation. The brain is a telephone exchange; we ring up when we want to remember, and when the exchange is working well we remember after getting through; when it is not we forget. To train the brain to give an instantaneous response is of course of great practical value.

Discernment and comprehension are the two most difficult qualities to apply to our mental equipment to discern the spirits of good & evil between the high and low, between the pure and evil; all qualities gone before are needed if we are to rise quickly between spiritual and physical aspects, especially comprehension in order to discern readily. Too often does it happen that the mind drifts, not discerning what is of real value.

Much psychic employment may be very exciting and interesting, but is, like toxicants, exhilarating while it lasts but with exhaustion in its train. Psychic work as such is nearly always dangerous, for it deals with the astral plane. The dark path of TAV, as we are told in one of the rituals – illusions, shells of the dead, empty things. Spiritualism may be doing good work in its way by uncovering some of the continuity of existence, but it deals only with its lowest planes on the other side of the veil and may hinder those who have passed on. But it is always possible to rise beyond the astral plane to great spiritual heights, and then we pass behind meditation in what we call contemplation ecstasy. Being like the greatest height of all. St. Paul, when speaking of rising to the seventh heaven, says that he heard works not lawful to utter; in other words things not comprehensible on the material plane. There is no language to correspond to what we see on the higher planes, hence the use of symbols. As long as your experiences are easy to describe you may take it that you are not very far advanced in your meditations.

Now we come to imagination and creation. Too often imagination is spoken of as if valueless and reprehensible, but actually in true exercise it is a god-like faculty. We may say that the creator imagined the world and it took form. Whatever you imagine is latent on some other plane; you cannot imagine that which does not exist. If you imagine vividly enough you create a thought form, which may be good or evil. An actual entity may be formed but you must be able to discern whether it be animated by good or evil before accepting its teaching. Evil spirits may desire to masquerade as spirits of light but hold them to the torch of truth – the name Jesus Christ – and they will reveal the true form.

When practising meditation it is well to use a mantra, creating as it were a wall that only the true and beautiful may pass. Beginners do not always see the evil and the pitfalls and tend not to notice the puddles. The path may be difficult but it leads upwards. On the plain you may be safe but your horizon is limited; it is from the mountain top you can see out – and it is to the mountain that Moses and Elijah came, not to the plain. As we go up we must be transfigured. Meditation is not an act of will and can never be too easy; the mind which wanders off is like a donkey which is always trying to get away even when tethered to a staff in a green plot, but the tether pulls it back.

When you have acquired the powers of meditation you have also acquired self-control – you have gained in concentration which can be used to advantage in other ways. It is those who know how to concentrate on what they are doing that find time to do things easily and quickly and with time to spare. One who is always too busy to do anything thoroughly is one who has not learned to concentrate.

HISTORY OF THE RR ET AC

Lecture of the Study Group of the Societas Rosicruciana[93]
Monday, 14th February, 5.30 pm.

Dr Felkin

Most worthy, supreme M.W. and Fratres,

I think a few preliminary remarks will be useful before coming to the main point of my address this afternoon, which is, as you know, upon Christian Rosencreutz, the founder of the Society to which we belong.

You must remember that many epochs have passed since man has inhabited this world, and that they are variously spoken of: but if we use the terms Lemurian, Atlantian, post-Atlantian, Egyptian, Persian and Indian and finally, the Christian Eras, the terms will suit our purpose.

Now in each of these epochs, a definite advance has been made in the knowledge and wisdom of mankind, and there have been certain advanced souls living in each epoch whose knowledge has far transcended that of their compeers, and who have after death formed distinct groups upon – let us say – the aura of the earth, or in other words, upon the Spirit plane contiguous to the earth.

These groups still persist, and a noteworthy point concerning them is this – that they are able upon the spiritual plane to follow the progress of civilisation, even up to the present time. Technically, individuals of this nature possess what we might term Etheric or Astral bodies.

We are all constantly surrounded by the residue of the Etheric bodies of the dead (to our weal or woe) and powerful influences are transmitted from Etheric bodies to the most advanced individuals amongst us.

Now Christian Rosencreutz was one of these beings, and he is able to function well, whether incarnated or non-incarnated, and what follows tries to explain some of his power.

In the restricted sense, the Rosicrucian movement had its rise in the thirteenth century, and for a hundred years or so the

---

93 This was circulated to Whare Ra members above the grade of 5=6 and is a presentation that Felkin gave to SRIA.

spiritual stream of wisdom appeared to receive marked impetus to manifest itself in a new way. This happened quite recently within the continental Theosophical movement.

In 1788, there appeared a book written by Henricus Matadamus Theosophus which was "The Secret Signs of Rosencreutz". You have a copy of this book in your library. This book indicated in a certain limited sense the Rosicrucian work which had taken place during the previous century. A hundred years later, certain Rosicrucian knowledge was given out through the medium of H.P.B. in "Isis Unveiled". In that book there is much wisdom although we must distinguish between the first and later editions.

For the origin of the newer Rosicrucian teaching, we must go back to the thirteenth century. At that time certain a nadir in spiritual life was reached. The generality of mankind had, to a great extent, lost all touch with the spiritual world, and it was at this time that a very spiritual group of men got together at a place – the name of which I am not allowed definitely to state – but it was in the South of Europe. Twelve men met together, who in themselves contained the sum of the whole spiritual knowledge of their time. Seven of them represented the seven traditions of the seven holy species; the other five represented the five sub-races of Culture Epochs since Atlantis. These twelve had thus between them all the Atlantian and post-Atlantian wisdom. One of them had all the current knowledge of his time, while the others, by direct indication or introspection, drew upon the memories of the earlier incarnations.

Now these twelve sought to initiate a new development, but they found that they could not make a synthesis of the knowledge they then collectively possessed. They felt, therefore, that it was necessary to add a thirteenth member to their number, and seeking about, they found a youth who was being educated in a monastery. By heredity he was a mystic. He had lived upon the earth at the time of the Crucifixion, and had prepared himself by further pious and tested lives for the mission to which he was called by the twelve in the thirteenth century. This man, as we shall see, was the person who called himself Christian Rosencreutz. His life name I know, and the place of his birth, but I am pledged not to reveal it.

He was a delicate young man, but readily consented to the training which was proposed to him by the twelve, and it reacted upon him, not only mentally, but physically. Entirely sheltered from all outside influences, he grew up in the midst of a college founded by the twelve.

Now these twelve were possessed or imbued by the idea that the Christianity of that period was only a distorted image. They were filled with the greatness of Christianity, yet they were forced at time to appear to be inimical to it as then practised. Their great aim was to procure a synthesis of all religions, not merely as a fraction, but also as a result of practical spiritual life; and they wished to elucidate, if possible, that Christianity was the culmination of all the various religious systems which had preceded it.

Now, to obtain this synthesis the education of this young man was directed. He was taught the knowledge possessed by all the twelve, and, during his training, his physical strength gradually faded, whilst his spiritual power increased in an extraordinary way. At last a point was reached when almost all communication with outward life ceased, and the young man finally rejected all nourishment and lay as one in a state of catalepsy or suspended animation. Then occurred one of those unique events which can only result when the macrocosmic forces work together, and the time is ripe for such an occurrence. The physical body of the young man became almost perfectly transparent and for many days lay as one dead. Around him the twelve assembled together at definite intervals of time, and it seemed as if all their wisdom streamed from them to him in short formulae – they appeared as concentrated prayers. The result was that a great change occurred in the young man's soul, but at the same time his body was vitalised in such a mystical manner that one can hardly describe it: and the twelve were then able to realise that he had now gone through a like experience to that which St Paul went through on the road to Damascus.

Then, as several weeks passed by, the young man gradually revived, was able to again to take nourishment, and, later on, all the knowledge he had received from the twelve he was able to give out in a concentrated form.

The revelation that he gave them was called by these twelve the true Christianity, the Synthesis of all Religions.

The young man died at an apparently early age. The twelve then occupied themselves with the task of depicting in symbolic hieroglyphs (because in this way only could it be done) the revelation which had been given them by the young man. It was in this way that the symbolic figures were produced which appear in the work of Henricus Matadamus Theosophus and which were practically given out by H.P.B.

This occult process must be so imagined that the results of the initiation of the thirteenth century are stored up in his Etheric Nucleus within the world's spiritual atmosphere. This Nucleus continued to act upon the twelve, inspiring them just as it also inspired their subsequent students, so that from them the Rosicrucian occult tradition could be propagated. But this nucleus worked on still further, for it subsequently penetrated or obsessed the Etheric Body of the young man when he again incarnated about the middle of the 14th century – on 14th September 1378. This time he lived for over 100 years. He was brought up in the circle of the pupils and followers of the twelve, but was not as isolated from the world as he had been in his previous incarnation. In his twenty-eighth year, he received a remarkable impulse which compelled him to travel and he went with a friend to Cyprus; his friend died there but he went on to Egypt and then to Mount Carmel, where he lived for a time, and at length arrived at Damascus, at which place there again occurred to him an experience similar to that which St Paul underwent. All the powers of that wonderful Etheric Body, which had remained intact, and which streamed out from him to the spiritual world, induced in him a desire to re-live once more the already experienced revelation. Exoterically it is to this personality, born in the 14th century, to whom we really point as the genuine Christian Rosencreutz, but esoterically, we can speak of Christian Rosencreutz as existing from the 13th century. It is the pupils of this Christian Rosencreutz of the 14th century who are the real Rosicrucians.

I may mention here that I am pledged not to reveal the name or real person who called himself Christian Rosencreutz, nor the place in which he was born, but I may say that, in 1914, I was on my way to his birth-place and also to see the vault in which he is buried, which still exists, although it is not in the place in which it is described as being, in any published account.

Christian Rosencreutz, after leaving his home, journeyed throughout the whole world, as then known, and it was easy for him in the course of his seven years' pilgrimage to acquire the total knowledge of that period. After this pilgrimage was completed, he adopted the most advanced pupils and followers of the Twelve as his pupils. It was in this way that the Rosicrucian work began.

Owing to influences which emanate from the Etheric Body of Christian Rosencreutz, a perfectly new view of the world could be initiated. The Maya of the material world could now be investigated. The Macrocosmos is just as much an Etheric Body as is the individual, and continuous transition takes place in the course of finer substances. If we direct our gaze to the boundary of the physical and Etheric substance, we become aware of a third substance which is contained in every other substance, or every other physical substance may be considered a modification of this one. It is the essence of all.

The object of the Rosicrucians was to perceive this substance clairvoyantly and the power to attain such vision they considered to be an exceptional development of the moral potency of the soul. This substance has been really discovered and investigated by the Rosicrucians.

They have found it, not only in the Macrocosm, but also in mankind. In the Macrocosm, they perceived it as a garment of the Macrocosm and in mankind, they saw it in the interchanged working between Thought and Will.

Will, they comprehended in the Macrocosm as thunder and lightning; thought as the Rainbow, or the Golden Dawn, and the power of this harmony between willing and thinking in their own souls, they sought from the Etheric Body of Christian Rosencreutz.

It was determined that all discoveries they made should remain secret for a hundred years, and that it was only after a hundred years had been spent in working at the subject that it became permissible to speak of it in any adequate manner.

In consequence of this Rosicrucian work, the Etheric Body of C.R.C. became increasingly powerful. Those who were absorbed in true theosophical study permitted themselves to be overshadowed by this Etheric Body which can act upon them whether C.R.C. is incarnate or disincarnate.

In the 18th century C.R.C. was again incarnated, in the body of Comte St Germain; only be it remembered, several other people were called by this name, so that everything which was said here and there about St Germain must not be considered to apply to the real C.R.C.

It was from out of this Etheric Body that there flowed the inspiration of H.P.B which was partly given out in "Isis Unveiled".

Imperceptibly, also, has it inspired Lessing in his "Development of the Human Race". In consequence of the rising flood of materialism, it has, of recent years, been very difficult to inspire the Rosicrucian tradition. Much of it could only be given out in very fragmentary streams.

Wiedmann, in 1851, was able to solve the problem of the immortal soul in the sense of reincarnation. His volume was crowned by the Academy. About 1850, Drasbach wrote "The Idea of Re-Incarnation from the Psychological Standpoint". Even during the 19th century the Rosicrucian tradition has continued to work. The termination of the small Kali-Yuga at the end of the 19th century permits a great revival of the true theosophical or Rosicrucian life. On this account, it is easier to-day for influences to penetrate the spiritual spheres. Great revelations may now be called forth from the Etheric Body of C.R.C. which has now become so extremely powerful to those who give themselves up to its influences. Up to the present time, the esoteric Rosicrucian preparation has been necessary for them. It is, further, the mission of the 20th century to enable the Etheric Body to become so mighty that it will be able to work exoterically. Those who are enabled to be absorbed in it may experience the same initiation which St Paul had on the road to Damascus. It is the work of the Rosicrucians to render possible the second coming of Christ on the Etheric plane. The number of those who will be capable of doing this will be repeatedly greater and greater.

ROSICRUCIAN WORK

The first act of this work, begun in the 13th century, continuing today, and which will continue to all eternity, was naturally that which we have been able to relate concerning the Initiation of C.R.C.

After C.R.C. was re-incarnated, in the 14th century, his work was chiefly that of instructing the pupils of the Twelve. These Twelve were really the only personas who learned to know and appreciate him. Indeed, he was not generally recognised at all, and apart from the Twelve, and a small group of students, no-one knew of his existence. It was, as a matter of fact, similar to the condition of things to-day, but his Etheric Body and its powers function in ever widening circles and, at the present time, there exists a very considerable number of people on the point of being drawn into the influence of the powers of his Etheric Body.

Those whom C.R.C. selects as his pupils are chosen by him for that purpose in a remarkable way.

The point to be considered is this: when anyone is chosen, his aspiration will very likely be started by the hearing of a voice and therefore persons who hear such a voice should carefully reflect upon their past life and pay special attention to one or two startling events which may have occurred.

What happens is briefly this: a certain person during his life arrives at a definite parting of the ways or, in other words, arrives at a Karmic crisis. For instance, a man may think he took some definite action on a given occasion and thereby escaped death. It might, for example, happen that he were within a few steps of a hidden precipice and he hears a voice saying: "Stop at once!" halts and, by so doing, escapes death. Now that person may be under the impression that it was a physical voice that struck his ear. Thousands of cases of this kind may occur. It is something external, but the most important part is the spiritual call. To this interior or intuitional call, the chosen person must respond, and, as a result of it, must undertake some study which, up to that time, he has paid no heed to, such as the study of theosophy or the like – anything which bears a definite relation to spiritual life.

The external experience is then something which the chosen pupil undergoes later. The voice came from the spiritual world and when the pupil is ripe to ascertain that it is not indeed a physical personality which has instilled an influence into his life, he recognises and becomes convinced that a spiritual world exists, from out of which the voice has addressed him.

Such events may occur once or many times. The influence that is produced upon the mind of the pupil is that he is impelled to say to himself "my former life was but labour in vain; it is true grace that a further span has been allotted to me; without this warning I must have died."

The event may have occurred years before my dealings with theosophy have commenced, but when such study is begun, the recognition of the definite events becomes evident. It is only necessary that the past life be sufficiently examined. This is the indication and the call to the higher students of the Rosicrucians.

The Difference between the Instruction of Rosicrucian Students in former times and at present: in ancient times, Rosicrucians were generally instructed in natural philosophy and nowadays it is rather in spiritual philosophy. Therefore in ancient times the processes of Nature and especially the science of Alchemy were constantly spoken of and discussed, and in so far as these processes were to be found external to the world, the science was called Astrology.

In the present day, we chiefly occupy ourselves with a consideration of spiritual things: we discuss, for instance, the great post-Atlantian Epochs and we can, from this consideration of Nature, begin to understand the invention (or development) of the human soul.

Rosicrucians of the Middle Ages investigated Nature in processes; that is to say, those natural processes as they could be seen in geological formations and so forth. We will briefly consider three of these natural processes.

First, then, let us consider the formation of Salt (precipitation). Everything in nature which separates itself off is precipitated from a solution, which the Rosicrucians in the Middle Ages termed Salt. In their chemical investigations, their perception of it was completely different from ours. Their idea of such processes must have acted like a prayer if they wished to understand the impression produced in their minds or souls. They endeavoured further to make it clear what must happen in their own souls when this process of Salt or precipitation should occur. They considered that human nature must be continually secreting itself through activity and the passions. They considered that our life was, in fact, a continual process of dying when we gave ourselves up to the passions. Now the protection against this dying is the development of pure thoughts.

The Rosicrucians of the Middle Ages knew perfectly well that if they gave way to their passions in one incarnation, they would enter into the next incarnation with a predisposition to disease and vice versa. The process of overcoming all the passions, the process of destruction through spirituality they called technically the Microcosmic Salt Formation or Precipitation. Looked at in this way, it is easy for us to comprehend how the processes of Nature may become a prayer. When the medieval Rosicrucians saw the formation of Salt in their laboratories, they said to themselves:

"Godly spiritual forces have for thousands of years worked in Nature exactly as pure thoughts work in us and we pry behind the Illusions of Nature to the thoughts of the Great Spirits."

"If we permit ourselves to be stimulated by Nature, we make ourselves resemble the Macrocosm; if we regard this process only as an external one, we cut ourselves off from the Great Spirits". It was thus that the minds of true alchemists were impressed.

The medieval Rosicrucians named anything which could dissolve anything else, Quicksilver or Mercury, and they asked themselves what property of soul acts in the same way as Nature acts through

Mercury. They recognised that Mercury in the soul represented all forms of love. They differentiated between the lower and the higher forms of love which exist. They said to themselves: "the Love of God has indeed worked externally just as love works in us."

We will now refer to Combustion:

The medieval Rosicrucians sought for a corresponding wider process and they found it in intense devotion to Godhead. They named anything which could be consumed in flames Sulphur. They saw in the development of Life the process of a magical, universal sublimation, just like the process of the combustion of Sulphur. They said to themselves: "All this is the work of the Great Spirits who raise all things to higher spirits. Now lower spirits sacrifice to higher spirits." So said they, as they watched the process of sublimation and when they proved the activity of the process, within themselves: "We do what the Great Spirits do when they sacrifice to those of higher rank", and they felt themselves permeated with the necessity of making such sacrificial offering. They gave themselves up, with religious enthusiasm to the formation of salt solution and the processes of sublimation and considered themselves, when at this work, bound thereby to the macrocosmic powers.

When they witnessed the process of the formation of salt they felt within themselves pure thoughts arise. When conducting the process of precipitation or solution, they felt themselves stimulated to love, and, at the process of sublimation, they felt themselves compelled to the service of sacrifice. If one looked clairvoyantly at the change which took place in the Aura of the operator during these processes one would notice how the Aura, which at the beginning on account of sin was of mixed colours, gradually becomes of pure colour. First, it became the colour of copper, then it took on a silver hue, finally it became like glistening gold and the alchemists then said to themselves, when this change had taken place, that they had transmitted the Aura of subjective silver to subjective gold.

Further, it followed that a man thoroughly penetrated with purity, love and devotion, produced by these alchemical processes, attained, as a result, a certain measure of clairvoyance. The medieval Rosicrucians could pierce with their glances the manner in which the spiritual existence was permitted to come into being, even to vanish behind the illusion of things, and therefore he was also able to see that large powers of functioning of the soul were capable of development and which were quite natural.

The law of ascent and descent became clear to them, and they were able to express the science acquired in this manner in symbolic hieroglyphs.

It was in this way that the Rosicrucian alchemists worked, from the fourteenth to the eighteenth century. Of this work we do not find, so to speak, anything printed. What has been written concerning alchemy refers to what the alchemists did for spiritual advantage, for, as the false alchemist set himself the task of forming substances, the true alchemist was really concerned with the interior experiences induced through the formation of matter.

It was for this reason that a strict law with those alchemists that the material substances produced by means of alchemical processes could only be parted with, as gifts, the only exception being that they were permitted to use a little of the gold produced for bare necessities, but not for luxuries.

The modern man can hardly comprehend that the medieval Rosicrucian could experience within his laboratory the whole drama of the soul, for instance, in the production of antimony. Those experiments must necessarily precede our labours in order that we to-day may work at spiritual science in the sense of the Rosicrucian tradition. What the medieval Rosicrucians had experienced through a sanctified natural philosophy in the ideas of sacrifice, joy and sorrow, prepared and set the conceptions of natural processes upon which all our mentality of to-day is based. How do we find these hidden forces? Through spiritual science and meditation. Later on, all investigations of Nature will again become a service of sacrifice and it will become possible to view the spiritual matter behind the veil, but in order to do this mankind must penetrate and fully comprehend the spiritual sciences.

THE CYCLE OF MEDITATION[94]
(With acknowledgement to the writings of Geoffrey Hodson)

PURPOSE: The purpose of meditation is to effect a unity between the lower mind and the higher spiritual nature of the Self. A necessary preliminary is the control of the body, emotions and thought. This in turn demands control of the actions, desires and speech.

PREPARATION: Relax the body and harmonise the emotions. Alert the mind and charge it with will. Establish a centre of awareness in the Higher Self.

DISSOCIATION: Mentally affirm: "I am not the physical body, I am the spiritual self. I am not the emotions, I am my spiritual self. I am not the mind, I am my spiritual self."

MEDITATION: Assert: "I am the Divine Self. Immortal. Eternal Radiant with spiritual light. I am that self of Light; that self am I. The self in me, the Atma, is one with the self in all the Paramatma. I am that self in all. That Self am I. The Atma and the Paramatma are One. I am that. That I am."

PERIOD OF MEDITATION: Five minutes at first, then lengthen gradually to 15 or 30 minutes. Best times are sunrise, mid-day and sunset. Cease meditating if any signs of a headache are felt.

CLOSING PHASE: Bring the centre of awareness:

(a) Into the formal mind, illumined and responsive to the intuition.

(b) Into the emotions radiated by the Spiritual Light.

(c) Into the body, empowered by the Spiritual Will, inwardly, vitalised and self-recollected throughout the day, remembering the Divine Presence within the heart, the inner ruler, immortal, seated in the hearts of all beings.

CONCLUSION: Now relax the mind and permit the uplifting effect of the meditation to extend into all other activities of the day.

---

94 You can see the Theosophical influence in this paper. Indeed when I was given this paper I was told to replace the words Atma with the "Higher Self" or the "son" and Paramatma with the Absolute or One Thing. It is possible to say "I and the Father are One" just as easily as it is to say "The Atma and the Paramatma are One."
However, this shows how sometimes Theosophical teachings and Indian systems found their way into Whare Ra.

REFERENCES

Abraham ben Simeon, and Mathers, S. (1975). *The book of the sacred magic of Abramelin the mage, as delivered by Abraham the Jew unto his son Lamech, A.D. 1458*. New York: Dover Publications.

Anon, (2015). [online] Available at: http://www.guild-of-st-raphael.org.uk/Publications/Chrism/2006-May.pdf [Accessed 22 Mar. 2015].

Bailey, A. (1971). *A treatise on the seven rays*. New York: Lucis Publishing Co.

Benham, P. (2006). *The Avalonians*. Glastonbury: Gothic Image.

Budge, E. and Budge, E. (n.d.). *The book of the dead*.

Case, P. (1989). *The book of tokens*. Los Angeles, Calif., U.S.A.: Builders of the Adytum.

Crowley, A., Symonds, J. and Grant, K. (1989). *The confessions of Aleister Crowley*. London: Arkana.

Dunn, P. (1999). Robert Felkin MD (1853-1926) and Caesarean delivery in Central Africa (1879). *Archives of Disease in Childhood - Fetal and Neonatal Edition*, 80(3), pp.F250-F251.

Ellwood, R. (1993). *Islands of the dawn*. Honolulu: University of Hawaii Press.

Ericson, E. (1983). *Master of the temple*. London: New English Library.

Farrell, N. (2011). *Mathers' last secret revised – the rituals and teachings of the alpha et omega*. [S.l.]: Rosicrucian Order Of The.

Farrell, N. (2012). *King over the water*. Dublin: Kerubim Press.

Farrell, N. (2014). *The Hidden Path of Initiation*. Rome: Lulu.

Fortune, D. (1929). *Occult Review*, December.

Fortune, D. (1957). *Psychic self-defence*. Wellingborough, Northamptonshire: Aquarian Press.

Howe, E. (1972). *The magicians of the Golden Dawn*. London: Routledge and K. Paul.

Inquire Within, (1930). *Light bearers of darkness*. London: Boswell Print. & Pub. Co.

King, F. (1970). *Ritual magic in England*. London: Spearman.

References

Mackey, A. and Clegg, R. (1921). *Mackey's symbolism of freemasonry.* Chicago: The Masonic history Company.

Meihuizen, N. (1998). *Yeats and the drama of sacred space.* Amsterdam: Rodopi.

Nzhistory.net.nz, (2015). *North Island influenza death rates – The 1918 influenza pandemic | NZHistory, New Zealand history online.* [online] Available at: http://www.nzhistory.net.nz/culture/influenza-pandemic/north-island-death-rates#eastcape [Accessed 26 Mar. 2015].

Pixley, O. (1969). *The armour of light.* Cheltenham, England: Helios Book Service.

Regardie, I. (1971). *The Golden Dawn.* St. Paul: Llewellyn Publications.

Regardie, I. (1984). *The complete Golden Dawn system of magic.* Phoenix, Ariz., U.S.A.: Falcon Press.

Richardson, A. and Hughes, G. (1989). *Ancient magicks for a new age.* St. Paul, Minn.: Llewellyn Publications.

Scott, E. (1890). *Stanley and his heroic relief of Emin Pasha.* Toronto: W. Bryce.

Sheringham, H. and Meakin, N. (1904). *The court of Sacharissa.* New York: Macmillan.

Sheringham, H. and Meakin, N. (1906). *The enemy's camp.* London: Macmillan.

Stratton-Kent, J. (2010). *Geosophia.* [Dover]: Scarlet Imprint/Bibliotheìèque Rouge.

The Hermetic Tablet Vol. One, Winter Solstice. (2015). Rome: The Hermetic Tablet.

Wikipedia, (2015). *Guild of St Raphael.* [online] Available at: http://en.wikipedia.org/wiki/Guild_of_St_Raphael [Accessed 22 Mar. 2015].

Zalewski, P. and Lisiewski, J. (1988). *The secret inner order rituals of the Golden Dawn.* Phoenix, AZ: Falcon Press.

INDEX

Abiegnus 137
Abram 130
Abramelin ritual 95, 96, 98, 245
acacia sprig 103, 121, 122, 145, 146, 187, 188, 190, 202, 205
Adam Kadmon 114, 146, 175, 176
African magic 25
Agrippa, Henry Cornelius 211, 212, 244
Albertus, Frater (Dr. Albert Richard Riedel) 78, 79
alchemy 78, 79, 180, 204, 272, 273, 274
Aldebaran 200-201
almond 164, 187, 188, 199, 202, 209, 211
Amentet 131
ankh 40, 127, 128
Antares 59, 201, 206, 209, 210, 214
anthroposophy 48, 75
Anubis 41, 213, 238, 239, 240, 241, 255
Apophis 38
Ara Ben Shemesh (The 'Arab Teacher') 42, 49, 54, 57, 58, 59, 63, 64, 65, 78
Archangel Gabriel 201
Archangel Michael 176, 201
Archangel Raphael 31, 50, 201
Archangel Sandalphon 176
Archangel Uriel 201, 254
Armour of Light exercise 58
astral contacts 18, 21, 28, 30, 31–32, 58, 65, 66, 73, 87, 220, 263
astral projection 63
Athena 126
Augustine of Hippo 207

Aura papers 32
Avernus 129
Azoth 80

Ba 131
Babe of the Abyss 233, 234, 239
Bad Pyrmont (Germany) 44, 48
Baha, Abdu'l 47
Bahá'í faith 46, 47
Bailey, Alice A. 30
Baldwin, King of Jerusalem 161
banishing ritual 90, 92, 96, 245, 249
Beeston (England) 22
Benham, Patrick 46
Bennett, Allan 14, 43
Berlin (Germany) 49
Berridge, Edward 43, 63
Biggs, Caroline 59
Binah, sphere of 68, 152, 200, 205, 234, 252
Bion, Wilfred Ruprecht 216, 217
Black Osiris 42
Blackwood, Algernon 14
blood 34, 35, 125, 126, 204
BOTA (Builders of the Adytum) 78–87, 91, 92, 94, 95, 98
Bristol (England) 60, 64, 77
British Empire 19, 23
Brodie-Innes, John 18, 27, 32, 33, 42–48, 56, 57, 60, 128, 135
Burden, Mike 94, 99, 100
Burry, Dr. Pullen 137

Caesarean birth 25, 26
Cairo 22, 42–48, 47
Campbell, Euan (Hugh) 68, 78, 95–99
Cape Kidnappers (New Zealand) 52

Index

Carnegie Dickson, John 60, 64
Carnegie Dickson, Mrs 60, 64, 77, 78
cartouches 135
Case, Paul Foster 14, 18, 79, 80, 81, 85, 99, 137
Chambers, Maurice 47
Chapman-Taylor, James Walter 54–55, 90
Chesed, sphere of 152, 205, 231
Chesterman, Joyce 78, 86, 87, 94
Chesterman, Will 86, 87, 91, 94
Chiah 127, 140, 165
Chokmah, sphere of 152, 202, 205, 234, 252
Christian mysticism 28, 32, 53–54, 59, 233, 234, 256, 266, 267
Cicero, Chic 88, 89
Collins, Mabel 58
Communion 130, 233
Congo 27
Conman, Joanne 141
crossing the Abyss 67, 68, 202, 204, 206, 233, 234, 235, 236, 237, 241, 244
Crowley, Aleister 14, 43, 49, 50, 63, 81, 82, 125, 132, 141, 218, 233, 236
cubical cross 159, 160, 162, 210, 245, 246

Da'ath 156, 157, 158, 233
dark night of the soul 113, 137, 200, 244
Davidson, John 29
Davies, Ann 79, 81–87
decans 141, 144, 145, 257
Dee, Dr. John 98
demons 34, 49, 125, 131, 132, 147, 233, 244, 245
Denderah (temple) 141
d'Olivet, Fabre 261
dweller on the threshold 66

Eastern teaching 30, 32, 42, 53–54, 207
Edom 135, 136

egregores 30 *(see also* Golden Dawn *and* Whare Ra)
Egyptian Book of the Dead 58, 131, 135, 138, 206
Egyptian magic 32
Egyptian Order (G.O.T.S.) 59
Elementals 32, 90, 160, 254
Eleusinian Mysteries 60
Ellwood, Robert 62, 72
Enochian Magic system 80, 81, 82, 85, 98, 99, 233, 245
Epopt 60
Equinox (magazine) 81
Extreme Unction 140

Farrell, Paola 100
Farr, Florence 14, 18, 59, 217
Felkin, Denys 28
Felkin, Ethelwyn 28, 54, 61, 63, 73, 75, 76, 82, 83
Felkin, Harriet (née Davidson) 26, 27, 42, 45, 54, 66, 72, 82, 83, 90, 91, 93, 221, 248, 256
  marriage 29
  channelling and prophesy 73, 83, 84, 85
  leadership of Whare Ra 29, 72–75
  death 30, 76
Felkin, Mary (née Mander) 27, 28, 29
Felkin, Robert 18, 19, 21, 22, 23, 83, 88, 90, 93, 128, 135, 139, 145, 200, 203, 212, 216, 218, 219, 256
  missionary work 22–27
  marriage 27, 29
  leadership of Golden Dawn 28
  search for secret chiefs in Europe 45, 57
  founding of Smaragdum Thallasses 56
  alcoholism 29, 71
  first visit to New Zealand 54–56
  emigration to New Zealand 61
  death 71
  posthumous contact as "The Chief" 73

279

First World War 18, 47, 57, 61, 63, 64, 65
Fitzgerald, Father Charles 53–54, 68–69
Flying Rolls 247
Fomalhaut 59, 200, 201, 202, 208
Forerunner, The (magazine) 53
Fortune, Dion 14, 56, 60, 74–77, 95, 96, 98, 247
Freemasonry 45, 48, 58, 70, 72, 145, 146
Fuller, Tony 32, 55–57, 56, 59, 60, 68–69, 69, 90, 93, 98, 203, 204, 220, 221, 247, 248, 252

Garden of Eden 254
Gardiner, Reginald 52, 69, 73, 75, 76
Gardiner, Rose 53
Gardiner, Ruth 53
Geburah, sphere of 15, 130, 132, 133, 135, 137, 150, 152, 168, 231
Geddes, Ros 94
Geographical Society 27
Geomancy 245, 254
Gethsemane 162, 163
Gilbert, Robert 50
Gilmore, W.G. 82
Girdle of Venus 127
Glastonbury (England) 46, 247
godforms 16, 17, 127, 130, 141, 144, 145, 204, 205, 213, 245
Goetic magic 91, 125, 128, 245
Golden Dawn
  Alpha et Omega (AO) temple 43, 56, 60, 78, 79, 80, 81, 247
  Amen-Ra Temple 27
  Amoun temple 28, 60, 63
  Bradford Temple 31
  Cromlech Temple (Solar Order) 28, 32, 56, 77, 78
  Edinburgh temple 29
  egregore 31, 217, 218
  established in New Zealand 54, 61, 77, 78
  grades 16, 17, 28, 80, 233, 235
  Hermetic Order of the 14, 28, 89, 99, 220
  internal revolt 28, 32, 50, 217
  Isis Urania temple 28
  lineage claims 15, 16, 45
  modern Orders 17, 88, 89
  Nottingham temple 99
  rituals 15, 16, 59
Gonne, Maud 14
Goodie, Frank 79
Gordon of Khartoum (Major-General Charles George Gordon) 19, 24
Grail 36, 234
Great Pyramid 33, 36–42
Guild of St Raphael 59, 60

Harpahkrat 205
Hartley, Christine 60
Hastings (New Zealand) 19, 51, 62, 65, 69, 86
Hathor 41, 141, 204, 205
Havelock North (New Zealand) 28, 29, 51, 52–53, 56, 62, 69, 71, 72, 75, 77, 78, 88, 92, 94, 100, 139
Havelock Work 52–53
Hawkes Bay (New Zealand) 61, 71, 79, 84, 89, 93, 100, 144
Hawkes Bay Herald Tribune (newspaper) 53
hazel 202
Hebrew letters 211
Heka 127
Hermes Temple 60, 77
Hidden Masters of the Sun 28
Higher Genius 73, 176, 251, 255
Hillary, Sir Edmund 72
Hinerakau 51
Hod (sphere of) 152
Horniman, Annie 14, 31
Horos, Madame 31, 50, 218
Horus 41, 204, 205
hot springs 248
Howe, Ellic 21, 44, 45, 50

Index

Hubbe-Schleiden, Dr 48
Hughes, Miss C.E. 60

initiation 16, 67, 91, 92, 99, 129, 158, 177, 219, 251
Inner Plane communications 18, 63, 79, 145
Inner Temple method 247
Io-Ana Temple 78
Isis 33, 41–46, 127

Jellicoe, John Rushworth 90
Jones, Betty 68, 69, 76, 87, 91
Jupiter room 54

Ka 127, 128
Kabbalah 32, 47, 79, 140, 165, 231, 232, 236
Kether, sphere of 152, 161, 200, 202, 205, 234, 244
Khartoum 23-25
Khert-neter 131, 206
King, Francis 18, 19, 21, 32, 33, 45, 59
King's Chamber 40
Kuntz, Darcy 19

Lantern, The (magazine) 73
Large, Harold 53
Larunda 128, 129
Leopold II, King of Belgium 27
Lesser Key of Solomon 125, 132
lineage 14, 15, 17–18, 31, 44, 88, 216, 218, 220, 221
Link ritual 14, 17–18, 58, 76, 93, 216–227
Livingstone, Dr David 22, 23
London (England) 44, 54, 60, 62, 63, 65, 77, 218
Lord of the Eventide 130
Lux E Tenebris (L.e.T) 31, 49, 50

Maat 132, 135
Machen, Arthur 14
Mackay of Uganda (Alexander Murdoch Mackay) 19, 22, 23

Magical Order of the Aurora Aurea (MOAA) 16, 17, 92, 99, 100, 134, 225
Malkuth (sphere of) 152, 244, 254
Māori tradition 51–52
Mars room 54, 145, 146
Martinism 49
Mathers, Moina 31, 56, 79, 80
Mathers, Samuel 18, 21, 25, 28, 29, 30, 31, 32, 33, 42, 43, 44, 49, 50, 56, 57, 60, 62, 91, 95, 98, 125, 135, 216, 217, 220, 225
Matrona 128, 129, 151
McDowell, Charles 75
McLean, Miss M.M. 53
Mead, G. R. S. 137
Meakin, Neville 29, 45, 46, 47, 49, 66, 138
medical missionaries 22, 23
medicine men (African) 25
Melchizedek 129, 130
Melusine 126
Mercury 129
Merlin Temple 60
Meyrink, Gustav 14
Middle Pillar exercise 58
Minerva 126
Mirfield fathers 27, 28, 53–54
Mithraism 32, 137
Monpel, Father Simon Lourdel (Père Mapeera) 26
moonstone 178, 186, 204
Mount of Olives 163
Muteesa I, King of Buganda 22, 23, 25, 26

Nairn, Barbara 74, 91, 100, 219
Napier Daily Telegraph (newspaper) 69, 94
Napier (New Zealand) 62, 69, 84, 94
nemyss 100, 130, 238
Nephthys 33, 41–46, 141
Nesbit, E. 14
Neshamah 127, 140, 165, 211
Netzach (sphere of) 152

Neuburg, Victor Benjamin 233
new moon 36, 96, 97, 258
New Thought movement 80
New Zealand 14, 18, 19, 21, 47, 51, 52–53, 55–56, 56–58, 57, 61, 63, 66, 70, 71, 72, 75–78, 77, 84, 88, 92, 94, 99
Nile, River 22, 24, 25, 27, 36

oath 15, 55, 89, 95, 132, 133, 134, 218, 219
Occult Review (magazine) 96
Old Vault (tomb of Christian Rosencreutz) 57
olive oil 125, 126, 165, 166
Order of the Table Round 46, 47, 65, 66, 67, 71, 76–77, 84, 85, 87, 93, 94, 95, 99, 100
Ordo Templi Orientis (O.T.O.) 49
Osborne, David 68
Osiris 37, 41–46, 131, 138, 141, 205, 214, 239

Pakipaki 51
Paris 31, 42, 49
Pasha, Emin 24, 25
pā sites. *See also* Māori tradition
Pattison, T.H. 31
pentagrams 134
Philae 33
pillars 127, 128, 132, 135, 203, 208, 209, 213, 214
planets 149, 153, 160, 161, 178, 211, 212, 213, 244, 245, 246, 248, 254, 255, 257, 258
Pole, Wellesley Tudor 46, 47, 48
portable vault 92
Portal ritual 29, 46, 74–77, 135, 162, 175
Poseidon 126
Prayer of the Hours 144
Prince of the Horizon 130
Processes (exercises) 58

Queen's Chamber 39, 40–45

Queen Victoria 25, 26

Radiant Health movement 72
Raison, Ron 85
Ramanathan, P. 43, 44
Regardie, Israel 14, 16, 18, 58, 82, 218
Regulus 200, 201, 209
Re-Horakhty 205
Renn, Beryl 78
Renn, Charles 77, 78
Ricca, Dr. Alfonso 146
rising in the planes 155, 156
Robe of Glory 129, 187, 210, 242
Rosencreutz, Christian 44, 47, 49, 57, 127, 218, 219, 222, 225, 265, 266, 267, 268, 269, 270
Rosicrucian adepts 32, 44, 45, 48, 49, 57, 58, 62, 64, 90
Rosicrucianism 28, 48, 216, 217, 218, 219, 220, 221, 226, 265, 266, 268, 269, 270, 271, 272, 273, 274
Ruess, Theodore 49
Russell, Andrew Hamilton 89

Sacred Names 35
sacrifice 34, 126, 131, 132, 139, 140, 162, 165, 173, 206, 208, 214, 273
Saint John of the Cross 169
Salem, King of 129, 130, 202, 203, 205, 206, 207, 214, 215
Salt, Frank 67, 69, 76, 90, 93, 99, 204, 220, 247
School of Radiant Living 72
Scot, Reginald 128
secret chiefs 18, 21, 30, 31, 32, 33, 44, 45, 46, 49, 50, 56, 58, 60, 87, 100, 216
Secret College 60
Sem-Priest 202
serpent 34, 37, 97, 126, 174
Servants of the Light 99
Seshat 205
Set 41

Index

Sharp, William 14
Shaw, Archie 76
Shekinah 125, 126, 128, 129, 145, 146, 148, 165, 166, 167, 168, 202, 203, 205, 208, 209, 210, 211, 214, 215, 255
Shri Parananda. *See* P. Ramanathan
Siers, Judy 55
silence 128, 129, 131, 132, 136, 138, 146, 177, 178, 179, 205, 208, 250
Sirius 200, 201, 205, 206
Smaragdum Thallasses 14, 16, 54, 56, 218, 221
Societas Rosicruciana in Anglia (Rosicrucian Society of England) 45, 60, 65, 265
Society (Fraternity) of the Inner Light 58, 60, 74, 89, 99
Society of the Southern Cross 53
solar eclipse 26
Sprengel, Anna ("Sprengel") 44, 45, 48, 49, 50, 220
Stanley, Sir Henry Morton 22, 24, 25, 27
star magic 200
Steiner, Rudolf 48, 49, 56, 57, 58, 59, 60, 61, 75, 83, 138, 139, 216, 221
Stella Matutina 16, 21, 28, 32, 33, 47, 54, 56–58, 60, 61, 63, 103, 200, 204, 216, 218, 219, 221, 235, 243
St Germain, Comte 269
Stoddard, Christina 21, 54–55, 57, 58, 59, 63, 64, 65, 68–69, 218
Stratton-Kent, Jake 125, 131
Studtmann, Dr. 44
sub-lunar 131
Sun Masters 32, 33, 42. *See also* Hidden Masters of the Sun
supernal triad 15, 35, 200
Sutcliffe, Dr Herbert 72
Sword Bridge 234

Tarot 28, 34, 66, 79, 80, 86, 134, 137, 138, 178, 179, 186, 205, 207, 208, 213, 231, 254
Tat (or Tet) 40, 128
Tatwas 32, 35, 36
Tauhara project 75, 83, 84, 87
Taupo (New Zealand) 75
Taylor, Catherine 67
Taylor, Jack 67, 73, 74, 75, 76, 77, 78, 81–84, 91, 92, 93, 95, 98, 100, 220, 221
Te Hau Valley (New Zealand) 52
TeMata Peak (New Zealand) 51, 100, 231
Temple of the Sphinx 36–41
Theosophical Society 27, 48, 89, 275
Theosophus, Henricus Matadamus 266, 267
Thiessen, Dr 49, 50
Third Order 28, 45, 203
Thompson, Viv 67
Thoth 134, 204, 205, 207
Thoth-Hermes Temple 93, 220
Tiphareth, sphere of 19, 130, 152, 156, 157, 158, 168, 169, 225
Tohunga 52
Tranchell-Hayes, Maiya 56, 247
Tree of Life 127, 129, 132, 154, 155, 157, 159, 165, 233, 251, 252, 253
Tudor family 46
Typhon 38

Uganda 22, 25, 26
Underhill, Evelyn 14
Underworld 125, 126, 127, 128, 129, 131, 132, 135, 139, 141, 245
University of Adelaide, Australia 29

van Leeuwen, Roel 79
von Dadelszen, John 67, 69, 72, 74, 75, 76, 77, 78, 86, 87, 88, 89, 90, 92
vowels 211, 212

Waite, A. E. 14, 28, 30, 42, 46, 47, 49, 57, 59, 60, 68–69
Wallace, Alistair 79, 81, 82–85
Wayfaring Man, A (biography) 26, 42, 62, 73
Westcott, William Wynn 18, 31, 44, 45, 48, 49, 50, 60, 63, 64, 80, 98, 220
Whare Ra
  foundation of 54, 66
  temple building 14, 54–55, 73, 87, 91, 92, 248
  adepts 15, 67, 68–69, 74, 76, 78, 91, 92, 95, 98, 99, 100
  egregore 216, 221
  grades 17, 67–68, 76, 85, 171, 203, 244, 255
  local community figures 68–70, 89
  Māori legend 52, 54
  red stockings 69
  secrecy 68–70
  training 95, 251, 255
  vault 54, 90, 91, 92, 203
  attempted BOTA merger 81–87, 94
  closure 87–93

White Temple 247
white triangle 15
Whitty, Michael James 80
Wilkinson, Percy 19, 69, 70, 74–77, 77, 85, 87, 92, 93, 94, 95, 99, 100, 103, 164, 251
Williams and Kettle 52
Williams, Charles 14
Woodford House, Havelock North 53

Yeats, W. B. 14, 16, 28, 46, 148, 203, 217, 235
Yechidah 127, 140, 165
Yesod (sphere of) 152
Yoga 43
Yorke, Gerald 33

Zalewski, Christine 73, 91, 93, 220
Zalewski, Pat 14, 15, 16, 17, 19, 67, 68–69, 74, 78, 91, 93, 94, 95, 99, 126, 127, 135, 139, 219, 220, 221
Zanzibar 27
Z-documents 247
Zoa 139, 165

ALSO BY THIS AUTHOR

Mather's Last Secret, by Nick Farrell, Rosicrucian Order of the Golden Dawn
King over the Water, by Nick Farrell, Kerubim Press
Magical Pathworking, by Nick Farrell, Llewellyn
Egyptian Shaman, by Nick Farrell, Mandrake
Magical Imagination, by Nick Farrell, Skylight Press
The Osiris Scroll, by Nick Farrell, Magical Order of the Aurora Aurea Press.
Shem Grimoire, by Nick Farrell, Magical Order of the Aurora Aurea Press
What My Hierophant should have told me, by Nick Farrell, Magical Order of the Aurora Aurea Press
Commentaries on the Golden Dawn Flying Rolls, (edited by Nick Farrell)
Making Talismans, by Nick Farrell, Mandrake
When a Tree Falls, by Nick Farrell, Immanon Press
The Druidic Order of Pendragon, by Nick Farrell and Colin Wilson, Thoth Publications.
Gathering the Magic, by Nick Farrell, Immanon Press